Living the Mystery of Jesus

LITURGY I

Living the Mystery of Jesus

Author and General Editor
Sister Loretta Pastva, S.N.D.

BENZIGER

Encino, California

Theological Consultants: Rev. Edward T. Francis, M.A., S.T.D.
Executive Director, Office for Pastoral Liturgy
Diocese of Cleveland, Ohio

Rev. James R. McGonegal, M.Div., M.A. Liturgics
Associate Director, Office for Pastoral Liturgy
Diocese of Cleveland, Ohio

Nihil Obstat:
The Reverend Paul J. Sciarrotta, S.T.L.
Censor Deputatus

Imprimatur:
The Most Reverend Anthony M. Pilla, M.A.
Bishop of Cleveland
January 6, 1981

The nihil obstat and imprimatur are official declarations that a book or
pamphlet is free of doctrinal or moral error. No implication is contained
therein that those who have granted the nihil obstat and imprimatur agree
with the contents, opinions, or statements expressed.

Scripture passages are taken from *The New American Bible*, copyright ©
1970, by the Confraternity of Christian Doctrine, Washington, D.C. All
rights reserved.

Benziger

17337 Ventura Boulevard
Encino, California 91316
Collier Macmillan Canada, Ltd.

Printed in the United States of America

ISBN 0–02–655840–8

3 4 5 6 7 8 9   87 86 85 84 83

Contents

Introduction

You may have heard a few mild complaints from your grandparents or other adults about the recent adaptations in the Church. Some people miss the solemn High Masses which were sung in Latin and which reminded them of things eternal. Many still speak lovingly about the strict Communion fast and fish-on-Friday rule that once identified the practicing Catholic to the world.

Many of the older generation may feel upset because, to them, the changes came too fast and because they think they missed an explanation for the new things happening in their parishes.

■ Name some changes that have taken place in the Church within your memory. Ask your parents or grandparents to name some. Ask them how they feel about the changes. How do they affect you?

As an American Catholic teenager growing to adulthood in the 1980s, you are very fortunate. More than fifteen years have passed since the deliberations of Vatican II launched the Church's new self-understanding.

Theologians and scholars have been busy writing books and articles on the aims of the Council and the meaning of its documents. The real impact of what took place is only now coming into focus. You are at just the right stage of life to receive the full benefit of this study.

One of the greatest breakthroughs of the Council was a new appreciation of the role of the laity in the Church. This means that without your involvement and unique contribution, the Church of the future will not become what it could be. It is crucial for you to be aware of what is going on in the Church so that you can participate intelligently in God's plan for his Church.

This book tells you how to involve yourself in worship, and also presents the rich historical and cultural developments that led to the kind of worship we have today in the Roman Catholic Church. Your reflection on sacramental worship, especially in the Eucharist and Penance, can result in a more perceptive grasp of the liturgy and a better appreciation of the liturgical year. This heightened awareness can be a source of deep, personal happiness and comfort in your life. Your study will also make you more knowledgeable, so that you will be better equipped to share your faith in God with all who may depend on your witness. In addition, your understanding of liturgy and your gentleness in sharing your insights can help those who have trouble adjusting to the changes in the ever-maturing Church.

■ Write any questions you may have on the liturgy or the sacraments and submit them to your teacher.

PART I

MYSTERY AND WORSHIP

Worship is not part of the Christian life; it is the Christian life.

(GERALD VANN)

What is natural mystery?

What is religious mystery?

How did ancient people worship?

How did the Hebrews worship?

Sacred Presence

Lord, our God, give your people the joy of hearing your Word in every sound and of longing for your presence, more than for life itself.

(*OPENING PRAYER*, TWENTY-FIRST SUNDAY IN ORDINARY TIME)

A SENSE OF MYSTERY

Two men lounged on a ship's deck, watching the sunset. One of them stood up and stretched. "I think I'll turn in," he yawned.

The other looked at him with disbelief. "I couldn't leave this if my life depended on it!" he said, motioning toward the flaming sky. "In moments like this I sense a mysterious Presence. It gives me courage to keep going."

- What is meant by a "mysterious Presence"?
- Name some times and places when you have sensed such mystery and Presence. What did it feel like?
- Did this sense of mysterious Presence change you in any way? If so, how?

NATURAL MYSTERY

Sherlock Holmes, Ellery Queen, Nancy Drew, and Columbo are popular heroes in a unique form of entertainment: the mystery. But while most people like mystery stories, many seem strangely uneasy with mystery itself. People tend to avoid facing things that can't be explained. Mystery shows or books that consistently featured unsolved cases would soon die. Whodunits must be challenging, but in the end they must also be solvable. People want to arrive at answers, not further questions. They are frustrated if any thread is left hanging.

Many people insist that every mystery can eventually be fully explained. They are trained to believe that every effect has a cause. These people seem to take it for granted that someone will find the missing link, the undiscovered virus, or the unknown quantity. After forty-six centuries, some people still expect to find the entrance to the Great Pyramid.

To others, there is something fascinating about real mystery, even though it somehow makes them admit their limitations. Magic shows, hypnotism, demonstrations of ESP, and other evidence of the mysterious exercise a strange power over this group. Realizing that some things may be beyond them stirs these people to awe and wonder.

The Great Pyramid was built by the Egyptian ruler Khufu (Cheops) in 2900 B.C.

ESP is an abbreviation that means extrasensory perception.

RELIGIOUS MYSTERY

The sacraments were once known as *musteria,* which is the Greek word for "mysteries." A *musterion* is not the kind of mystery that one investigates in order to find a solution. Originally, the word was used in connection with pagan initiation rites. A candidate seeking entrance into a secret religious society was required to reenact the story of a particular deity in order to become a member. In performing the rite, the person became united with the god or goddess. All knowledge gained

Initiation rites are ceremonies that introduce a new person into a group.

by initiation was to be kept strictly a secret—that is, a mystery.

The Christian mysteries, or sacraments, differed from the pagan cults in two ways. First, those who had been initiated into Christianity were to proclaim their faith, not keep it secret. Second, it was not primarily the actions of the candidate that brought him or her into the Christian community, but a special call from God. The Christian religion was seen as the response of people to the actions of God.

When Saint Paul used the word *mystery,* he meant God's secret plan to save the human race, a plan God freely revealed in the course of history. Hidden in God's mind for all eternity and gradually revealed in the Old Testament, this mystery was made fully known in Jesus—a visible, touchable, audible person who revealed God in human life.

The mystery of Christ—his becoming human, his life of service, his friendship with sinners, his death, resurrection, and continuing presence in the Holy Spirit—cannot be grasped in an entire lifetime. Only gradually do people learn to understand all that Christ means. They enter into Christ's mystery insofar as they allow him to touch them and become central in their lives.

The Christian liturgy reenacts the mystery of Christ. Each year, Christians sacramentally relive the Christmas, Easter, and Pentecost mysteries. In doing so, they deepen their relationship with God and confirm their belief in his active loving presence.

- Name some things you don't understand about your religion. Can these beliefs be understood completely or someday be solved? Or are they mysteries that cannot be entirely grasped by the human mind?
- Tell what happened in each of the following events: Christmas, Easter, and Pentecost. Why is each considered to be a mystery?
- Try to imagine life without Christ, the Church, the sacraments, and feasts like Christmas and Easter. What would it be like?

EIGHT NATURAL MYSTERIES

Most people are familiar with the eight unsolved natural mysteries described below. Identify as many as you can by matching them with the following descriptions.

_____ Pyramid of Cheops   _____ Loch Ness Monster
_____ Stonehenge   _____ Easter Island Statues
_____ Nazca Lines   _____ Bermuda Triangle
_____ UFOs   _____ Yeti

1. These are two hundred long-eared Caucasian sculptures. Some are three stories high and weigh sixty tons. They were discovered two thousand miles west of the coast of Chile in 1722.
2. Its construction involved transporting stones that weighed up to thirty-five tons a distance of twenty-four miles without modern machinery. Without the aid of telescopes, this structure was precisely placed to correlate with the position of the sun and moon.
3. Its construction involved moving two-and-one-half-ton stones without modern machinery.
4. This is an area bounded by Florida, Puerto Rico, and Jamaica in which planes are reported to disappear without a trace.
5. These are strange objects, supposedly from outer space, flying individually or in groups.
6. These "abominable snowmen" are upright creatures with pointed heads and humanoid features. Their twelve-to-twenty-inch-long footprints have been photographed.
7. This giant sea slug or newt was first seen in a Scottish lake by an abbot in A.D. 565. Nearly two hundred other people have since seen this creature.
8. These forty-mile-long drawings are in the Peruvian desert. From the air, they portray geometric figures, animals, insects, flowers, and gods.

ANCIENT PEOPLE AND THE SACRED

The terms ancient people *or the* ancients *are here used to refer to all the various tribes of peoples, including the descendants of Abraham (the Hebrews), who lived in the southwest section of Asia (between Egypt and Syria) about 2,000 to 1,500 years before Christ.*

When Christians become aware of God's active presence in their lives, their natural response is to address God intimately and confidently. They adore and thank God, and, as Christ encouraged, ask God's help for their lives. But did you ever stop to wonder how ancient people, who never heard of the Bible, thought of God? Their encounters with God had, of necessity, to be different from those of people who have lived after Christ and who possess his revelation.

And yet, ancient human beings were, in some ways, much like people today. They lived close to the earth and found their world charged with sacredness and mystery. They were awed by the majesty of towering mountains and the magic of moonlight on a dark lake. They feared the danger of rushing waterfalls, violent thunderstorms, fire, and wild animals. The vastness of the sky and the unending cycle of birth, growth, death, and rebirth seemed to cast a spell over them. They understood the power of sun and rain to nourish as well as to destroy life. All these experiences spoke to them of a great power or force in and beyond nature.

Worship is something basic to human nature. When ancient people encountered mystery, they associated it with the divine. They linked experiences of wonder with the gods. They engaged in ceremonies and sacrifices to contact the gods, gain their favor, and ward off disaster. Their worship was not offered to the gigantic

boulders, the blazing sun, or the wild animals, but to the gods beyond or within these things. Because these people did not separate the mystery from particular objects, they had a sun god, a water god, a moon goddess, a mountain god, an earth goddess, a harvest goddess, a monkey god, a tree god, and even deities of such human activities as childbearing and death.

Like people of today, ancient people needed to make sense of their lives. Often they found life contradictory. It seemed full of hope on such occasions as marriage, the birth of a child, or springtime and the rebirth of nature. But life also seemed threatened by despair in such experiences as death, disaster, and human disharmony. To express their interpretation of the mysterious forces at work in the universe, ancient people created and handed down myths of their gods and heroes. Sometimes they spoke of their first ancestors, whose actions, struggles, sufferings, deaths, and resurrections established the basic patterns of nature.

Myths are fictional stories that explain, through the actions of gods, heroes, or ancestors, what a society thinks about itself and its world.

In rhythm with the seasons, the ancients dramatized their stories of creation and eternal rebirth. They enacted rituals built around the mysterious life-giving and death-dealing qualities of water. Through the dances of their witchdoctors and the offerings of their best fruits and animals, they tried to appease the gods and win healing. They celebrated meals in which partaking of consecrated food united them with the gods or strengthened them for the return to a lost paradise. Ancient people held wedding feasts and funeral banquets to solemnize the peak moments of life and death. Although they never arrived at the knowledge of God as a person or savior, they recognized the presence of the sacred and responded to the distant call of God to union with himself.

To be *consecrated* means to be set apart for sacred purposes.

- Does modern technology take the mystery out of life? Explain.
- Several years ago, some people acquired "pet rocks." These objects held personal meaning for them. Have you ever treasured something inanimate? If so, what?

THE CHOSEN PEOPLE

For centuries, ancient people searched for God. But gradually the Hebrew people began to understand that God came in search of people. They began to believe that God manifested himself through inspired words of prophets and through specific historical events as well as through nature.

See Genesis 12:6

To the Hebrews, God's first direct revelation was an appearance to Abraham at the sacred tree of Moreh. Abraham heard God speak to him inwardly, calling him to move to another land. Abraham's "moment of truth" was so real to him that he risked everything to respond to God's call.

Abraham's experience of the divine presence was an event of saving power in his life. It set in motion a chain of events that resulted in the birth of a son, Isaac, which not only saved the elderly Abraham and Sarah from the misfortune and disgrace of childlessness, but also insured that God's promise of descendants would be fulfilled. God's revelation also resulted in a kind of material salvation: Abraham and his clan grew prosperous.

Christians and Jews believe that in calling Abraham, God was preparing a people for himself. To them, God's saving power has always worked through a visible human community—whether that community be the Israelites who were the descendants of Issac or, as Christians uniquely believe, the Apostles who gathered around Jesus.

When Abraham and his descendants realized that God revealed his plan in visible signs, they made their response of faith visible. They externalized it by building stone altars and by actually living a particular life style. The Israelites believed that they were the Chosen People and that God required them to be faithful to the Covenant they had made with God. They were to perform the prescribed actions, blessings, anointings, and sacrifices as an expression of their interior faithfulness.

Jesus, a faithful Jew, visibly expressed his faith in God's call. He asked to be baptized, he preached God's kingdom, and he showed his love by dying on the cross. The early Christians showed their faith by requesting baptism and the sacrament of the Spirit and by participating in the Eucharist. Today, Christians still externally express their faith by associating themselves with the visible Church community and by actively celebrating the sacraments.

- Have you ever sensed God "speaking" in your life? If so, when? What did you hear God telling you?
- How are you responding to God's call in your life?
- Name some ways you visibly express your faith.

DEALING WITH THE SACRED

The book of Genesis, written by the descendants of Abraham, contains stories of prehistoric times dealing with creation and the entry of sin into the world. These stories describe the way ancient people interpreted God's plan for the world. Natural disasters such as famine, earthquake, and volcanic eruption were considered punishments from heaven for the growing moral corruption of the people. This corruption was seen in hatred between family members, divisions and rivalries among tribes, wars between nations, and sexual perversions.

Enoch, Noah, and Abraham represent those people who responded to God, insofar as he could then be known. The stories of the safety of Noah's Ark and of Abraham's escape from the destruction of Sodom and Gomorrah present a humanity that strayed far from God and a God who constantly brought new beginnings out of rampant evil.

Though mixed with superstitious practices, the natural inclination of these earliest peoples was to reach out toward the divine. They responded to God's dimly perceived presence with the following basic elements of worship:

Intuition of a superior being. Prehistoric people sensed the existence of a power greater than themselves as the source and controller of nature. It was not until God's revelation to Abraham that the power behind nature began to take on a face and become a Someone. Even in the later and more advanced civilizations of Greece and Rome, many philosophers could not reason to the fact that the "highest" god was Someone who created, cared about, and came very close to his people.

Recognition of this being's transcendence. Although early people associated their gods with specific things or places like rocks and mountains, they believed that the sacred presence originated outside of the natural world. In this, they had the beginnings of an insight into the true identity of God as one who is wholly other, or transcendent.

Response in hope of salvation. By responding to this nameless, faceless power in rituals and sacrifices, ancient people established a saving relationship that they believed restored and increased their vitality, well-being, and favor with the divine.

Through their response to the manifestation of God in nature, the ancient people were able to find salvation.

Transcendence is the condition of being above and independent of the material universe.

LITURGY

In these people, God was already preparing the soil of humanity to receive the seed of his Word.

The *Word* of God is Jesus.

The experience of the ancient peoples shows that all humanity has received the call of God to communion with himself. Those who never receive his revelation in Christ are able to find wisdom when they respond to his presence in creation or natural revelation. Nature, then, is sacramental in the broad sense, because through it God extends a call of salvation to which people are capable of responding.

Sacramental means having the power to mediate God's grace or help.

Even when, by ignorance or by deliberate choice, people try to cut themselves off from God, God shows an active concern. Throughout history, he has sent religious leaders to point a clear and definite course leading to his divine love. This revelation is referred to as divine revelation. From the beginning of time, then, God has created ways to discover his presence. These ways increased in clarity until God directly revealed himself in the person of his Son, Jesus.

An Indian Prayer

O Great Spirit,
    whose voice I hear in the winds,
    and whose breath gives life to all the
      world, hear me!
    I am small and weak; I need your
      strength and wisdom.
Let me walk in beauty, and make my eyes
      behold the red and purple sunset.
Make my hands respect the things you have
      made and my ears sharp to hear your
      voice.
Make me wise so that I may understand the
      things you have taught my people.
Let me learn the lessons you have hidden in
      every leaf and rock . . .
Make me always ready to come to you with
      clean hands and straight eyes,
So when life fades, as the fading sunset,
      my spirit may come to you without
      shame.

SUMMING UP

Use the following questions to help you review the main themes of this chapter.

1. Why are people sometimes uneasy with mystery?
2. How does religious mystery differ from natural mystery? How are the two mysteries similar?
3. What are the "Christian mysteries"? How do they differ from the pagan mysteries?
4. What is meant by the expression "mystery of Christ"?
5. Where in nature did the ancient people encounter God? Were these experiences religious? Why or why not?
6. What elements of worship were found in the ancient peoples' response to the divine presence in creation?
7. What is the difference between natural and divine revelations?
8. Give some examples of the following statements: God always works through a group or community; God always gives visible signs of his invisible presence; God requires an exterior response.

Words to Know

natural mystery, religious mystery, musterion, initiation rites, cults, ancient people, myth, transcendence, natural revelation, divine revelation

Think/Talk/Write

1. Someone has said that the trouble with not having a goal is that you spend your life running up and down the field without getting a touchdown. How can an awareness of God's presence help you establish goals in your life? How would an awareness of God affect the ways you attempt to achieve your goals?
2. Ancient people celebrated in order to honor the gods and to ask for help in the successful capture of a mammoth. After the capture, the people thanked the gods for the food, clothing, and tools provided from the mammoth. On what occasions do you pray in order to

"psych yourself up" for the accomplishment of some goal? Which of these goals, if any, are religious in nature? What are some kinds of thanksgiving celebrations?

3. Make a list of all the reasons why someone would worship God. Compare your list with others in the class, and then try to rank these reasons in order of importance.

Activities

1. Make a survey of TV programs shown during prime time. Record all references to prayer, God, church, or religion on a chart and tell how often religious themes were treated and in what way.
2. Using slides from your school library or from your own collection, put together a visual presentation of scenes that might stimulate meditation on the presence of God. For something different, you might try to choose scenes that are not from nature—for instance, children playing around a water hydrant in an inner-city environment. Show your presentation to the class.
3. Bring to class a recording that helps you feel the presence of God. Before playing it for the class, present a prayer or other explanation that points to the inspirational elements it contains.

What kinds of places have special meaning to you?

When does a special place become a sacred place?

How do the sacred places of Moses affect you?

Why is Jesus like a sacred place?

Sacred Places

When the Lord saw Moses coming over to look more closely, God called out to him from the bush, "Moses! Moses!" He answered, "Here I am." God said, "Come no nearer! Remove the sandals from your feet, for the place where you stand is holy ground."

(EXODUS 3:4–5)

KINDS OF PLACES

Consider how certain places can make you feel lost or found. Practically every day you lose things and find them. Once in a while, you even get lost yourself. Being lost is a matter of becoming separated or "unglued" from the right place—the place where you are supposed to be, the place where you feel all together.

The strange thing is that places themselves have the power to make you feel found or lost. Although some people may enjoy changing their environment frequently, there is something satisfying about being able to kick off your shoes and feel at home in a particular place. Certain places make you feel more at home because they bring back comforting memories. They are places where important events of your life happened: the place where you were born, where you spent your first day at school, your grandparents' house, the farm where you had a carefree summer, a beach where you met someone you like.

- Name some places that are full of memories for you. Explain why they are important in your life.
- If you've ever gone back after some time to a place that held good memories for you, were you able to capture the original feeling it gave you? Why or why not?

The sad fact is that you can't count on the places where you once experienced happiness to give you that feeling again. For one thing, they often change: they become shabby, are redecorated, or are even torn down. And if they remain the same, you have changed. The high swing or the corner sandbox where you spent so many happy hours of your childhood turns out, when you've grown a little, to be quite small and ordinary. The trouble with memorable places is that you can't stay in them always, and you can't carry them around with you.

SACRED PLACES

Since ancient times, people have recognized that certain places possess an unusual power to bring deep peace. The power of these places does not depend on one's mood or on personal memories, but on something more real and unchanging—a special presence of God.

You've heard of, or perhaps even experienced, what might be called a moment of truth. It happens when you encounter something or someone greater than yourself. It gathers together everything inside you and makes you feel complete. It resembles the moment of relief and joy that came to you when, after the panic of being lost, you first glimpsed your parents heading toward you.

The patriarchs of the Old Testament experienced such moments of truth when they encountered God. Just as lovers carve trees to mark the place where they enjoyed one another's company, the patriarchs placed stone markers at the sites where they had experienced

A *patriarch* is a father or male leader of a tribe. Abraham, Isaac, Jacob, and Jacob's twelve sons were all patriarchs.

See Genesis 28:18–22

In the Old Testament, oil was often used to consecrate things or persons.

God. Recognizing them as sacred places, they sometimes poured oil over the stones to consecrate them to God's worship.

- Where do you worship God?
- Is this place sacred because you worship there, or do you worship there because it is sacred? Explain your answer.
- There are many different churches. Do you think all of them are holy places?
- Describe some places where you feel at home.
- What do you think this "at home" feeling has to do with one's ability to pray?
- Look up the following references from the book of Genesis and find the names of the places where stones (altars) were set up to mark where God had revealed himself: Genesis 12:6–8; 13:3–4, 18; 21:31–33; 26:23–26; 28:10–22; 33:18–20; 35:9–15.

MEETING GOD

Mountains, woods, seashores, and deserts can become sacred space. But, because of their consecration or special blessing, churches are recognized as special places for meeting the divine. A church is a house for the People of God. When you enter, the door acts as a divider. It separates you from the changing world and transports you to a place where you can more easily encounter God.

In some cultures, sacred places actually contain a second door in the form of a roof opening that symbolizes God's entrance from the world above. Smoke vents in the yurts of certain Central Asian herdsmen have this function. In other cultures, ceremonies that focus on a person's head indicate that the crown of the head is the door that leads into sacred space. This custom suggests that meeting God is more a matter of what goes on inside a person than of being in a particular place.

We do not *necessarily* encounter God in a sacred place. It is easy to become distracted and to enter a sacred place somewhat unthinkingly. For a genuine experience of meeting God, we must prepare ourselves. Only then can God be encountered.

The reason for certain ritual actions that often accompany our entry into sacred places is to stir up faith. These actions can remind us of the sacred and actually initiate us into the sacred. Moses was asked to remove his shoes before approaching the burning bush where God revealed his presence. Different religions require bowing, removing footwear, donning headgear, lowering veils, prostrating, kneeling, turning in a certain direction, or signing oneself with blessed water upon entering a sacred place.

Yurts are circular, dome-shaped portable tents used by the Mongols of Siberia.

To *don* something means to put it on.

MOSES AND SACRED PLACES

Isaiah 2:3

When God spoke to Moses in the burning bush (about 1200 B.C.), he revealed himself by name. From that moment, God was known to his people as a definite person, "Yahweh," which means "I am." But Moses had only heard a voice. In the strange bush that burned and was not destroyed, he could not see God as you see others. Later, in the desert, God's presence was both revealed and hidden in the pillar of fire and the luminous cloud.

Throughout the Old Testament, the privileged encounters with God are described as occurring on mountains because the early peoples associated the mystery of divinity with the vast heights of the sky. "Come, let us climb the Lord's mountain, to the house of the God of Jacob," writes Isaiah. The mountain encounter with God was an experience of deep happiness. Moses' meeting with God on Mount Sinai was far superior to what the ancients had experienced in nature. This encounter on Sinai resulted in a spelled-out, mutual contract in which God and his People agreed, through the mediation of Moses, to be faithful to each other. The Book of Exodus says that the face of Moses was so radiant when he descended Sinai that he had to veil it.

See Exodus 34:33

The one difference between the self-communication of God to his Chosen People and his communication through creation to people of other cultures is that God now took the initiative. He started the action. Moses was not looking for God in the burning bush; God attracted Moses' attention in order to speak to him. The Chosen People didn't reach God by their own efforts of meditation or penance. He reached into their everyday lives, just as he had done for Abraham. It is true that they needed faith to recognize God's intervention, but he acted in ways they could see and feel—through physically destructive plagues, blood on doorposts, a safe passage through the sea, and the conquest of their enemies.

Most astonishing of all, God communicated with Moses, revealing his identify and plans. His revelation

LITURGY

was concrete and specific, and based in history. And it was always expressed in terms that people could grasp easily.

All God's saving interventions were for one purpose: to build a people through whom his plan could be safely carried out and eventually transmitted to all other nations.

As a visible sign of his special presence among the Chosen People, God instructed them to build a sacred place—the ark of the covenant—which was to be placed in the tent of meeting. God determined everything about the ark: its measurements, its construction, its adornments. It was to be a portable chest of acacia wood overlaid with gold inside and out, about three feet nine inches by two feet three inches by two feet three inches. A gold plate, called the "mercy seat," rested on the top of the ark. Two cherubim faced each other on either side so that their wings overshadowed the seat.

See Exodus 25:21–22

The Israelites often recalled God's wondrous deeds to them in songs and ceremonies celebrated around the ark. Whenever a decision was needed as they moved through the desert, the Israelites prayed to Yahweh at the ark. It was the ark that was placed in the forefront of the whole column of people during their many years in the desert. It was the ark, too, that was carried first across the Jordan when the Chosen People entered the Promised Land.

The two stone tablets of the commandments, a vessel of manna, and the rod of Aaron were kept inside the ark. They symbolized the concern God had shown to his People in the past. The ark was a reminder of the deepest purpose of Israel's existence—that God cared in a special way. By means of this sacred place, the Israelites addressed God whenever they wanted. This portable symbol reminded them of God's nearness.

- Where are the places you meet God?
- Name some times when you felt God taking the initiative in your life.

SACRED POLES

A *nomad* is someone who is homeless and who wanders from place to place. The *bush* is unexplored territory.

Reverence for God's presence has not been limited to the Israelites. Some nomadic hunting tribes who were recently discovered in the bush of Australia carry around with them a long, consecrated pole hewn from a giant tree. Other people in Indonesia keep a thirty-five-foot cedar pole, more than half of which projects out of their ceremonial house.

These tribal peoples believe that their ancestors climbed these poles into the skies, the place of the gods. The poles are symbols of the ability to pierce "the heavens." The poles supposedly enabled their ancestors to share the divine power they found when they entered the "sacred space" of the upper regions. There they learned the purpose and meaning of their lives, and they were assured that the gods cared.

To these tribal peoples, the sacred pole is the pillar of the universe. It is the center or axis of their world. Without it, they cannot live. When their pole breaks or is stolen, the people are known to lose interest in everything. They refuse to eat; some simply let themselves die.

■ Why do you think sacred places are important to human life?

THE MONARCHY AND SACRED PLACES

When the Israelites formed themselves into a kingdom, King David saw the ark as the symbol needed to unify the northern and southern tribes. He had the ark brought to Jerusalem (about 1000 B.C.), which was to serve as the capital and sacred center of the nation. David had hoped to build a fitting temple there to house this ark, but through the prophet Nathan he was told that though the time was near for building such a sacred See 2 Samuel 7:1–17 place, he would not be the one to do it.

David's son, Solomon, fulfilled his father's dream by building the magnificent Temple of Jerusalem (about 950 B.C.). The ark was placed in the Holy of Holies inside the Temple. There, in the one Temple of Israel, the Israelites worshiped Yahweh. It was every Israelite's goal to visit this most holy place at least once in the course of his or her lifetime. The psalmist composed special songs for pilgrimage to Jerusalem, the Holy City.

I rejoiced because they said to me,
    "We will go up to the house of the Lord."
And now we have set foot
    within your gates, O Jerusalem—
Jerusalem, built as a city
    with compact unity.

To it the tribes go up,
    the tribes of the Lord,
According to the decree for Israel,
    to give thanks to the name of the Lord.

The construction of the Temple was completed in A.D. *67, only three years before its total destruction in* A.D. *70.*

The Israelites believed that God was present in Palestine, the Promised Land. They believed that God had chosen Jerusalem as the center of the earth and that the Temple was the privileged place of God's presence. From this sacred place, Yahweh's saving Word, in all its power, pulsed out to the rest of the world. There, in the sacrifices of animals, the Chosen People thanked Yahweh for his favors and made offerings to him to atone for their sins.

Today, none of our holy places—Saint Peter's Basilica in Rome, the Dome of the Rock in Jerusalem (the holy shrine of the Muslims), the Holy Sepulchre in Jerusalem—have the same vital meaning that the Temple had for the Israelites. When Solomon's Temple was destroyed at the time of the Babylonian Captivity (587 B.C.), the people as a nation almost perished. Only with the help of God did some few—a remnant—remain loyal to the Covenant. The first thing they did on returning from captivity to Jerusalem fifty years later was to rebuild the Temple.

Even though the Israelites believed they had been chosen from among all the nations on earth to receive God's self-revelation, they knew God's Covenant with them was incomplete. Two prophets, Jeremiah and Ezekiel, foretold the day when God would make a new covenant with Israel. The Israelites gradually began to expect a Messiah, a king who would lead the people in the ways pleasing to God.

JESUS, THE NEW MEETING PLACE

In a sense, Jesus is himself a sacred place. He is the place where the divine meets the human. On certain occasions, Jesus used place words to describe himself. When the Pharisees challenged Jesus for allowing his disciples to pick wheat on the Sabbath, Jesus responded by saying, "I assure you, there is something greater than the Temple here." Jesus later said to the priests who questioned his authority in driving out the money changers from the Temple, "Destroy this Temple, and in three days I will raise it up." Matthew 12:6 John 2:19

In these two statements, Jesus made the greatest revelation ever to be granted to the human race. In effect, he is saying, "I myself am the true Temple—the sure place where God and human beings meet. I am *the* sacred place where all the world can unfailingly find meaning and salvation."

Three of Jesus' Apostles began to understand this message one day when Jesus led them to a high mountain. There, he was transfigured before them. He revealed to them that he was the Messiah, the Promised One. He assured them not only of God's existence, but of his love for them.

Peter's reaction is reflected in his comment to Jesus: "How good it is for us to be here!" Peter was only on an ordinary mountain, but because he had truly experienced God's presence in Jesus, he felt a "rightness" about everything. He felt so good at being there that, the Gospel says, he wanted to build three tents and remain always. He was so overwhelmed that he wasn't making much sense. Mark 9:5

Somehow, Peter and the others actually touched eternity—the place of no space and no time. Unlike the ancients who had sensed a sacred presence in the mountains, sun, and sea, the three Apostles were truly in a sacred space when they were with Jesus. They knew themselves to be in personal contact with God. Unlike the ancients whose knowledge of God came through nature, and unlike the invisible presence of

God in Israel, the Apostles were able to recognize that, in Jesus, God himself had entered human history. In loving Jesus, the Apostles were actually united with God.

KNOWLEDGE AND POWER

See Matthew 16:15–17

One of the most important questions ever asked is the one Jesus put to his Apostles at Caesarea Philippi: "Who do you say I am?" When Peter answered, "You are the Messiah, the Son of the living God," Jesus praised him, saying that this knowledge had come to him directly from the Father.

But salvation does not consist of knowledge alone. In their contact with Jesus, the Apostles not only learned about the kingdom, they received power, courage, and the ability to live according to God's plan. By their experience of Jesus on the mountain, the Apostles were able to make it through the very difficult days of the passion. They were given entry into sacred space, not to get away from the real world but to return with divine power.

For twentieth-century Christians, being "found" by God in sacred space does not depend on God's presence in nature, though he may still be sensed there. It does not depend on gifts, talents, intelligence, or the "right" mood—although it does require a living body and a living faith. Today, sacred space is where the People of God encounter the risen Lord in the sacraments, in Scripture, in prayer, and in love for one another.

God has chosen to "find" us in these forms. Through them, we worship him and become holy like him. Since the coming of Christ, sacred space is wherever two or three persons gather in Christ's name—in the Christian community and in celebrating the Eucharist.

Jesus' cross is the only sacred tree with power to keep people from despair. It speaks the truth about the meaning of life—that humans are worth God's sacrifice. It makes each person complete by giving him or her a place or home in the kingdom of eternal life.

God's presence in Jesus is far superior to that experienced by the ancients or by the devout Jews who awaited the Savior. Yet, it remains a mystery to be grasped only by faith. The risen Christ is an inexhaustible mystery. His presence in the Church, the presence of his saving action in the sacraments, and Christians' participation in divine life are all mysteries.

Psalm 84

How lovely is your dwelling place,
    O Lord of hosts!
My soul yearns and pines
    for the courts of the Lord.
My heart and my flesh
    cry out for the living God.
Even the sparrow finds a home,
    and the swallow a nest
    in which she puts her young—
Your altars, O Lord of hosts,
    my King and my God! . . .
I had rather one day in your courts
    than a thousand elsewhere;
I had rather lie at the threshold of the
      house of my God
    than dwell in the tents of the wicked.

SUMMING UP

Use the following questions to help you review the
main themes of this chapter.

1. What is a "moment of truth"? How does it relate to an encounter
   with God?
2. How did Abraham's encounter with God "save" him?
3. What were some visible signs that God gave to the Israelites as proof
   of his continuing presence?
4. In what important way did God's revelation to Moses differ from that
   offered to peoples of other cultures?
5. Why do societies and individuals lose hope without some kind of
   relationship with the divine?
6. Briefly outline God's gradual revelation of himself through the history
   of the Chosen People.
7. Why did Israel almost disappear as a nation when its Temple was
   destroyed?
8. How can modern people meet God today?
9. Why is Jesus called "the meeting place of God"?

Words to Know

patriarch, revelation ("moment of truth"), consecrate, ark of the covenant, Temple

Think/Talk/Write

1. Look up these Scripture passages: Genesis 12:6–7; Exodus 3:11–15,
   25:8–30; 2 Samuel 7:2–7; 1 Kings 6:1–14; Psalm 84:1–3; Isaiah
   1:12–20; John 2:19–21; 1 Corinthians 11:23–24. Write a composition
   telling the story of how God broke into time to communicate with
   his Chosen People. Trace how he gradually revealed himself. Incorporate at least five of the passages.
2. Find these passages in Saint John's Gospel in which Jesus applies
   the name "I am" to himself: John 6:35; 8:12, 58; 10:11; 11:25; 14:6;
   15:5; 17:24. What is John trying to say by having Jesus use this phrase?

3. Someone has said that the Lincoln Memorial is a waste of money. Sidney Waugh, an artist, says that the same Lincoln Memorial has more real meaning for the common person that a hundred volumes of political theory. Do you think monuments or other works of art are a waste? What Christian works of art are you familiar with in this country or in other parts of the world? Look up information about one of them. Do you think the money spent to build and maintain this work is wasted?

Activities

1. Robert Frost, in his poem "Stopping by Woods on a Snowy Evening," tells about a man driving along the edge of a woods on a cold, snowy night. Becoming absorbed in the sheer beauty and quiet of the snow, he experienced a strong desire to stop and watch the woods fill up with snow. The poem concludes with these lines: "The woods are lovely, dark and deep,/But I have promises to keep, and miles to go before I sleep." Write a letter to the late Mr. Frost explaining what benefit might have come to the man in the poem by lingering a while in that sacred place.
2. If you draw, do a cartoon strip or a series of drawings developing the ideas of the first exercise in Think/Talk/Write.
3. Write a composition or arrange a collage to show Christ as the fulfillment of all meaning through these symbols: rock (stone), way (gate), cross, eternal dwelling place (home).

THREE

How do we communicate with signs and symbols?

What is the difference between simple and complex signs?

How are sacraments symbolic actions and words?

How can we prepare to encounter sacramental symbols?

Signs and Symbols

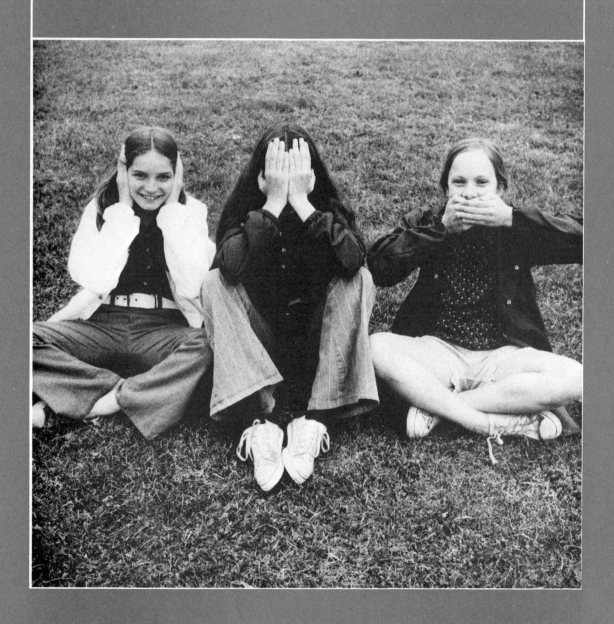

The thing which becomes a symbol retains its original form and its original content. It does not become, so to speak, an empty shell into which another content is poured; in itself, through its own existence, it makes another reality transparent which cannot appear in any other form.

(G. SCHOLEM, MAJOR TRENDS IN JEWISH MYSTICISM)

SIGN LANGUAGE

Hermine woke with a start. "Bud Bosiglove . . . Bud Bosiglove . . ." The name rolled around in her mind a while before she was awake enough to remember that Bud Bosiglove was the new student who had been admitted to her history class the week before.

Hermine glanced at her clock. Its illuminated dial showed 2:30. Why did she have so strong a sense of Bud Bosiglove at 2:30 in the morning? She had hardly said a word to him since giving him his text and an outline of the course. "Maybe he's in trouble," Hermine thought. She whispered a quick prayer for him, rolled over, and fell asleep again.

The next morning there was a flurry of excitement in the teachers' lounge. Everyone was talking about how Bud Bosiglove had been killed in an auto crash. Hermine turned pale.

"When?" she murmured, almost afraid to ask.

"His car went out of control, hit a guard rail, and

exploded sometime around seven last night," Jim Hoover, the geometry teacher, answered.

Hermine relaxed slightly.

Then Jim added, "He died at 2:30 this morning."

- Do you think this story could be true? Why or why not?
- How would you have felt if you were Hermine? Why?

Although some people communicate by ESP, it certainly is not the ordinary way people get across to others what is in their minds and hearts. Communicating without the use of the senses may work for angels, but for humans, ideas and emotions are nontransferable unless they are embodied. They must be packaged in signs that can be unwrapped by others' eyes, ears, taste, smell, or touch.

A sign is something that suggests the existence of something else that cannot be known exactly. For example, if you want to let others know you're tired, you have to make sounds and signs such as saying "I'm tired," yawning, slouching, or sleeping.

Human beings are expert sign-makers. Daily they make hundreds of body-signs and action-signs: they wave, drum their fingers, salute, and eat. They make many sound-signs: they speak, whistle, or give a cheer. They make written signs: they record messages on walls, clay tablets, papyrus, wood, glass, plastic, and metal. They use objects as signs—objects such as poison, wine, diamonds, statues, candles, or firecrackers.

- What other signs do people use to communicate?
- Choose any five signs from the examples above, or those that you've mentioned, and tell what they suggest. (For example, saluting signifies respect.)

SIMPLE AND COMPLEX SIGNS

All signs point to something beyond themselves. A *simple sign* conveys a single idea to the mind in a one-to-one relationship. Once the sign gets its message across, its work is finished. A traffic light, a barber pole, and a "wet paint" sign are some examples of simple signs. The "wet paint" sign is not wet, and the sign itself may remain posted long after the paint has dried.

- Name some other simple signs.
- What are the signs of a cold? Fear? Rain? Sorrow? Spring? Joy?

The second kind of sign, a *symbol,* is richer in both its meaning and what it can do. It represents something else by association or resemblance. Like a simple sign, a symbol is a form of communication that points to something outside itself. But unlike a sign, a symbol also contains within itself something of the meaning it conveys. A symbol somehow brings about what it represents. Your body, for example, is a symbol of your invisible spirit. It outwardly shows your interior poise or nervousness, love or hate.

A sign appeals to the mind. A symbol stimulates the imagination by carrying with it a whole background of feelings, memories, and sense experiences. A sign conveys an idea; a symbol conveys an experience. Your school jacket is an example.

To people who are not well acquainted with your school, your jacket is, first of all, a sign. It identifies the name of the school you attend. But if your school has just won the state championship in football, that jacket becomes the symbol of everything your school stands for: discipline, achievement, courage, excellence, school spirit, self-control, responsibility, initiative, and leadership. Its colors will remind you of your school years for the rest of your life. Because many people in the school wear a school jacket, you feel a oneness with them. If you paid for the jacket yourself, wearing it gives you a sense of independence. In some ways, the jacket is part of your own identity, and its symbolism has the power to stir up all sorts of feelings and memories. If the losing team were to drag it through the mud or set it on fire, you would feel it very personally.

THE MEANING BEHIND SYMBOLS

Symbols can grow in meaning. For example, your school jacket may mean more to you as a senior than it did when you were a sophomore. Long after graduation, seeing a picture of yourself wearing the school jacket may bring back the joys, excitement, and fun of high school. Symbols grow as you grow. Their value may also change. If, for some reason, during your high school years you got into trouble with the administration or were expelled from your school, the sight of your jacket might arouse bitterness, rebellion, or shame.

- On a piece of paper, write the word "flame." Think about any ideas it generates. Next, place a lit candle in a darkened room. Experience it.
- What difference did you notice between this experience of a flame and the first experience on a piece of paper? Which was more alive for you?
- Which of the following do you think a burning flame symbolizes? Why?

zeal	creation
love	knowledge
hate	peace
punishment	friendship
an old person	the Spirit
wisdom	patience
self-giving	goodness
courage	jealousy
fear	faith
youth	prayer

You may have found yourself disagreeing with others over some choices. This is because symbols contain deep and almost endless meanings. Some of these meanings are built up by personal experience, training, culture, and history.

- Name some symbols cherished by your family that might not be special to another family. Explain.

SACRAMENTAL SYMBOLS

You have seen that human beings have always used symbols to express their faith. After some time it became clear that nature was not to be worshiped because God has his own existence apart from his creation. God became so distinct in his identity that under his inspiration the Chosen People constructed symbols like the ark and the brazen serpent in order to experience his specialized presence. Natural and man-made symbols continue to speak today of God's presence, goodness, beauty and creativity.

The brazen serpent was a bronze serpent that Moses held up on a pole in the desert. All who looked on it were cured of deadly snakebite. See Numbers 21:4–9.

■ Take a few moments to ponder one of the following symbols. What does it reveal to you about God?

a sunrise	the grass
the moon	a bird
ice	a rose
water	a mountain

Sacraments are rich symbolic actions that make use of words, symbols, and simple signs. For instance, the sanctuary light is a sign of Christ's presence The paschal candle is a symbol of Christ. The celebration of the Eucharist, with all its gestures, is the richest symbolic action human beings can ever experience. Yet you may be confused by the fact that sacraments are sometimes called signs even though they are not simple idea-bearers, such as a green light. When applied to a sacrament, the word "sign" is used in a broader sense to mean its total action, words, gestures, prayers, symbols, and signs.

If you have seen *Fiddler on the Roof,* you may have been struck by the intimate friendship the Jewish people have with God. They bring God into every cranny of their lives, whether in the joy of a wedding, the anguish of exile, or the routine of their daily work. The many ceremonies and blessings of the Jews are symbolic. Jesus brought the Jewish symbols and rituals to an even fuller development by his gift of the sacraments, especially the Eucharist.

LITURGY

Sacramental symbols can have layer upon layer of meaning. Bread, for instance, has a symbolic tradition reaching back to the beginning of recorded time. Bread has nourished billions of people since creation. For Christians, the Eucharistic bread symbolically reflects the traditions of Israel going back to Melchizedeck's blessing of Abram, the unleavened bread eaten in haste by the Hebrews on the night of Passover, and God's great gift of manna that saved the Israelites in the desert. Eucharistic bread also reminds Christians of the times Jesus fed the thousands with a few loaves, and of Jesus' last meal, when he consecrated the bread as his own body.

See Genesis 14:18; Exodus 12:37–39, 16:1–8

Then, too, the Christian community has a two-thousand-year tradition of sacred bread. Countless Eucharistic meals have been celebrated from the time of the Apostles—in the private homes of the early Christians, in the catacombs, in the great medieval cathedrals, in small country churches, in large parishes, at formal high Masses, in secret hiding places, in the glorious setting of the Vatican, and in the foxholes of war.

Besides all these associations, each Christian has his or her own personal memories of Eucharistic bread. There are memories of special occasions such as First Communion, Confirmation, Matrimony, Religious Profession, or Ordination. There are also memories of intimate, peaceful communions of ordinary days, and the soul-shaking liturgies of the high feast days.

- Which Eucharistic celebrations are most vivid in your life?

The concrete symbols used in the sacraments—water, bread, wine, and oil—are laden with meaning and associations. But the entire action of each sacrament, from beginning to end, is a sign with rich symbolic overtones as well.

- Recall your own associations with and memories of each of these symbols: water, wine, bread, oil.
- What actions of Jesus symbolize God's love? What actions of the liturgy celebrate these events?

SYMBOLIC ACTIONS

Sirach 43:33

When God revealed himself to his Chosen People, he and his prophets described him through symbols. As one prophet wrote, "Who can see him and describe him? Or who can praise him as he is?" God came to his People *through* visible actions that actually saved them from different kinds of evil: slavery in Egypt, starvation in the desert, defeat by enemies, and idolatry. All these actions symbolized a God who was gracious to his Chosen People without any merit on their part.

Above all, the Chosen People kept sacred the memory of the Covenant God had made with them. Through rituals—the symbolic actions of what God had done for them—the Israelites reminded themselves again and again of his faithful love. In this way, they recalled the past. Over the centuries, their liturgies continually renewed the memory of God's saving acts. These actions helped them to receive God's deliverance in their present lives. They also provided a way for the Israelites to look ahead with the expectation that God would send a Savior to end their hardships forever.

A *liturgy* is a public act of worship.

■ Read the following passages from the Old Testament that speak of the worship of the Chosen People, and then match the type of worship with the correct Scripture readings.

Scripture Passages
Genesis 1:1–2, 4a; Leviticus 23:33–44; Exodus 23:16, 34:22; 1 Kings 8:31–40

Types of Worship
Thanksgiving feasts for barley and wheat harvests that saved the people from starving.

Seven-day Festival of Booths to worship God for sheltering his people while they were in the desert.

Prayers in the Temple to beg God for punishment of enemies, forgiveness of sin, rain for the crops, and protection from plague and epidemics.

The weekly Sabbaths that celebrated God's act of creation.

SYMBOLIC POSTURE

Each Muslim believer sits and kneels on a small, beautifully designed rug during the five required daily prayer rituals. Each prayer ritual, called a *rakah,* consists of seven body positions and six prayers.

1. *Position:* The worshiper stands facing Mecca with hands raised along the side of the face. The fingers point upward. *Prayer:* Allahu Akbar—God is most great!
2. *Position:* Hands are placed on stomach, right on top of left. *Prayer:* Praise be to Allah, Lord of the Worlds, the Beneficent, the Merciful.
3. *Position:* Hands are placed on knees, while the worshiper bows. *Prayer:* Glory be to my Lord, the Great!
4. *Position:* The worshiper stands, letting arms dangle at his or her sides. *Prayer:* Glory be to my Lord, the Great!
5. *Position:* Worshiper kneels, touching rug with forehead, nose, palms of hands, knees, and toes. *Prayer:* Glory be to my Lord, the Most High!
6. *Position:* With hands on top of knees, the worshiper, still kneeling, sits upright on heels. *Prayer:* Allahu Akbar—God is most great!
7. *Position:* Repetition of positions five and six, with face turned to the right. *Prayer:* Peace be with you.

The morning prayer of a Muslim requires two *rakahs,* the noon prayer four, the midafternoon prayer four, the sunset prayer three, and the evening prayer four.

- What bodily postures and hand gestures do Catholics use in their worship?
- What is the reason that all religions engage the body for the expression of interior religious sentiments?

SYMBOLIC WORDS

Words are symbols. Because they are personal and direct, they are clearer than objects and events. They make the meaning of symbols specific. Many people don't like to be asked to explain their meaning when they speak because they expect words to be plain. But they don't mind being asked what symbols mean because symbols can be ambiguous.

Ambiguous means vague.

An angry wife might interpret the bouquet of roses sent by her estranged husband on their anniversary as a bitter mockery of the roses he brought her on their first date. By his addition of the four small but powerful words "I still love you," the intended meaning of the roses cannot be mistaken.

Estranged means separated or become like strangers.

The inspired words of the prophets in the Old Testament clarified the meaning of God's symbolic actions in Israel. Over and over, the prophets repeated how God had chosen and saved his People and how, even in calamities like the destruction of their Temple, God was blessing his People.

■ Describe the action and the meaning Jesus gives to it by his words in these passages: Luke 18:15–17, 19:1–10, 22:17–20; John 13:1–17.

SACRAMENTAL WORDS

Because the Hebrews considered God as one, they could not separate the communications of God from God himself. He *was* his Word. Therefore, when God spoke, he himself came to his People in his Word.

The word of the sacraments is God's Word, even though it is spoken by the human voice. It makes the symbols and symbolic actions of the sacraments definite and clear. What is more, God himself comes through this Word. But the word of the sacraments is more than God's presence. When God speaks, his Word always makes things happen. The Word of God is the vehicle and cause of God's power. The prophet Isaiah explains it thus:

Isaiah 55:10–11

> For just as from the heavens
> > the rain and snow come down
> And do not return there
> > till they have watered the earth,
> > making it fertile and fruitful,
> Giving seed to those who sow
> > and bread to those who eat,
> So shall my Word be
> > that goes forth from my mouth;
> It shall not return to me void,
> > but shall do my will,
> > achieving the end for which I sent it.

Word and act are one in God. As the Book of Sirach states, "At God's Word were his works brought into being; they do his will as he has ordained for them." God both speaks and acts through the word of the sacraments, and he both speaks and acts through the actions of the rite. God's Word is expressed in the human word and in the human action.

Sirach 42:15

A *rite* is the set words and actions that make up a sacrament or other religious ceremony. One traditional definition of *sacrament* is a visible sign of inward grace (God's favor) that accomplishes what it signifies. A more modern definition is a symbol of Christ's saving action reenacted by the Church.

- ■ How is God shown to have created the world in the first chapter of Genesis?
- ■ Find the words of God Saint Paul speaks of in the following texts: 1 Corinthians 1:18; Acts of the Apostles 13:26; 2 Corinthians 5:18. In each case, what synonym do you find for "word"?

HOW TO ENCOUNTER SYMBOLS

The Statue of Liberty, which raises its lamp of freedom and justice over the New York harbor, has stirred hopes and dreams in the hearts of thousands of immigrants. Most Americans who witnessed the telecast of the planting of the Stars and Stripes on the moon were moved with emotions of patriotism. Symbols greatly enrich life. But they speak only to those who listen.

Because they are capable of many possible interpretations, symbols ask us to use our imaginations. They require faith in their power to call forth our deepest human emotions. A gift of flowers or a single dew-trimmed blade of grass has no symbolic meaning at all unless we actively exercise our belief in the reality of the love that someone (or Someone) means to express by it.

To experience symbols fully, we need to cultivate openness and imagination. Being too scientific or too logical can make us miss their many dimensions. Instead of thinking too precisely about symbols, analyzing and dissecting them like frogs in a biology lab, we need to cultivate a sense of wonder and alertness to the possibilities of things. We need a readiness to let their meaning penetrate our hearts. Sometimes we may completely overlook a breathtaking sunset or the magic of a starlit sky simply because we're too busy to give it our attention.

In other words, symbols are empty and lifeless when we are unwilling to take the risk of faith, when we are closed or negative to their many possibilities, or when we refuse to let them into our hearts. If we approach symbols with the simplicity of children and allow ourselves to respond to them freely, they can become bridges between each of us, and between us and the Spirit at work in the world.

- Do you think Americans are good at responding to symbols? Do they show their response to symbols publicly?
- Do most Catholics pay attention to and really participate in the ceremonies at religious services? Why or why not?
- Rate your own involvement in Sunday worship on a scale of one to ten, ten being a great degree of involvement and one being no involvement.
- Some thinkers have said that the emphasis in the past century on scientific fact, industrialization, and computerization, together with a lack of interest in history, make the modern generation unsuited for symbolic communication. Others claim that because of these impersonalizing trends there is a renewal of involvement with symbolism. It is shown in an upswing of interest in new religions, the occult, dream interpretation, prayer, and Pentecostalism. Which position would you agree with? Why?

Psalm 23

The Lord is my shepherd; I shall not want.
    In verdant pastures he gives me repose;
Beside restful waters he leads me;
    he refreshes my soul.
He guides me in right paths
    for his name's sake.
Even though I walk in the dark valley
    I fear no evil; for you are at my side
With your rod and your staff
    that give me courage.

You spread the table before me
    in the sight of my foes;
You anoint my head with oil;
    my cup overflows.
Only goodness and kindness follow me
    all the days of my life;
And I shall dwell in the house of the Lord
    for years to come.

SUMMING UP

Use the following questions to help you review the
main themes of this chapter.

1. Why do human beings need to communicate by signs?
2. What is the difference between a simple sign and a symbol?
3. Why are symbols known as "experience-bearers"?
4. How can symbols grow and change? What "layers" do the Christian sacraments have?
5. What are symbolic actions? What was the purpose of ritual in Israel?
6. What does the spoken word add to everyday actions?
7. In what way is God's Word different from ordinary words?
8. How can you learn to experience symbols better?
9. What is the difference between a simple sign and a sacramental sign?

Words to Know

sign, symbol, sacrament, ritual, liturgy, rite

Think/Talk/Write

1. What do each of the following symbols represent to you?

lilies	lamb
mistletoe	turkey
butterfly	jack o'lantern
candle	valentine

2. At John F. Kennedy's grave, his widow lit an "eternal flame." What did she mean the flame to symbolize?
3. Why is a flame a good symbol for the risen Christ?
4. Explain this statement: "There are two ways of spreading the light— to be a candle or the mirror that reflects it."
5. Explain this passage (John 1:1–3):

   > In the beginning was the Word;
   > the Word was in God's presence,
   > and the Word was God.

He was present to God in the beginning.
Through him all things came into being,
and apart from him nothing came to be.

What is the Word of God? What is the relationship between God's Word and his action?

6. How can the birth of Jesus be symbolized as light coming into darkness? Why can it be said that the darkness did not overcome the light?

7. For each of the following liturgical seasons, create your own symbols (words, colors, actions, objects): Advent, Christmas, Lent, Easter. Explain what the symbols mean.

Activities

1. Review Saint John's Gospel, the Book of Psalms, or the first fifteen chapters of Exodus. What symbols are used to describe God? What do the symbols mean?

2. Ask a Jewish friend or rabbi to explain the symbols of Hanukkah (Feast of Lights).

3. Make a list of signs that appear around your school. Then make a list of symbols. Compare these with the lists of others in your class.

4. Write a poem or short essay, using a symbol to explain your present experience of God.

5. Look through religious art books. How is Christ drawn in each century? What do you think the artist was saying through such symbolism?

What is a celebration?

What is a Christian celebration?

Why is Jesus the Sacrament of God?

Why is the Church the sacrament of Christ?

Roots of Worship

They went to the temple area every day, while in their homes they broke bread. With exultant and sincere hearts they took their meals in common, praising God and winning the approval of all the people.

(ACTS OF THE APOSTLES 2:46–7)

CELEBRATION

Most people would rather hear a voice over the phone than get a letter. But more than that, most people would like to see and be with their friends. People are happier in the actual presence of friends than with any gift or message sent in their place.

And yet, mere physical nearness isn't what people long for. You would be disappointed if your friends were asleep or consistently refused you attention whenever you visited them. You want to feel their interest and affection. You value the love in their eyes and the smile on their lips. But more than anything else, you feel the need to communicate with them personally and intimately.

- Why do so many families gather on Thanksgiving or other holidays?
- Why do the reunions so often center on a meal?
- Why do people like to talk about "the good old days" when they get together?

A celebration is a time out from the daily grind, a pause for the purpose of rediscovering who you are and what you are about. For example, the routine of countless classes, the pages of notes, the cramming for exams, the trips to your locker, the dreaming out the window in spring—all end in the "time out" of graduation. This is a celebration of the fact that you did what was required to become free to read, to write, and to think on your own.

It is right that you celebrate this event in the company of all who made the day possible. There are special robes, long speeches, processions, music, and awards in a ceremony at which everyone gathers to acknowledge your good fortune. There are further parties, gift-giving, and good food at home to emphasize the significance not only of what you've become but of what your achievement promises for the future.

■ What other achievements do people celebrate?

It is typical to mark the important occasions of life with celebrations: birthdays, anniversaries, passing tests, winning games and awards. These occasions are milestones of growth into the person you are meant to become. It is likewise typical to celebrate what gives you your deepest identity—your relationship with God.

Since the beginning of history, people have celebrated their religious identity. To celebrate their special closeness with God, the Israelites annually held a Passover festival that extended over a full week. The center of the feast was a meal of lamb and, later, unleavened bread, which brought to mind the original event of the Passover. This commemoration was more than a simple retelling of the story; it was a reenactment of the event, and the Jewish people actually felt God's saving power among them in the symbolic actions. For example, they left the door open and a seat empty to make room for the possible return of the prophet Elijah.

Every week, this feast was celebrated in miniature at the Sabbath supper. As time went on, other feasts were added to bring out different aspects of the great and complex Passover event. The Feast of Weeks, or Pentecost, commemorated the Covenant with God. During the Festival of Tents, the Israelites thanked God for feeding and caring for them in the wilderness.

CHRISTIAN CELEBRATION

Christian celebration centers around Christ. Christians worship the Father through Christ in the Holy Spirit. They recognize the source of their special relationship to God in the Passover of Jesus from his sacrificial death to his resurrection. This is known as the Paschal Mystery. In this world-shaking event, Christ joined himself forever to the human race. Because he is human, he redeems the world. Because he is divine, he makes all persons children of God.

After Pentecost, with the help of the Spirit, the early Church understood the Last Supper as a new Passover meal to commemorate Jesus' saving action on Calvary. Jesus' followers broke bread together on the first day of every week, the Lord's Day, to bring into their midst his death and resurrection. They not only recalled the Paschal Mystery; they actually made it *present*.

The Lord's Day, the day on which Jesus rose, was Sunday.

LITURGY

Foremost among the sentiments of the first Christians was thanksgiving. They were grateful to God for his continued presence and saving acts, first for creation, but above all for the gifts of redemption through his Son and the Holy Spirit.

To show their wholehearted participation, the assembly of the early Church would enthusiastically stamp their feet, shout glad alleluias at the conclusion of the Eucharistic Prayer, and sing out the Great Amen. Something of this spontaneous spirit can be seen today in the applause of a congregation when a new member is added to the Church by baptism, when a couple is married, or when a minister is ordained, a bishop consecrated, or a new Holy Father elected.

The singing of songs and hymns played a large part in the early liturgies. When the first Christians sang Christ's own prayer, the Our Father, they stood with arms extended to praise God with their whole bodies as well as their voices. Their enthusiasm was infectious. The great happiness shown in the assemblies of these early communities attracted many new converts.

Eventually, each Sunday became a small paschal celebration. The early Christians called these celebrations *ministry*—that is, "official service." At the season of the Passover, Christians remembered Jesus' paschal sacrifice and victory over death in a special way.

In the centuries that followed Jesus' departure from earth, the weekly and annual Easter celebrations were the only liturgies of the Christian communities. As time marched ahead, Christians understood more and more what Jesus had accomplished by his life and death. As their realization became clearer, the Church added daily celebrations of praise and joy that extended through the entire year.

The word *Eucharist* is based on a Greek verb meaning "to give thanks."

- You may have experienced or read about charismatic Masses. What are they? Share any knowledge or experience you have of them with the class.
- What do you think attracts converts to the Faith?

KEEPING THE BUDDHA CENTRAL

The world's 267 million Buddhists center their religious practices around the life and teaching of their founder, Siddhartha Gautama, a rich prince who renounced his kingdom to search for truth.

In festivals, parades, and dances, they honor Buddha—the Enlightened One—who, while meditating under the Bodhi tree, discovered, and then spent his life teaching, the meaning of life.

In a community ceremony, young boys are dressed in princely clothes such as those worn by Siddhartha before his conversion, only to strip them off as a sign of rejection of the world. In imitation of the original Buddha, the boys put on the tea-colored robes of the strict monks with whom they live and through whom they hope to learn the truth and the path of the Buddha.

On the days of the Buddha's birth and death, April 8 and February 15, his followers make offerings to his altars in their homes and temples. The daily reading of the *sutras,* the Buddhist scriptures, and the saying of grace before and after meals are other practices that keep devout Buddhists mindful of the Buddha and his teachings.

Some Japanese sects hold thanksgiving worship in the *hondo* (temples) every Sunday morning. When they enter, they make a *gasho* (bow), offer incense, and take their places at the sound of a gong. The priest reads scripture and gives a sermon. They wrap *ouizu* (prayer beads) around their folded hands, especially during *gasho.* By their worship and by living in accord with the way of the Buddha, believers hope to reach *nirvana,* the place of perfect peace.

■ In what ways do Christians center their lives around Christ and his teachings as the Buddhists do around Siddhartha Gautama?

MEAL CELEBRATIONS

Some Scripture scholars believe that the Last Supper was the last of a long series of meals Jesus took with his friends. It was characteristic of him to join others at table and, over the breaking of bread, to instruct them about the kingdom. This can be seen in the story of Jesus inviting himself to dinner at the house of Zacchaeus, the tax collector. During the meal, Jesus declared that his coming to eat with "sinners" brought them salvation.

See Luke 19:1–10

■ Reread these Gospel stories: the anointing at Bethany, John 12:1–7; Simon the Pharisee, Luke 7:36–50; the Lord's Supper, Mark 14:22–24; the multiplication of the loaves, John 6:1–15; the apparition to the disciples, Luke 24:36–49; the apparition by the lake, John 21:12–19. Notice Jesus explaining and showing his saving power at meals.

Being a gregarious people, the Jews centered their festivities around the banquet table. Elements of table fellowship appear as far back as Abraham, when hospitality was shown in the offer of refreshments. Even today, the offer of food is a sign of friendship in the East.

Gregarious means enjoying the company of others.

See Genesis 18:4–8

LITURGICAL CELEBRATIONS

Originally, *liturgy* meant any work undertaken for the welfare of the whole people—a public work. As Christianity flourished, liturgy came to mean the public worship the People of God offer in union with Christ. The Eucharist celebration was the main liturgical action, but the Jewish converts added the morning and evening psalms and other prayers of Judaism to their official liturgy. These prayers became known as the Liturgy of the Hours, or Divine Office. Their aim was to officially worship God throughout the day.

Liturgy is from the Greek words *leiton* (people) and *ergon* (work).

Christian liturgy was not just public prayer offered by a few members of the Christian community. Even those Christians who had died were commemorated. Since liturgy was the official worship of the Church, the unbaptized, who had not yet been incorporated into the Church, were not permitted to participate fully.

Because he is God, Jesus' sacrifice on the cross is eternal divine worship. In his risen humanity, Jesus "lives forever to plead with God" for the human race. He ceaselessly bears humanity's thanks to the Father and in return continually sends his Spirit to fill the earth. By sharing in Jesus' risen life, Christians mysteriously become his very body, continuing through time his mission of perfect and unceasing praise. Although the language and prayers of worship may change from time to time, Christian worship does not change, for "Jesus Christ is the same, yesterday, today, and forever."

See Hebrews 7:25

Hebrews 13:8

- What changes in the liturgy have you witnessed in your lifetime?
- What answer would you give to people who say that nothing is the same as it used to be in the liturgy?

LITURGY

SACRAMENTAL PRESENCE

Love is the unique power that makes us different from the rest of creation. Animal love does not involve the deep mutual exchange found in human love. The capacity to share ourselves intimately with others is perhaps the source of the greatest satisfaction. Through the power of intimacy, God gave us the possibility of union with him and of our fullest development as human beings. Revelation teaches that we are most human when God is our friend.

See John 15:15

God provided a way for us to share his friendship, despite the insurmountable difference between the divine and the human. He bridged the gap by acting sacramentally—that is, by showing his action through things that we can see and touch. Any objects, actions, or persons that bring us into contact with God or his saving power are, in a general sense, sacraments. As stated before, *sacrament* translates as the word *mystery*—the secret plan and ability of God to bring people to their proper destiny. The plan includes all the ways that God used and still uses to reach out to humanity and for humanity to respond to his love.

JESUS AS SACRAMENT

God used more than symbols or prophets to show people the way to true peace and salvation. He gave his own Son to reveal his intention. In Christ, God's plan was no longer secret, but fully revealed. In Christ, that plan was also fully achieved. By Christ's death and resurrection, the human race is now liberated. Sin is overcome and people are free to become their true selves in Christ.

Jesus is the full expression of the invisible God. "Whoever has seen me has seen the Father," Jesus tells Philip at the Last Supper. "I am in the Father and the Father is in me." In Christ, God encounters humanity and humanity meets God directly.

John 14:9–10

Being God, Christ communicated the gift of divine life from the Father by his visible words and actions. At the same time, being the most perfect human ever to be created, he offered in all humanity's name the perfect response to the Father. Through Christ, all sacraments are given form and power. For these reasons, Christ is called the first and greatest Sacrament.

Encounters with Jesus of Nazareth were encounters with God. When Jesus cured people, the love of God was visible in his human actions. When Jesus was friendly with Mary and Martha, and when he patiently taught Nicodemus in the middle of the night, God's personal love for human beings was no longer hidden as in a sunset or pillar of fire. Yet none of these actions so clearly revealed the incredibly selfless and other-centered love of the Father as did the Paschal Mystery—Jesus' death on the cross and his resurrection. In loving the human race with the last drop of his blood, Jesus expressed God's infinite yearning to share his life and love. His resurrection was the greatest sign of God's intention and power to give eternal life.

Jesus' risen and glorified presence among his Apostles ended with his return to the Father. Yet he did not come to serve as the Sacrament of God only to those few who had the privilege of living with him. Before Jesus' resurrection, he, like you, could be personally present in the fullest sense only to the people he met and talked to. When he left the earth to take his rightful place at the Father's side, his risen humanity became present in the Holy Spirit. From the moment of his glorification, Jesus' range of contact became unlimited. He received the power to be personally present in the Spirit to everyone who believes in him to the end of time.

- Before his ascension, Jesus said, "I will be with you always to the end of the ages." How can someone "go away" and yet remain?
- How can Christ be the Sacrament of God to those who live after his return to the Father?
- How many ways can you name in which Christ is present to you today?

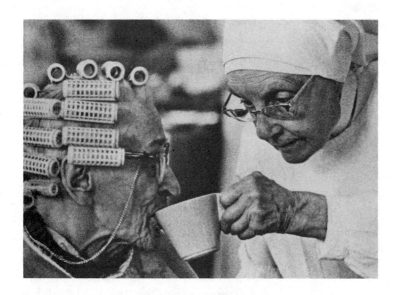

THE CHURCH AS SACRAMENT

Christ's presence in the world today is a living presence based on a unity of hearts—a unity of love and life in the Holy Trinity. Christ lives in the world today through the Church.

At Pentecost, when Christ poured out the Holy Spirit on those gathered in the upper room, he made them a mysterious embodiment of his risen life through time. Just as Christ is the Sacrament of God (God made visible in Christ), the Church is the Sacrament of Christ (Christ made visible in his Church).

Christians, members of Christ's mystical body, together with the risen Christ, are the *sign* of God's plan. Their faith is the route by which God comes to the world, as well as the way by which humanity can respond to him. At the same time, the Church has the power to bring about the close union that she is the sign of. Christians are enabled by baptism and missioned in confirmation to do what the risen Lord does: they praise God for his goodness through the perfect worship of the Eucharist. They also continue his work of spreading his kingdom by building up the community of life and love, by deepening their own holiness which is union with him, and by going out into the world to spread the Gospel.

God wants everyone to enjoy his intimate friendship. The Church's work is to continue to build God's kingdom until one day all nations join the Body of Christ. The life of the Holy Trinity, a relationship of eternal love, will then permeate all things. Saint Paul puts it this way:

Colossians 1:17–20

> He is before all else that is. In him everything continues in being. It is he who is head of the body, the Church; he who is the beginning, the first-born of the dead, so that primacy may be his in everything. It pleased God to make absolute fullness reside in him and, by means of him, to reconcile everything in his person, both on earth and in the heavens, making peace through the blood of his cross.

Followers of Jesus don't merely symbolize Jesus, nor do they only suggest or represent his presence. They *are* Jesus to the world, by both their presence and the power of their example to lead others to God. The Church can be defined as a visible union of those who publicly say to the world, "We are Christ for you today." Every individual Christian, too, is a visible sign of Christ. You might even define a Christian as "a sacrament of Christ in the world." This means that when you serve your neighbors, you are Christ serving people today. And whatever you do to others, as Jesus said, you do to him.

See Matthew 25:40

- In what ways can you be Christ to others at home? At school? At work? At play?
- At the Last Supper, Jesus asked his Father for unity between himself and his followers. Saint John stresses this unity at the beginning and end of his Gospel. Tell the point he makes in each of these passages: John 1:12, 14, 16; 14:23; 15:4, 7; 17:21, 23.
- Write and act out for the class a skit in which a Catholic is (obviously or subtly) Christ in an office, classroom, club, party, neighborhood, or other ordinary situation.

ETERNAL LIFE THROUGH THE SACRAMENTS

The Church continues Christ's risen life through all her various actions. Among the most important of these actions are the sacraments. A sacrament is an encounter between a person and the risen Christ brought about by Christ through the symbolic action of the Church. In these encounters, Christ acting in his Church saves us by bestowing eternal life. But since life has many needs, each sacrament produces the particular effects that it symbolizes. The seven sacraments serve the main life processes of the Church: bringing forth new members, offering means of nourishment and growth, building up the community of faith, and blessing her members in death.

Sacraments dispense God's life, but they also need the People of God. They need the cooperation of those who participate in them. Christ may come to someone who communicates at Mass, but if the person inwardly rejects Christ, the effect of the sacrament will not take place. Sacraments also express the faith of the community. If there is only one person present to perform a sacrament, there is usually no sacrament. If the sacrament is not carried out in the symbolic form recognized by the entire Church community, there is no sacrament.

Because the sacraments are personal actions of Christ who lives in eternity, as well as of the Church which lives in time, they have elements of time and of eternity. Each sacrament contains three time elements:

1. It calls into the present the *past* offering that Christ once made in the one Paschal Mystery.
2. It is an encounter with the risen Christ in the *present* to bring his saving action to the participant.
3. It is a pledge and an actual bringing about of *future* glory and eternal salvation.

   ■ Compose a song, poem, collage, or drawing that expresses your understanding of the practical meaning of the past, present, and future tense of one of the sacraments.

INSTITUTION AND NUMBER OF THE SACRAMENTS

Did Jesus institute seven sacraments? Yes. By the mystery of his death and resurrection, Christ made us sharers in divine life. In this he is the author and source of the sacraments. But the word *sacrament* does not appear in Scripture. There was no such thing as a sacrament before the time of Christ, and although Jesus performed many saving actions, he did not prescribe the formulas and gestures used in the sacraments today. The infant Church was quick to recognize that certain of Jesus' actions were more purposeful than others. Some of these were his baptism by John, his miracle at the wedding feast at Cana, and his blessing of bread and wine. The young community carried out the commission of Jesus to continue his mission by beginning at once to perform these "signs," or symbolic actions, in memory of him. They did this to bring his saving presence into their midst.

If you consider every personal encounter with the risen Lord as a sacrament, there are more than seven sacraments. But the Church has come to identify seven vital saving actions in her liturgy as especially powerful bearers of divine life. Of these, baptism and Eucharist are the most important, although the others cannot be dismissed. The form of the sacraments may have changed somewhat through the centuries, but their power has not.

- Connect each of the life processes mentioned above with a sacrament.
- Does it disturb you to find that Jesus did not determine the exact words and actions of the sacraments? Why or why not?

SACRAMENTALS

If you wear a medal or observe Lent, you are aware that the Church offers other ways to grow in union with

Christ in the *sacramentals.* These, too, are sacred signs—actions, objects, places, times of the Church year—but they differ from the sacraments. Their power comes from the prayers of the Church rather than from Christ's direct presence. In reminding us of Christ, things like crucifixes, medals, rosaries, statues, and the sign of the cross provide opportunities to grow in union with him. Vestments, candles, blessed water, and hymns help us to worship better. Blessings for our homes, cars, and crops open the everyday aspects of life to the influence of Christ. Through devout use of the Advent wreath, blessed ashes, and fasting, as well as the observance of the solemn feasts and sacred times, we mark and sanctify the various seasons of the Liturgical Year. The sacramentals, like the sacraments, lead to a greater love of Christ.

- What actions, besides the specific actions of the sacraments, are sacramental? An example is giving the sign of peace.
- What sacred seasons of the Church year do you find put you in the mood for a feast? How and why do they do this?

Prayer

Lord Jesus Christ,
you gave us the Eucharist
as a memorial of your suffering and death.
May our worship of this sacrament of your body
and blood help us to experience the salvation you
        won for us . . .
May we who faithfully proclaim your death and
resurrection in these sacramental signs
experience the constant growth of your salvation
in our lives . . .
Renew us at your table with the bread of life.
May this food strengthen us in love
and help us to serve you in each other.
We ask this in the name of Jesus the Lord.
Amen.

From the Rite of Eucharistic Worship
Outside Mass

SUMMING UP

Use the following questions to help you review the
main themes of this chapter.

1. Why would Jesus naturally have chosen a supper at which to leave
   a memorial of the Paschal Mystery?
2. What were the first Christian celebrations like?
3. How does the memorial of Christ's passion differ from other memorials?
4. What is the difference between the liturgy and other kinds of devotional services?
5. What is the essential meaning of Eucharist?
6. What effect should Christian liturgy have on your life?
7. How is the fact that human beings are fulfilled by close personal
   relationships connected with your relationship with God?
8. What is meant by God expressing himself "sacramentally"?
9. What is meant by the statement: "Christ is the Sacrament of God."
10. What does the expression "The Church is the Sacrament of Christ"
    mean?
11. When do Christians become sacraments of Christ to the world?
12. Explain how we can say that Jesus instituted the sacraments.
13. Explain the three elements contained in each sacrament.

Words to Know

celebration, Passover, Paschal Mystery, the Lord's Day, ministry, liturgy,
Christ as Sacrament, Church as Sacrament, sacramentals

Think/Talk/Write

1. Someone has said that there can be no salvation for us unless we care
   for the salvation of others. Someone else put it this way: "No one
   goes to heaven or hell alone." Do you think that is literally true?
   Write out or discuss your answer.
2. What are some of the real hindrances to recognizing Christ as the

Sacrament of God, members of the Church as sacraments of Christ, and the sacraments as actions of Christ? What remedies would you propose?

3. Someone has said, "Who does not know the Church, does not know Christ." Would you agree or disagree? Why?

Activities

1. Prepare a puppet show, a skit, or a closed-circuit TV clip showing how a group of teenagers transformed their ho-hum parish liturgies into vibrant, "involved" celebrations. Show the liturgies before the changes, the transforming process with its frustrations, and the liturgies after the changes.
2. Write a poem or prayer expressing the meaning of any sacrament to you.
3. Create a poem, story, or painting that shows what Christ, the Sacrament of God, can do for your life.
4. Spend a specified amount of time each week giving service in one of the following areas: volunteering in a hospital; helping in nursing homes; visiting the elderly in their apartments; tutoring younger or less gifted students; collecting food or clothing for the poor; assisting teachers with routine jobs; acting as a camp or playground counselor. Share your experience with the class.

People have always found the world charged with mystery. In creation, one can dimly perceive the hidden presence of God. Although in his holiness God is far beyond time and space, he decreed to reveal himself more directly at particular times and places to the Israelites. Both these ways of meeting God—in nature and in history—are sacramental in the wide sense that, through each, God can be embodied and communicated.

But God revealed himself most fully in the person of Jesus, his Son. For Christians, Jesus is *the* place of sacramental encounter with God. The climax of revelation occurred in Christ's death and resurrection. His total self-offering was both a sign of God's love and of humanity's total response to it.

Since Jesus' resurrection, his Holy Spirit is at work in the Church, his Mystical Body, which is now the sacrament—or continuing visible sign—of God's sacred presence in the world. Through words, signs, and symbols, Christ and the Church offer God public worship (the liturgy) by celebrating the Eucharist and other sacraments and by reciting the official prayer of the Church. It is through our sacramental participation in the Paschal Mystery that God continues to be perfectly worshiped and communicates himself to us and, through us, to other Church members and the world.

PART II

THE SACRAMENT OF UNITY

A meeting can be described as a sharing rather than a contact. Whenever a real meeting between an "I" and a "Thou" actually takes place, there is always the hidden presence of "another." It always takes three to unite two.

(MARTIN BUBER)

Why did Jesus use table fellowship to unite his followers?

What is the meaning of the Passover meal?

How did Jesus give the Passover meal a new meaning?

How did Jesus fulfill the Passover hopes?

Table Unity

The celebration of the Eucharist nourishes the faithful with Christ, the Bread of Life, in order that, filled with the love of God and neighbor, they may become more and more a people acceptable to God and build up the Christian community with the works of charity, service, missionary activity, and witness.

(NATIONAL CATECHETICAL DIRECTORY #121)

THE POWER OF TABLE FELLOWSHIP

One of the most natural moments of the day to feel unity with others is during mealtime at the dinner table. People seem instinctively to sense the close association of food with friendship. Wherever two or three of them are gathered, food almost seems to make a miraculous appearance. But because of the rush of modern life, few people know the satisfactions that leisurely eating can provide. A four-hour multicourse dinner in a European restaurant, an evening meal served formally on banana leaves in a Brahmin household in India, or a traditional tea ceremony in Japan would demonstrate the love and worship that a meal can be.

Brahmins are members of the highest caste, or class, of society in India.

- If you have experienced any kind of elaborate meal, tell the class about it. What ceremonies accompanied the meal? What did they mean?
- Where do you find yourself most readily opening up to others? While working with them? While

eating together? During hours of recreation? During class discussions? At meetings? Or at some other time?

Jesus could have chosen to deliver his message of love by gathering people around him as a teacher gathers students in a class or as a corporation holds its committee or sales meetings. But he was working toward something more than mere instruction. In carrying out his mission, Jesus often ate with others because eating together creates a feeling of unity. It has greater possibility for the experience of love than does a class or a meeting.

Around a table, Jesus—besides explaining his teachings—allowed others to get to know him. Over good food, he laughed, listened to complaints, discussed local opinions and national affairs, and shared what was on his mind and in his heart. At the meals he shared with his Apostles, there is no doubt that he was even more intimate and self-revealing than when he was with other groups. It was probably at mealtime when Jesus and his closest followers were most conscious of themselves as a "family."

The Eucharist is the most powerful means of unifying individuals, both within themselves and with one another, because it brings Christ's actual presence to their relationships. The warm fellowship of the Last Supper was a culmination of Christ's entire mission. He brought a great heart to that momentous meal with his closest friends because he had made a practice of loving and serving others all his life. He had always been able to think of the needs of others before his own. This night was no different. Despite his own heaviness of heart, Jesus put his Apostles first. He showed them the depths of his great desire to be one with them and with all humanity.

- Skim the texts given below to find examples of Jesus, who, while eating or drinking with others, listened to their complaints, shared his thoughts, and was aware of the thoughts and feelings of those present: Matthew 9:9–13, 16:5–12, 26:6–13; Mark

2:13–17, 8:14–21, 14:3–9; Luke 5:27–32, 7:36–50, 19:1–9; John 12:1–8, 2:1–12, 4:1–26.

■ In Luke 11:29–32, the Jews ask Jesus for a sign. What sign does he say will be given them? Do they accept it? What is the connection between that sign and the Eucharist?

THE PASSOVER MEAL

Every November, the United States observes the national holiday of Thanksgiving, which celebrates the blessings of freedom and plenty that came together in a festive meal of turkey, cranberries, and pumpkin pie—food the Pilgrims supposedly ate at their first Thanksgiving. While remembering the past, Thanksgiving Day also celebrates God's continued gifts to the country as symbolized by the abundant food on the table.

Similar to Thanksgiving, the Passover was the most sacred annual festival for the Jews in Jesus' time. The high point of the feast was a family meal commemorating the great historic events of the past. The family recognized God's continued blessings in the food they enjoyed together, and their meal symbolically expressed their reliance on God's faithfulness and their hope of receiving even greater blessings in the peace of the Messianic Age to come.

The Passover meal was not a Hebrew invention. Many religions hold sacred meals of worship. The origin of this particular feast was an ancient spring festival common to the agricultural peoples of the East. Nomadic peoples believed that they needed to restore the life given by the gods to their herds in order to ensure fertility in their fold. Accordingly, they offered the first and best lambs, which, to them, held the most vibrant life. After slaughtering and roasting the lambs, the people shared in the food offered to the gods as a sign of the divine acceptance.

The Jewish Seder celebration rang with the theme of liberation. Early in the meal, the youngest member of the family asked, "What is so special about this night?" The leader or head of the family then joyfully proclaimed God's mighty deeds in the history of their ancestors and their deliverance from bitter Egyptian enslavement.

"Passover" is a complex word that has many associations. Basically, it refers to the liberation or salvation the Israelites won from their oppressors when God's vengeance slayed the eldest born of the Egyptians while passing over and sparing their own firstborn sons (1230 B.C.). It also recalls the Israelites' safe passage through the Sea of Reeds when the Egyptians, pursuing them in royal chariots, were drowned. It includes the Covenant on Sinai that God made with his People through Moses, as well as the religious ceremony of the sealing of the Covenant in blood. The Passover was a remembrance of God's guidance through the barren desert to the Promised Land (1200 B.C.). Finally, in the years just preceding the coming of Christ, the Passover commemorated the Israelites' release from exile after the Babylonian Captivity (587 B.C.)

Another name for the Passover was the Feast of Unleavened Bread. Because of the pressure on the night

The *berakah* (BEAR-eh-kuh) was a prayer of praise which began with "Blessed be God."

the Jews had escaped from Egypt, they could not wait for their bread dough to rise before they ate it. Called the "bread of affliction," the unleavened loaves, which were eaten with bitter herbs at the Passover meal, reminded the Jews of their suffering in Egypt. Eventually, leaven came to symbolize evil. Unleavened bread was the sign of the Israelites' willingness to do God's will.

■ In what ways was the Passover meal a celebration of unity?

The memory of these unexpected liberations called forth in the Jewish people a feeling of exaltation at God's power to bring their impossible dreams to realization by his Word. They became convinced that they were special, a chosen race, loved above even the greatest nations. They were filled with awe and gratitude that, although their God was high above them in holiness, he had entered their lives to make them more livable and more human.

In blessing God for past favors, the Jewish people felt his saving power in their midst again, strengthening them in their present trials. At the same time, the Passover meal expressed their eager hope and longing for the final coming of God's kingdom, the time of peace foretold by the prophets. When they blessed and drank the customary cups of wine, they launched a week-long celebration of joy and thanksgiving. The Passover meal consisted of three main parts:

Blessing and Remembering. The meal always began with the *berakah* over the cup of wine. A dish of bitter herbs was then served, but not eaten. There followed a washing of hands and the breaking of bread, after which an explanation of the reason for the feast was given by the head of the family. A second cup of blessed wine was shared.

A Sharing in the Sacrifice of Praise. The main dish was the Passover lamb, which had been sacrificed in the temple. It commemorated the lamb whose blood, sprinkled on the doorposts of the Israelites at the time of the Exodus, saved them from the destroying angel. It also recalled Moses' sealing of the Covenant by sprinkling the blood of the sacrificed animal.

LITURGY

A Closing Blessing. The meal closed with a blessing said over a third cup of wine and the singing of hymns.

- What two parts of the Jewish Seder correspond to the Liturgy of the Word and the Liturgy of the Eucharist?
- Do you notice any other similarities between the Mass and the Seder?
- What connection do you see between the "bread of affliction" and the Eucharistic bread? Between the Paschal lamb and Christ? Between the Passover's memory of the Covenant and Jesus' action in every Mass?
- What in Jesus' life corresponds to the Israelites' oppression in Egypt, their wandering in the desert, and the Babylonian Captivity?

Pasch is another name for Passover.

THE MOST MOMENTOUS MEAL

It was in the consciousness of this heritage that Jesus and the Twelve sat down to table the night before his death. According to the Gospel of Saint Luke, Jesus sent Peter and John ahead to make the customary preparations for the feast. The Apostles certainly expected to follow the form of the meal they were familiar with since childhood, but the evening began with an unusual occurrence.

See Luke 22:7–13

Ordinarily, servants washed the feet of the guests who had just come in from the dusty roads. But at the beginning of this meal, Jesus did a most extraordinary thing. Like a servant, he, the host, removed his cloak, tied a towel around his waist, and washed the feet of his Apostles. Jesus insisted that unless his followers let him do this for them, they could have no part with him. Jesus added, "But if I washed your feet—I who am Teacher and Lord—then you must wash each other's feet." This action was a vivid parable of the theme that runs through the final hours of Jesus' life: loving service to others. At the same time, it is a continuation of what Jesus had been doing all his life.

John 13:14

The meal itself opened in the ordinary way, but once
again Jeses introduced something new. The Gospel accounts say that while giving thanks, he took the unleavened "bread of affliction," broke it, and said, "Take
this and eat it. This is my body, which will be given
up for you."

Jesus did the same with the cup of wine. After the
supper, using the "blood of the grape," which, according to Jewish ritual, was always red, he said, "This is
the cup of my blood, the blood of the new and everlasting covenant. It will be shed for you and for all, so
that sins may be forgiven."

The intention is clear. The Hebrews had always offered real lambs and bulls, not mere signs of them. This
bread and wine was not to be a sign only, but the true
body and blood of Jesus, who would soon be sacrificed

on the cross. Bread—either in itself or as a symbol—could hardly have been "given for you," nor could regular wine be "shed" for the forgiveness of sin. Only by becoming Jesus could this bread and wine have been connected with the events of Calvary. Only the real, personal presence of Christ, the lamb of sacrifice, could make this meal a way of uniting worshipers with their God.

Jesus' gift to the Apostles and to all his followers was not something he had made or bought. It was himself, his body and blood, his very life. As Jesus himself explained, "There is no greater love than this: to lay down one's life for one's friends." This meal was to be the way Jesus' closest friends would celebrate for all ages to come his greatest act of love: his passion, death, and resurrection.

John 15:13

At that Passover meal with his disciples, Jesus devised a way for his followers to remember how he had given himself. In the Eucharist, they were to commemorate not only his death but also what his death won: God's acceptance as shown in the resurrection, ascension, and sending of the Holy Spirit. Jesus commanded that his followers together celebrate his self-gift "in memory" of him to the end of time.

The Church has taken Jesus' words very seriously. It is obvious from the entire setting of the Mass—the bread and wine, the plate and cups, the table with its covering, the priest as host, the congregation as invited guests, the great Eucharistic prayer of thanks, and the reception of the food—that the Eucharist is basically a meal commemorating the Last Supper. It contains the main rituals of the Passover meal: a retelling of God's saving deeds in the Scripture readings, a solemn prayer of thanksgiving in the Eucharistic Prayer, and the sharing of food in Communion.

Despite the solemnity of the occasion, at the Last Supper Jesus presented no theology or lengthy explanations about the Eucharist. He gave only a few words and actions. He simply gave himself as food as a sign of unity with God and others.

NAMES FOR THE LORD'S SUPPER

See 1 Corinthians 11:20 and Acts of the Apostles 2:42, 46; 20:7.

At the beginning of the Church, the Mass was known as the "Lord's Day," the "Lord's Supper," or the "breaking of the bread." This was because it continued what Jesus did with bread and wine at the Last Supper. At first an entire meal was celebrated, with the bread and cup introducing and closing the celebration, but soon the essential actions connected with special blessings were separated from the eating of the main dish.

Before long, the word frequently used for the Mass was *eucharistia,* a Greek word meaning "thanksgiving," which referred to the Jewish *berakah.* The early Christians followed the Jewish custom that Jesus had used at the Last Supper of pronouncing the *berakah* over the bread and wine, which represented all things in creation. The first prayers over the gifts in the Liturgy of the Eucharist today closely imitate this *berakah.*

By using bread and wine, Jesus sanctified the natural world. His actions said that everything in creation is holy because it can become a means of nourishing divine life. However, the Christian religious meal goes far beyond the offering of human symbols and prayers. It is the offering of Christ's own perfect love of the Father, which was shown in his loving acceptance of death.

Saint Augustine lived between A.D. 354 and A.D. 430.

By the time of Saint Augustine, the Mass was given the Roman name *sacrificium laudis,* a "sacrifice of praise," an act offering something pleasing as a gift to God. Other words that conveyed the same meaning of approaching God with a gift were *oblatio* (oblation) and *korbono* (reserved for God's use).

Some names for the Eucharist which stressed that the Mass is a celebration of the entire Christian community were *collecta* (a gathering together) and *processio* (a marching forward together). As a sign of being pilgrims, the people formed a procession to enter the Church. *Liturgia* (work or service performed with or for the people) was the word the Greeks settled on to call the Mass. This was because the people shared Christ's priesthood in offering Christ's sacrifice and because it was offered for all the people.

In occasional use were early terms like the Lord's celebration, the table of the Lord, the holy thing, service, divine service, offering, the holy sacrifice of the Mass, the sacrificial banquet, and High Mass.

The word *Mass* itself became popular around the fifth century. It was practically the only term used for the Lord's Supper until this century, when the reform of Vatican II reintroduced *Eucharist* or Eucharistic Liturgy.

Originally, *missa* (*missio, dismissio*) meant "dismissal" or "being sent out." At first, the presbyters were sent out to the surrounding parishes with a particle of the bishop's Eucharistic bread. It was to be dropped into the local chalices as a sign of the unity of all the people with the bishop. This action suggested Christ's one sanctifying action spreading through the world.

The *missa* also referred to the continuing action of the celebration, which usually involved the blessing with which the Christian was "sent out." Either the blessing or the entire celebration itself would be called *missa*.

As time went on, the word *missa* referred only to the Eucharistic celebration to signify the blessing it offered for all human life. Today, because people no longer use Latin in the Mass, the word seems less appropriate than Eucharist, which names the main action of the celebration.

A *presbyter* was an elder or priest in the early Church.

- Which of the names of the Mass seems most meaningful to you? Why?
- If you could give the Mass a new name, what would it be?

THE PASSOVER FULFILLED

Considering the meaning that Jesus gave to the Passover meal, it is little wonder the Apostles did not grasp the significance of his words immediately. Even after the terrible events of the next day, the Apostles did not understand what Jesus had done. It took the Resurrection and the sending of the Spirit to open their eyes in real understanding.

In his words of blessing over the bread and wine, Jesus fulfilled and, at the same time, entirely changed the meaning of the Jewish Passover supper. He made it clear that he was the Messiah for whom the Jewish families had waited.

Christ's offering is far superior to that of the Old Law. The Passover lamb commemorated Moses' offering of an animal as worship to God. Christ freely laid down his own divine/human life with the greatest possible love. Total and final, this covenant is infinitely pleasing and acceptable to the Father. No other sacrifice or covenant can ever replace it.

■ What does it mean to you to know that your sins are forgiven and God is your Father?

Just as the Passover was a memorial of God's saving actions in the history of Israel, a celebration of his goodness in the present, and a looking forward to the future, so the Eucharist has a threefold extension in time. It commemorates the past sacrifice of Calvary, celebrates God's unifying action presently taking place on the table, and awaits the future moment of union with him.

Saint Paul wrote, "Every time you eat this bread and drink from this cup you proclaim the Lord's death until he comes." Actually, in proclaiming Christ's death, the Eucharist also proclaims his resurrection, ascension, and sending of the Spirit. In God's view, these are all one and the same Paschal Mystery. Only because people need time to absorb each element of the Paschal Mystery does the Church separate the celebrations of the individual phases.

1 Corinthians 11:26

LITURGY

It is more than a coincidence that so many events over the course of thousands of years were so well summed up and brought to completion in Jesus' life. Only by a divine arrangement could so long a stretch of history have been made so clear a preparation for the coming of God's Son.

Another practical effect of understanding Jewish history is to see more clearly that the Eucharist is a unifying meal. Not to partake of Communion is not to participate fully in worship. It would be like attending a banquet, sitting down at the table, and then refusing to eat. It shows a lack of comprehension of what is really going on.

It is liberating to realize that, through the centuries, God created the Eucharist as an ingenious way to unite humanity with himself and all people with one another.

Prayer

I will bless the Lord at all times;   Psalm 34:1–9
    his praise shall be ever in my mouth.
Let my soul glory in the Lord;
    the lowly will hear me and be glad.
Glorify the Lord with me;
    let us together extol his name.

I sought the Lord, and he answered me
    and delivered me from all my fears.
Look to him that you may be radiant with joy,
    and your faces may not blush with shame.
When the afflicted called out, the Lord heard,
    and from all their distress he saved them.
The angel of the Lord encamps around
    those who fear him, and delivers them.

Taste and see how good the Lord is;
    happy are they who take refuge in him.

SUMMING UP

Use the following questions to help you review the main themes of this chapter.

1. Why is the Eucharist the great sacrament of unity?
2. Why did Jesus give his followers the Sacrament of Love in the form of a meal?
3. Why is it beneficial for Catholics to understand the Jewish Passover?
4. What three "times" entered into the Passover meal?
5. What added meaning did Israel give the pagan ritual? What were the main actions of the Passover meal? How did the custom of offering a lamb originate?
6. What meanings are connected with Passover? Which is the main one?
7. What two unusual changes did Jesus make in the Passover-supper customs?
8. What new and radically different meaning did Jesus give this "bread of affliction" and "blood of the grape"?
9. How does the ritual of the Eucharist today compare with the form of the Last Supper?
10. How does Jesus continue and fulfill the Passover supper?
11. What is the essential difference between the offering of the spring lamb and the offering Christ made?

Words to Know

berakah, pasch, Seder, unleavened bread, bread of affliction, *missa,* Eucharist

Think/Talk/Write

1. What is the reality behind the symbols in the following passages: John 2:13–21 (the temple, Christ's body); John 3:1–21 (water, wind); John 4:5–42 (water, food); John 6:1–15 (bread); John 9:1–41 (blindness).

2. As Jesus fulfilled and replaced the Mosaic covenant, he fulfilled the Old Law, substituting for the ancient commandments a call to the highest perfection. The Eucharist provides the spiritual strength needed to live Christ's challenge. Describe the relationship between these passages from the Sermon on the Mount and the sacrament of Christ's love: Matthew 5:16, 21–24, 27–30, 38–42, 43–48; 6:1–4, 14–15.

3. Refresh your memory of that historic night by reading the accounts of the Last Supper (1 Corinthians 11:23–26; Matthew 26:17–29; John 13:1–30; Mark 14:12–25; Luke 22:7–23) and answering the following questions:

   ■ Why do you think each account makes a reference to the betrayal of Judas?
   ■ When does the Last Supper take place? Why was it set in this background?
   ■ The excerpt from Saint John ends with the sentence "It was night." What does the image of night suggest to you?
   ■ What are the similarities among all the passages?
   ■ What are their differences?

4. In recent years, the Church has made an effort to encourage both the divorced and those separated from the Church to return to Eucharistic participation. What do you think about this trend?

5. The Last Supper was an event of such tremendous significance that Christ prepared his followers for it all during his years with them. Because of the faith and love demanded by the Eucharist, he postponed giving it until the very end of his life, making it the climax of his relationship with his closest friends. Describe how each of the following events was a preparation for the Last Supper: Matthew 14:13–21; Mark 6:30–44; Luke 9:10–17; John 2:1–12, 6:1–15, 16–21, 26–65, 66–71.

Activities

1. In the manner of a passion play, dramatize the Last Supper using action, dance, and music.
2. Find out what Byzantine Catholics call the Mass. Which Protestants have the equivalent of Mass? By what names are their rituals called?
3. As a class, attend a Passover celebration or prepare a Seder meal according to the Jewish ritual.

SIX

What was Mass like in the early Church?

What are the books used by the Church for liturgy and prayer?

Why do the priests wear vestments at Mass?

How are the readings for Mass chosen?

What are the parts of the Mass?

What is the Liturgy of the Word?

Liturgy of the Word

This is what we proclaim to you: what was from the beginning, what we have heard, what we have seen with our eyes, what we have looked upon and our hands have touched—we speak of the word of life.

(1 JOHN 1:1)

LITURGICAL ROOTS

More and more people today are interested in tracing their roots. In the Church, too, there has been a trend toward studying the first days of its existence. The basic shape of today's Mass seems to have been set before the end of the first century. One of the earliest known written records of liturgical custom comes from the pen of Saint Justin the Martyr, who summarized a second-century Sunday liturgy in his *First Apology.*

Saint Justin lived between A.D. 100 and A.D. 165.

Apologia I, 65–67.

The celebrant at the Eucharist was called the president.

Until the seventh century, the prayers of the Mass were spontaneous.

On the day named after the sun, all who live in city or countryside assemble, and the memoirs of the Apostles or the writings of the prophets are read for as long as time allows. When the lector has finished, the president addresses us, admonishing us and exhorting us to imitate the splendid things we have heard. Then we all stand and pray, and, when we have finished praying, bread, wine, and water are brought up. The president offers prayers of thanksgiving, according to his ability, and the people give their assent with an "Amen!" Next, the gifts over which the thanksgiving has been spoken are distributed, and each one shares in them, while they are also sent via the deacons to the absent brethren.

The wealthy who are willing make contributions, each as he pleases, and the collection is deposited with the president, who aids orphans and widows, those who are in want because of sickness or other cause, those in prison, and visiting strangers; in short, he takes care of all in need.

- What parts of present-day liturgy do you recognize in this description of the early Eucharistic celebration in the Church?
- What ministries or roles do you recognize?

LITURGICAL BOOKS

In the earliest days of Christian worship, the only book used was the Bible, from which readings were taken. The president signaled the reader when to stop reading. Other prayers were offered by the president of the assembly to the "best of his powers." It seems that he did prepare the prayers in advance.

The first written evidence of a formula for liturgical prayers appeared around A.D. 235. After A.D. 313, a systematic liturgy was developed and incorporated into separate books of prayers, lessons, homilies of the Fathers, psalms, chants, musical phrases, and hymns. Directions for gestures, at first minimal, gradually became precise and were recorded in the ordinals.

The Fathers of the Church were early Christian writers such as Saint Jerome and Saint Augustine.

An *ordinal* (also called the ordo) is a book of instructions or procedures for daily liturgical services.

In the ninth century, the Sacramentary—the book of all liturgical functions—was divided into three books: one for bishops, one for priests, and the missal, with all the parts for the celebrant, minister, choir, and people. The breviary was another book that held a brief version of the Divine Office, which is the official prayer of the Church. All persons in holy orders and certain other religious communities are obliged to pray this

prayer. It is composed of psalms, readings, and prayers, and is arranged in eight parts called "hours." These correspond to the times of day when they are ideally recited.

A reform of the Council of Trent in the sixteenth century abolished all liturgical rites of shorter duration than two hundred years. There were no further reforms until 1911 (by Pope Pius X) and 1955 (by Pope Pius XII). Vatican II, in the 1960s, called for further liturgical reform.

The Sacramentary is also known as the Missal of Paul VI.

Today there are five official liturgical books. The Sacramentary has all the prayers for the Eucharistic celebration except the readings. The Lectionary contains the readings for the Mass. These readings cover the most important parts of the Bible by using a three-year cycle for Sundays (A, B, C) and a two-year rotation plan (I, II) for weekdays. The Ritual provides prayers, directions, and explanations for the celebration of the sacraments. The Liturgy of the Hours, also known as the Prayer of Christians, contains the Divine Office. The Pontifical is the book of ceremonies and prayers used by the bishop.

■ Ask a priest, sister, or brother to see the Prayer of Christians. What is its structure?

LITURGY

HOW TO FIND THE CYCLE OF READINGS

The readings for Sundays and feastdays are in a three-year cycle, labeled Year A, Year B, and Year C. Both the New Testament readings and the Gospel readings are in a semicontinuous arrangement. The New Testament reading may or may not relate directly to the Gospel. The Old Testament reading complements the Gospel.

The Church year, and each new cycle of readings, begins with the first Sunday of Advent. Regardless of the day or year, it is possible to determine which cycle of readings you should be using.

If, in the year A.D. 1, you started with cycle A, then in A.D. 2 you would be in cycle B, and in A.D. 3 you would be in cycle C. To remember which year is which cycle, add up the individual numbers in that year. If the total is divisible by three, you are in cycle C. If there is a remainder of one, you are in cycle A. If there is a remainder of two, you are in cycle B.

For example, if it is the week before the first Sunday of Advent in 1981, you add $1 + 9 + 8 + 1 = 19$ and divide by 3. Your answer is 6, with a remainder of 1. Therefore you are in cycle A. Beginning with the first Sunday of Advent in 1981, you calculate according to the next year, 1982: $1 + 9 + 8 + 2 = 20$, divided by 3. Your answer is 6, with a remainder of 2. You have thus started cycle B.

Weekdays are planned in a two-year cycle, known as Year I and Year II. If the year (before the first Sunday in Advent) ends in an odd number, you are in Year I. If the year (before the first Sunday in Advent) ends in an even number, you are in Year II. For example, before the first Sunday of Advent in 1981, you are in Year I. After that, in 1982, you are in Year II. In 1983, you return to cycle I.

LITURGICAL DRESS

Until the fourth century of Christianity, the dress worn by the clergy for liturgical functions was the same as the ordinary clothes worn by the people. The regular dress of the Greco-Roman civilization at that time consisted of an undergarment fastened at the neck, a tunic (a loose-fitting garment with or without sleeves and extending to the knees), and the mantle (an ample outer garment wrapped around the body). When fashions changed during the barbarian invasions, the clergy kept the old styles. These styles became symbolic, much as the uniforms of airline attendants, nurses, and the military are today.

In the Middle Ages, vestments became so ornate and heavy that their size had to be reduced. Although there has been a reduction in the number of pieces to be worn since the 1950s, there has also been a return to the free-flowing, ample styles of earlier times. Contemporary vestments like the chasuble—the outer vestment—are made of light materials.

■ What are the names of each of the vestment pieces worn today?

Originally, the stole—the long band of material worn around the neck by priests—was the mark of a deacon. The deacon wore the stole around his neck crossed from his left shoulder to the right waist. This custom is still observed by deacons. Apparently adopted in the East from the distinguishing bands worn by those in service of the emperor, stoles appeared in Spain in the seventh century and spread throughout the Church by the twelfth century. Today, stoles are made to extend to the hem of the alb (the vestment worn under the chasuble) on either side, and are worn as they were originally—over the other vestments—as a visible symbol of the priest's spiritual power.

In many places, a short, lacy surplice is now worn over the cassock on occasions when the chasuble is not required. Originally, this surplice was a dignified alb-like garment of heavier material used to cover a fur-lined or fur-trimmed cassock. After the development of the European lace industry in the eighteenth century, the entire garment was made of lace and drastically shortened. Designers are beginning to restore the surplice, or ceremonial alb, to its original flowing and dignified appearance.

Concerning the color of the priest's vestments, the Church has been careful to use colors appropriate to the spirit of the different celebrations. White, gold, or silver express the joy of feasts of our Lord, our Lady, confessors, and virgins. These colors are also used on Sundays during the Paschal Season. Red, which symbolizes love, fire, and blood, is used for Pentecost, Good Friday, and feasts of the Apostles and martyrs. Violet brings out the penitential spirit of Advent and Lent, the vigils of certain feasts, and the Feast of the Poor Souls. Green, the color of hope, is worn on Sundays after Epiphany and Pentecost. Black, which was customary for funerals, has now been replaced by white to signify the hope of the Resurrection.

- Which contemporary liturgical garments correspond to the original undergarment, tunic, and mantle?
- Do the priests of your parish wear the full or the abbreviated stole? Do they wear it over or under the chasuble?
- Which version of the surplice is used by the priests of your parish?
- What is your favorite church color? How and where could it be used in a liturgical celebration?

LITURGICAL FURNISHINGS

Because of the danger of persecution in the early Church, the altars were wooden tables that were moved by the deacons to and from the place of the liturgy. As Christianity gained acceptance, the norm became small, fixed altars of stone just large enough for the chalice, bread, and book.

In the first centuries of the Church, the Mass was celebrated near the tombs of the martyrs. Eventually, Christians built altars over the tombs, as in the case of Saint Peter's Basilica in Rome. When new churches were built, relics of the martyrs were brought to the altars and installed in their base, sometimes with a window to permit viewing of the relic. Later, these reliquaries, some very large, were built into the rear of the altars. Churches without first-class relics were sometimes given a backing for the altar. This backing gradually became larger and more ornate, including carving and statues.

The Blessed Sacrament was reserved in different places throughout Church history. In the earliest years of the Church, it was placed in the sacristy (a "sacrament house") or in a vessel near or hanging above the altar. In the sixteenth century, the Blessed Sacrament began to be housed in a tabernacle on the main altar. With the tabernacle assuming the prominence originally given to the reliquaries, the relics were cemented into an altar stone in the altar table.

The Blessed Sacrament is still often reserved in a tabernacle either on the main altar, on a minor but outstanding altar, or in another properly adorned part of the church. The trend in new churches is to place the Blessed Sacrament not on an altar but in a niche or on a dignified pedestal.

The reform of Vatican II has suggested that the altar of sacrifice should be the most noble, the most beautifully designed, and the most well-constructed table the community can provide. Since it symbolizes the Lord, it should not be used as a resting place for papers, notes, cruets, or even candles or flowers. With or without relics, it is the main focus of attention in the sanctuary and the center of the action of the liturgy. It is covered with a simple altar cloth and, during Eucharistic celebrations, should hold nothing but the chalice, the book, and the bread. Ideally, the altar should be large enough for only one celebrant.

Perhaps the best word to describe the present thinking in liturgical furnishings is simplicity. The celebrant's chair should have a place of prominence in the sanctuary, and the placement of pews (or chairs) should foster a spirit of community. Each person in the congregation should have a clear view of all the movements of the celebration, as well as of other members of the community.

The ambo, or lectern, is the stand from which the readers proclaim God's Word. It should be dignified in design and, like the altar, constructed of fine materials. This stand should be used only for reading the Word of God and preaching. Another lectern may be used by commentators and song leaders for giving directions to the congregation or making announcements.

- Of what materials and shape is the altar of sacrifice in your parish?
- Where is the tabernacle in your church?
- Where is the celebrant's chair in your parish sanctuary?
- How are the pews in your church arranged?
- What provisions are made in your church for proclamation of the Word and for announcements?
- Of the churches you have been in, which is your favorite? Why?

LITURGICAL LANGUAGE

The earliest liturgical language in the Church was Aramaic, the language of the Apostles, of their first converts, and of Jesus himself. As Christianity spread to the cities where the common, or *koine,* Greek was used, Greek became the language of the liturgy.

Because the language of the invading barbarians in the West was not sufficiently developed for the liturgy, Latin became the official language as the Roman Empire moved north into Europe. The chief Eastern native languages such as Syriac, Coptic, and Armenian lent themselves well to the liturgy, and so Greek did not replace them. While the Eastern Church has always used many languages, the West, from about A.D. 360, used Latin, which was the language of educated people for a thousand years.

The *vernacular* is the standard native language of a country.

When the Protestant reformers introduced the vernacular into their worship, the Western Church held onto Latin as its sacred and unifying language even though the people no longer understood it. Missionary countries were allowed certain exceptions. With the reforms of Vatican II, the vernacular was allowed for all sacraments, sacramentals, and the Divine Office. However, Latin, so long a part of the Western liturgy, is still preserved as an option in the Roman rite.

ACTION OF THE EUCHARIST

The Eucharist, or the liturgy, is a single action that has as its purpose union with God through worship. It brings God to us and takes our offering of Christ and ourselves to God. God's self-revelation and our response is expressed through the Liturgy of the Word, which is preceded by a brief introductory rite. Our offering to God and his communion with us is accomplished through the Liturgy of the Eucharist. The following outline shows each major division of the Mass and its subdivisions.

INTRODUCTORY RITE
Entrance Song
Greeting
Penitential Rite
Lord, Have Mercy
Glory to God
Opening Prayer

LITURGY OF THE WORD
First Reading
Responsorial Psalm
Optional Second Reading
Gospel Acclamation
Gospel
Homily
Profession of Faith
General Intercessions

LITURGY OF THE EUCHARIST
Gift Procession
Preparation of Altar and Gifts
Prayer over the Gifts

> *Eucharistic Prayer*
> Preface
> Holy, Holy, Holy
> Eucharistic Prayer
> Memorial Acclamation
> Concluding Doxology and Great Amen

> *Communion Rite*
> The Lord's Prayer
> Doxology
> Sign of Peace
> Breaking of Bread
> Communion
> Communion Meditation
> Prayer after Communion

CONCLUDING RITE
Greeting
Blessing
Dismissal

About the Introductory Rite

In some parishes, provisions are made for the people to gather before the service to greet one another. Before Mass begins, it is the function of ushers to help everyone find a place in the Church and to feel at home in this place of worship. A commentator may explain what particular feast or theme the community will celebrate in the Mass.

The entrance song is a call to worship and a means of focusing the congregation's attention on the celebration at hand. A joyous song may be sung as the priest and ministers process to the sanctuary. If no song is sung, a leader may lead the congregation in reciting the entrance antiphon, a short verse or psalm that has the same function as a song. If a song is sung, the antiphon should not be recited.

It is the celebrant's right and duty to greet the People of God as they come together with him to worship. One official greeting is "The Lord be with you," to which the people respond "And also with you." This greeting acknowledges the presence of the congregation and reminds everyone that the Mass is not simply the actions of the priest by himself. Christ is present where his People pray.

- Some churches are being built with large lobbies in which parishioners can socialize before services. What do you think of this trend?
- What part does the entrance song play in setting the mood of the Mass?
- What symbolism do you see in the entrance procession?

People often fail in their attempts to be loving. The penitential rite is a time in the Mass for reconciliation with others and with God. There are different options for this rite. One calls for silent reflection and contrition. Another calls for the common saying of the *confiteor* ("I confess to almighty God . . ."). In the penitential rite, there are also several forms of the litany "Lord, have mercy."

Prepared now for worship, the congregation joins in praying or singing the glory to God, a hymn of praise for God's goodness. This hymn, which may be omitted on weekdays and on Sundays during Lent, is included in the Masses on Sundays and feastdays.

The opening prayer of the priest comes from the Sacramentary. This prayer reminds the people once again of the theme of the Mass and focuses their attention on the reason they have gathered together. The prayer also helps us in preparing to open ourselves to truly listen to God's Word.

About the Liturgy of the Word

The main part of the Liturgy of the Word is composed of readings from Scripture and chants between the readings. The homily, profession of faith, and general intercessions (prayers of the faithful) complete the Liturgy of the Word. In the readings, God speaks to the community about the mystery of salvation. The priest's homily then explains what these readings mean. Through the chants (responsorial psalm and Gospel acclamation) and the profession of faith, the People of God formally accept God's Word. Having reflected on this Word, they then pray for the needs of the Church and of the world.

On Sundays and feastdays, there are three readings: the first from the Old Testament, the second from the writings of the Apostles, and the third from the Gospels. There is an order of ascending importance in these readings. Like a family record, the first reading reaches far back into the history of Israel to show how, for centuries, God prepared for the coming of his Son. The New Testament reading is usually a comment on the meaning of what God did for humanity in Christ. The Gospel proclaims the good news of Jesus himself.

The reading of all three texts is strongly encouraged on Sundays and feastdays. One of the first two readings, however, may be omitted for good reasons. On weekdays, there are only two readings, the first from either the Old Testament or the writings of the Apostles, the second from the Gospels. Normally, the weekday readings are proclaimed, unless it is a special feast or solemnity such as the Ascension or the Immaculate Conception. Then, the readings should respond to the needs of the group. The *General Instruction of the Roman Missal # 313* gives the following guidelines:

> The pastoral effectiveness of a celebration depends in great measure on choosing readings, prayers, and songs which correspond to the needs, spiritual preparation, and attitude of the participants. This will be achieved by an intelligent use of the options. . . . In planning the celebration, the priest should consider the spiritual good of the assembly rather than his own desires. The choice of texts is to be made in consultation with the ministers and others who have a function in the celebration, including the faithful.

The Old and New Testament readings should be read by a lector or subdeacon with great reverence. The first reading is followed by a response from the people and is known as the responsorial psalm. This response should be directly related to the first reading. The response may be spoken, sung, or silent.

■ Read the following Scripture passages (first column) and match each passage with the psalm (second column) you think best responds to it:

Jeremiah 23:1–6	Psalm 56:10–14
Exodus 20:1–17	Psalm 19:8–11
1 Corinthians 15:35–37	Psalm 24:1–6
1 Thessalonians 1:2–5, 8–10	Psalm 23:1–6
Revelation 7:2–4, 9–14	Psalm 149:1–6

After the second reading, an alleluia, or Gospel acclamation, prepares the people to hear the Gospel. This acclamation is also called an "alleluia," which comes from the Hebrew words *hillel* (praise) and *Yah* (Yahweh, or God). If there is only one reading before the Gospel, the congregation can respond with both a responsorial psalm and an alleluia, use either the responsorial psalm or the alleluia, or use only the responsorial psalm. The alleluia should be sung. If not, it should be omitted.

During Lent, when alleluias are not sung, other Gospel acclamations may be used. Some suitable acclamations are: (1) Praise to you, Lord Jesus Christ, King of endless glory, (2) Praise and honor to you, Lord Jesus Christ, (3) Glory and praise to you, Lord Jesus Christ, and (4) Glory to you, Word of God, Lord Jesus Christ.

The Gospel should be read by a deacon, the celebrant, or a priest other than the celebrant. This reading may be enhanced by the placement of two candles on either side of the reader and the incensing of the Lectionary. The congregation stands to acknowledge that God is really present in his Word.

In the prayers of the faithful, the people exercise their priestly powers by praying for all humanity. In general, the types of intentions that should be included are the needs of the Church and of civil authorities; the salvation of the whole world, including the oppressed and those in any kind of need; and the needs of the local community. The priest usually introduces and concludes the petitions. The community responds vocally or silently after each petition.

- Read Matthew 13:4–8 and 19–23. What are some of the "rocks," "heat," and "thorns" that prevent you from hearing God's Word in the Mass?
- What are some constructive ways you can improve the way the Word of God is proclaimed so that people can hear it better and act on it more easily?

Prayer

O Sacred Banquet!
In which Christ is our food.
The memory of his passion, death, and
    resurrection is renewed.
We are filled with divine life and light
And are promised a share in his glory.

SUMMING UP

Use the following questions to help you review the
main themes of this chapter.

1. How far back do the actions and prayers of the Mass go?
2. What was the original book used at Christian liturgies?
3. Name the five official liturgical books, and explain what they are.
4. When did priests first wear vestments?
5. What are the liturgical colors? When are they used during the Church year?
6. What was the original liturgical language of the Church?
7. Explain the structure of the Mass. Into what two main sections is it divided?
8. List five understandings about any part of the Mass that have become clearer to you in this chapter.
9. What is the purpose of the entrance song?
10. What is the purpose of the penitential rite? What are some options for this part of the Mass?
11. At a Sunday liturgy, how many readings are there, and what are their sources?
12. What is the purpose of the homily?
13. What are the options in responding to the first reading?
14. What is the purpose of the Gospel acclamation?
15. Explain both the Sunday and the weekday cycles of readings.
16. What kinds of petitions should be included in the general intercessions?

Words to Know

Sacramentary, missal, Lectionary, Liturgy of the Hours, ordinal, chasuble, stole, ceremonial alb, altar of sacrifice, celebrant's chair, lectern (or ambo), introductory rite, penitential rite, Liturgy of the Word, responsorial psalm, Gospel acclamation, prayers of the faithful

Think/Talk/Write

1. Some people believe that Latin preserved a sense of mystery and reverence in the Mass. Others say that English makes the Mass more meaningful. Organize a debate on the pros and cons of celebrating the Mass in a universal language such as Latin as opposed to a vernacular language such as English.
2. What are some positive ways you could work to make the Liturgy of the Word in your parish more meaningful?
3. Some people criticize the recent Catholic emphasis on the Liturgy of the Word by saying that it is "too Protestant." What role does the Liturgy of the Word play in the Eucharistic celebration? How does it relate to what Jesus did at the Last Supper?
4. Jesus did not wear vestments at the Last Supper, and during the first four centuries of the Church priests did not wear vestments. Do you think priests today should wear vestments? List the advantages and disadvantages of wearing or not wearing vestments.

Activities

Choose one of the following Mass themes and then do one of the activities below using your chosen theme.

> Praise God for his abundant goodness
> Justice throughout the world
> Thanksgiving for friendship
> Searching for reconciliation
> Request for help in making a decision
> Openness to respond to God's will
> Better communication with others
> Appreciating and using one's talents

1. Design and make a set of vestments. Explain why you chose the particular colors and style.
2. Design and make banners or posters that reflect the theme.
3. Choose appropriate readings (two or three), a responsorial psalm, and a Gospel acclamation.
4. Choose three or four appropriate songs to go along with the theme and readings.
5. Compose five or six intercessions.

What is the Liturgy of the Eucharist?

What are the parts of the Eucharistic Prayer?

How do Catholics prepare for and participate in the Eucharist?

Eucharistic Liturgy

If you do not eat the flesh of the Son of Man and drink his blood, you have no life in you. They who feed on my flesh and drink my blood have life eternal, and I will raise them up on the last day.

(JOHN 6:53–54)

LITURGY OF THE EUCHARIST

In the Liturgy of the Eucharist, Christians give thanks for both God's Word and his actions. The Liturgy of the Eucharist has three main parts: the Preparation of the Gifts, the Eucharistic Prayer, and the Communion Rite. During the Liturgy of the Eucharist the sacrificial and meal aspects of the Mass become apparent.

- Read John 6:1–5. In what ways is this passage similar to the accounts of the Last Supper? In what ways is it different?
- In what ways does this passage resemble today's liturgy? How does it differ?
- In your church, is Communion given in the form of both bread and wine, or just bread?

PREPARATION OF THE GIFTS

The preparation of the gifts is also commonly known as the offertory. Earlier in Church history, great emphasis was placed on the bread and wine as sacrifices Christians offered to God. Today, the bread and wine are seen as God's gifts to his People, for which they give thanks. These gifts also symbolize the total dedication of the worshipers to Christ. During this part of the Mass, the gifts are placed on the altar. They should not already be on the altar, but at some other place. The gifts may be brought to the altar by an acolyte or may be presented by members of the congregation in a procession.

An *acolyte* is a minister of table service.

In times past, the offertory procession was a high point in the liturgy. People brought chickens, lambs, bread, eggs, and other items to be left at the altar. Today, a monetary offering symbolizes our self-gift and our willingness to support the work of the Church. This procession has reduced importance today, and the emphasis is once again where it belongs: on the Eucharistic Prayer.

Recent directives on the Eucharist have restored the important practice of the people receiving communion from the chalice. The chalice is the only vessel mentioned in all four Scripture accounts of the institution of the Eucharist. Early chalices were two-handled, similar to the bowl-like Roman drinking vessels then in everyday use. They were made of any metal, as well as of glass, wood, or horn. Since the ninth century, only precious metals have been used for chalices. Gradually a stem was introduced between the bowl and the base, and then a knob was introduced in the middle of the stem for easy holding. In the Middle Ages, the base was enlarged and the bowl was made smaller. The base grew even larger and more ornate, and the cup resembled a lily. Precious stones, enameled medallions, and pearls were also incorporated.

Present-day chalices are being made to resemble those of the early Church, and gracefulness, balance, and functional design replace added ornamentation. They may be of gold, silver, tin, glass, enamel, and even wood. But the interior must be plated with gold or rhodium to honor the precious blood of Christ.

■ Of what shape and material are the chalices in your parish?

Originally, the paten was a very large dish of metal or wood used to distribute the Eucharist or unleavened bread. When people stopped receiving frequent Communion, the paten's size was reduced so that it was only slightly larger than the large host which rests on it at Mass.

In the last part of the preparation of the gifts, the priest prays over the bread and wine. He asks the people to join him in praying that these gifts—this Eucharistic sacrifice—may be acceptable and pleasing to God.

THE EUCHARISTIC PRAYER

The Eucharistic Prayer begins with a prayer known as the preface. The preface is a prayer of glory. Full of thanks and praise, it sets the tone for the most solemn part of the Mass when Christ, in his sacrifice, becomes personally present in the midst of his People. The Holy, Holy, Holy imitates the spirit of the crowd who welcomed Jesus in his triumphal entry into Jerusalem. At the same time, it recalls the vision Isaiah had of the holiness of God that filled the whole Temple. This beautiful hymn of praise has undertones of the high glory of God as well as of the fickleness and betrayal of the mob who, a few days after praising him, shouted, "Crucify him!"

A *preface* is something that goes before or precedes another thing.

Isaiah 6:1–4

■ Why do you think the liturgy at this point recalls the betrayal of the crowds?

There are four official Eucharistic Prayers from which to choose, and they may be said at any Mass. Before Vatican II, there was only one Eucharistic Prayer. This, also known as the Roman Canon, has been retained as Eucharistic Prayer I. Eucharistic Prayers II, III, and IV were added after Vatican II. There are three other Eucharistic Prayers that may be said in Masses for children. There are also two more Eucharistic Prayers for Masses of reconciliation.

The Eucharistic Prayers are based on the ancient Jewish *berakah* prayers of praise and blessing. They consist of eight parts: Thanksgiving (the preface); the people's Acclamation of Praise (Holy, Holy, Holy); the Epiclesis (the invocation of the Holy Spirit to bless the gifts and the members of the Church); the Narrative of the Last Supper, instituting the Eucharist (consecration); Anamnesis, the memorial prayer expressing faith in Christ's Real Presence); an Offering of the Sacrifice to God; Intercessions for the whole Church; and a Doxology of praise.

Pronounced an-am-NEE-sis

A *doxology* is a short hymn of praise to God.

The four Eucharistic Prayers, with the prescribed prefaces for Prayers II and IV, are included here. Find the eight parts in each Eucharistic prayer.

Priest: We come to you, Father, with praise and thanksgiving, through Jesus Christ your Son. Through him we ask you to accept and bless these gifts we offer you in sacrifice.

We offer them for your holy Catholic Church; watch over it, Lord, and guide it: grant it peace and unity throughout the world. We offer them for N. our Pope, for N. our bishop, and for all who hold and teach the Catholic faith that comes to us from the Apostles.

Remember, Lord, your people, especially those for whom we now pray, N. and N. Remember all of us gathered here before you. You know how firmly we believe in you and dedicate ourselves to you. We offer you this sacrifice of praise for ourselves and those who are dear to us. We pray to you, our living and true God, for our well-being and redemption.

In union with the whole Church we honor Mary, the ever-virgin Mother of Jesus Christ our Lord and God. We honor Joseph, her husband, the Apostles and martyrs Peter and Paul, Andrew and all the saints. May their merits and prayers gain us your constant help and protection.

Father, accept this offering from your whole family. Grant us your peace in this life, save us from final damnation, and count us among those you have chosen. Bless and approve our offering; make it acceptable to you, an offering in spirit and in truth. Let it become for us the body and blood of Jesus Christ, your only Son, our Lord.

The day before he suffered he took bread into his sacred hands and looking up to heaven, to you, his almighty Father, he gave you thanks and praise. He broke the bread, gave it to his disciples, and said: Take this, all of you, and eat it: this is my body which will be given up for you.

When supper was ended, he took the cup. Again he gave you thanks and praise, gave the cup to his disciples, and said: Take this, all of you, and drink from it: this is the cup of my blood, the blood of the new and everlasting covenant. It will be shed for you and for all so that sins may be forgiven. Do this in memory of me.

Let us proclaim the mystery of faith:

People: (A) Christ has died, Christ is risen, Christ will come again.

(B) Dying you destroyed our death, rising you restored our life. Lord Jesus, come in glory.

(C) When we eat this bread and drink this cup, we proclaim your death, Lord Jesus, until you come in glory.

(D) Lord, by your cross and resurrection you have set us free. You are the Savior of the world.

Priest: Father, we celebrate the memory of Christ, your Son. We, your people and your ministers, recall his passion, his resurrection from the dead, and his ascension into glory; and from the many gifts you have given us we offer to you, God of glory and majesty, this holy and perfect sacrifice: the bread of life and the cup of eternal salvation.

Look with favor on these offerings and accept them as once you accepted the gifts of your servant Abel, the sacrifice of Abraham, our father in faith, and the bread and wine offered by your priest Melchizedek.

Almighty God, we pray that your angel may take this sacrifice to your altar in heaven. Then, as we receive from this altar the sacred body and blood of your Son, let us be filled with every grace and blessing.

Remember, Lord, those who have died and have gone before us marked with the sign of faith, especially those for whom we now pray, N. and N. May these, and all who sleep in Christ, find in your presence light, happiness, and peace.

For ourselves, too, we ask some share in the fellowship of your Apostles and martyrs, with John the Baptizer, Stephen, Matthias, Barnabas, and all the saints. Though we are sinners, we trust in your mercy and love. Do not consider what we truly deserve, but grant us your forgiveness. Through Christ our Lord you give us all these gifts. You fill them with life and goodness, you bless them and make them holy.

Through him, with him, in him, in the unity of the Holy Spirit, all glory and honor is yours, almighty Father, forever and ever.

People: Amen.

EUCHARISTIC PRAYER II

Priest: The Lord be with you.

People: And also with you.

Priest: Lift up your hearts.

People: We lift them up to the Lord.

Priest: Let us give thanks to the Lord our God.

People: It is right to give him thanks and praise.

Priest: Father, it is our duty and our salvation, always and everywhere, to give you thanks through your beloved Son, Jesus Christ. He is the Word through whom you made the universe, the Savior you sent to redeem us. By the power of the Holy Spirit he took flesh and was born of the Virgin Mary. For our sake he opened his arms on the cross; he put an end to death and revealed the Resurrection. In this he fulfilled your will and won for you a holy people. And so we join the angels and the saints as we say:

People: Holy, holy, holy Lord, God of power and might, heaven and earth are full of your glory. Hosanna in the highest. Blessed is he who comes in the name of the Lord. Hosanna in the highest.

Priest: Lord, you are holy indeed, the fountain of all holiness. Let your Spirit come upon these gifts to make them holy, so that they may become for us the body and blood of our Lord, Jesus Christ.

Before he was given up to death, a death he freely accepted, he took bread and gave you thanks. He broke the bread, gave it to his disciples, and said: Take this, all of you, and eat it: this is my body which will be given up for you.

When supper was ended, he took the cup. Again he gave you thanks and praise, gave the cup to his disciples, and said: Take this, all of you, and drink from it: this is the cup of my blood, the blood of the new and everlasting covenant. It will be shed for you and for all so that sins may be forgiven. Do this in memory of me.

Let us proclaim the mystery of faith:

People: (A) Christ has died, Christ is risen, Christ will come again.

(B) Dying you destroyed our death, rising you restored our life. Lord Jesus, come in glory.

(C) When we eat this bread and drink this cup, we proclaim your death, Lord Jesus, until you come in glory.

(D) Lord, by your cross and resurrection you have set us free. You are the Savior of the world.

Priest: In memory of his death and resurrection, we offer you, Father, this life-giving bread, this saving cup. We thank you for counting us worthy to stand in your presence and serve you.

May all of us who share in the body and blood of Christ be brought together in unity by the Holy Spirit.

Lord, remember your Church throughout the world; make us grow in love, together with N. our pope, N. our bishop, and all the clergy. Remember our brothers and sisters who have gone to their rest in the hope of rising again; bring them and all the departed into the light of your presence.

Have mercy on us all; make us worthy to share eternal life with Mary, the virgin Mother of God, with the Apostles, and with all the saints who have done your will throughout the ages. May we praise you in union with them, and give you glory through your Son, Jesus Christ.

Through him, with him, in him, in the unity of the Holy Spirit, all glory and honor is yours, almighty Father, forever and ever.

People: Amen.

EUCHARISTIC PRAYER III

Priest: Father, you are holy indeed, and all creation rightly gives you praise. All life, all holiness comes from you through your Son, Jesus Christ, our Lord, by the working of the Holy Spirit. From age to age you gather a people to yourself, so that from east to west a perfect offering may be made to the glory of your name.

And so, Father, we bring you these gifts. We ask you to make them holy by the power of your Spirit, that they may become the body and blood of your Son, our Lord Jesus Christ, at whose command we celebrate this Eucharist.

On the night he was betrayed, he took bread and gave you thanks and praise. He broke the bread, gave it to his disciples, and said: Take this, all of you, and eat it: this is my body which will be given up for you.

When supper was ended, he took the cup. Again he gave you thanks and praise, gave the cup to his disciples, and said: Take this, all of you, and drink from it: this is the cup of my blood, the blood of the new and everlasting covenant. It will be shed for you and for all so that sins may be forgiven. Do this in memory of me.

Let us proclaim the mystery of faith:

People: (A) Christ has died, Christ is risen, Christ will come again.

(B) Dying you destroyed our death, rising you restored our life. Lord Jesus, come in glory.

(C) When we eat this bread and drink this cup, we proclaim your death, Lord Jesus, until you come in glory.

(D) Lord, by our cross and resurrection you have set us free. You are the Savior of the world.

Priest: Father, calling to mind the death your Son endured for our salvation, his glorious resurrection and ascension into heaven, and ready to greet him when he comes again, we offer you in thanksgiving this holy and living sacrifice. Look with favor on your Church's offering, and see the Victim whose death has reconciled us to yourself.

Grant that we, who are nourished by his body and blood, may be filled with his Holy Spirit, and become one body, one spirit in Christ.

May he make us an everlasting gift to you and enable us to share in the inheritance of your saints, with Mary, the virgin Mother of God; with the Apostles, the martyrs, and all your saints, on whose constant intercession we rely for help.

Lord, may this sacrifice which has made our peace with you advance the peace and salvation of all the world. Strengthen in faith and love your pilgrim Church on earth; your servant Pope N., our bishop N., and all the bishops, with the clergy and the entire people your Son has gained for you. Father, hear the prayers of the family you have gathered here before you. In mercy and love unite all your children wherever they may be.

Welcome into your kingdom our departed brothers and sisters, and all who have left this world in your friendship. We hope to enjoy forever the vision of your glory, through Christ our Lord, from whom all good things come.

Through him, with him, in him, in the unity of the Holy Spirit, all glory and honor is yours, almighty Father, forever and ever.

People: Amen.

EUCHARISTIC PRAYER IV

Priest: The Lord be with you.

People: And also with you.

Priest: Lift up your hearts.

People: We lift them up to the Lord.

Priest: Let us give thanks to the Lord our God.

People: It is right to give him thanks and praise.

Priest: Father in heaven, it is right that we should give you thanks and glory: you alone are God, living and true. Through all eternity you live in unapproachable light. Source of life and goodness, you have created all things, to fill your creatures with every blessing and lead all men to the joyful vision of your light.

Countless hosts of angels stand before you to do your will; they look upon your splendor and praise you, night and day. United with them, and in the name of every creature under heaven, we too praise your glory as we say:

People: Holy, holy, holy Lord, God of power and might, heaven and earth are full of your glory. Hosanna in the highest. Blessed is he who comes in the name of the Lord. Hosanna in the highest.

Priest: Father, we acknowledge your greatness: all your actions show your wisdom and love. You formed man in your own likeness and set him over the whole world to serve you, his creator, and to rule over all creatures. Even when he disobeyed you and lost your friendship, you did not abandon him to the power of death, but helped all men to seek and find you. Again and again you offered a covenant to man, and through the prophets taught him to hope for salvation. Father, you so loved the world that in the fullness of time you sent your only Son to be our Savior.

He was conceived through the power of the Holy Spirit and born of the Virgin Mary, a man like us in all things but sin. To the poor he proclaimed the good news of salvation, to prisoners, freedom, and to those in sorrow, joy. In fulfillment of your will he gave himself up to death; but by rising from the dead, he destroyed death and restored life. And that we might live no longer for ourselves but for him, he sent the Holy Spirit from you, Father, as his first gift to those who believe, to complete his work on earth and bring us the fullness of grace.

Father, may this Holy Spirit sanctify these offerings. Let them become the body and blood of Jesus Christ our Lord as we celebrate the great mystery which he left us as an everlasting covenant.

He always loved those who were his own in the world. When the time came for him to be glorified by you, his heavenly Father, he showed the depth of his love.

While they were at supper, he took bread, said the blessing, broke the bread, and gave it to his disciples, saying: Take this, all of you, and eat it: this is my body which will be given up for you.

In the same way, he took the cup, filled with wine. He gave you thanks, and giving the cup to his disciples, said: Take this, all of you, and drink from it: this is the cup of my blood, the blood of the new and everlasting covenant. It will be shed for you and for all so that sins may be forgiven. Do this in memory of me.

Let us proclaim the mystery of faith:

People: (A) Christ has died, Christ is risen, Christ will come again.

(B) Dying you destroyed our death, rising you restored our life. Lord Jesus, come in glory.

(C) When we eat this bread and drink this cup, we proclaim your death, Lord Jesus, until you come in glory.

(D) Lord, by your cross and resurrection you have set us free. You are the Savior of the world.

Priest: Father, we now celebrate this memorial of our redemption. We recall Christ's death, his descent among the dead, his resurrection, and his ascension to your right hand, and, looking forward to his coming in glory, we offer you his body and blood, the acceptable sacrifice which brings salvation to the whole world.

Lord, look upon this sacrifice which you have given to your Church; and by your Holy Spirit, gather all who share this bread and wine into the one body of Christ, a living sacrifice of praise.

Lord, remember those for whom we offer this sacrifice, especially N. our pope, N. our bishop, and bishops and clergy everywhere. Remember those who take part in this offering, those here present and all your people, and all who seek you with a sincere heart. Remember those who have died in the peace of Christ and all the dead whose faith is known to you alone.

Father, in your mercy grant also to us, your children, to enter into our heavenly inheritance in the company of the Virgin Mary, the Mother of God, and your Apostles and saints. Then in your kingdom, freed from the corruption of sin and death, we shall sing your glory with every creature through whom you give us everything that is good.

Through him, with him, in him, in the unity of the Holy Spirit, all glory and honor is yours, almighty Father, forever and ever.

People: Amen.

- In the Eastern Church, the Epiclesis (invocation of the Holy Spirit) after the consecration is considered essential to the Mass. In Eucharistic Prayers II–IV, find these invocations both before and after the consecration. Pronounced ep-ih-KLEE-sis

- What does each Eucharistic Prayer ask for before the consecration? Who is prayed for at this time in the first Eucharistic Prayer?

- Which scriptural liturgical formula do the Eucharistic Prayers follow for the words of consecration? See Matthew 26:26–29; Mark 14:22–25; Luke 22:19–20; 1 Corinthians 11:24–25.

- The anamnesis or memorial prayer occurs right after the consecration. What is remembered?

At the end of the Eucharistic Prayer, the people respond with a heartfelt "Amen!" This amen is called the

Great Amen, because it affirms everything that has taken place throughout the Eucharistic Prayer. For the Jews and early Christians, a prayer was not complete or "validated" unless it ended with an "amen." This is another reason why the Great Amen is considered so important and should have a place of prominence in today's liturgies.

EUCHARISTIC GRAMMAR

Hardly anyone pays much attention to grammar these days, but sometimes it can make a great deal of difference. In a legal document, such as a will, the addition of one small adverb like *not* can mean that someone will be cheated out of an inheritance.

In the liturgy, the prepositions used are of tremendous importance. In many prayers of the Eucharistic celebration, the prepositions follow this order: from, through, in, to. *From* God the Father, *through* Christ, *in* the Holy Spirit, back *to* the Father.

This order may not seem important, but it expresses God's entire plan for the world. Every good thing comes from the pure goodness of the Father, through Jesus the great mediator. Without Jesus, no one can receive anything from the Father or even approach him. The Holy Spirit, sent by Christ and the Father, is present personally with his gifts. It is in the Spirit that we are united with Christ. Our response to the Father works in reverse order: it is by the presence of the Spirit within that we return back to the Father, through Christ.

- Look for any of the four key relationships—from, through, in, to—as expressed in Ephesians 1:3–14. Do the same for Ephesians 2:4–5 and 18–22.
- Find evidence of this plan of salvation in the prepositions you find in the concluding doxology of the Eucharistic Prayers and the first paragraphs of the prefaces of Eucharistic Prayers II and III.

THE COMMUNION RITE

The Communion rite begins with the Our Father. Even in Communion services outside of Mass, the Our Father is included as a preparation for reception of the Eucharist.

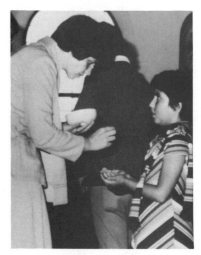

Matthew 5:23–24

- Why is the Our Father a good preparation for Communion?
- What are the seven petitions included in the Our Father?

The sign of peace occurs after the Our Father, but may occur anytime throughout the Mass preceding the reception of Communion. This gesture of reconciliation is based on Jesus' instruction to his followers, "If you bring your gift to the altar and there recall that your brother has anything against you, leave your gift at the altar, go first to be reconciled with your brother, and then come and offer your gift."

- What are some ways to offer the sign of peace?

Just before Communion, the priest breaks the bread and drops a small part into the chalice. This action is known as the fraction rite. At this time, the priest may also break up the bread into smaller pieces for Communion. The priest then reminds the people that Jesus is the Lamb of God who takes away the sin of the world. The faithful then approach the altar to receive Communion, the body and blood of Christ.

FULL EUCHARISTIC PARTICIPATION

Religious practices have a way of moving back and forth between extremes. Following Christ's ascension, when initiated Christians gave thanks to the Father for the gift of Christ through the Eucharist, their participation in the Mass reached its high point when they partook of the bread and the cup. Their liturgical participation always involved this sign of full communion with Christ.

As time passed, this ideal situation changed in a variety of ways. People came to eat and drink, without due reverence for Christ. As early as A.D. 54, Saint Paul taught that full participation in the Eucharist required certain standards of behavior. He reprimanded the Corinthians for getting drunk and for not sharing their food. "Whoever eats the bread or drinks the cup of the Lord unworthily sins against the body and blood of the Lord. A man should examine himself first; only then should he eat of the bread and drink of the cup."

In the fourth century, when the Arian heresy denied Christ's divinity, Christians began placing such emphasis on his divinity that people soon felt unworthy to partake of Communion. For centuries, Christians approached the altar only a few times a year at the high feasts.

By the Middle Ages, the Eucharist had developed into a sacrament to be adored and looked at rather than eaten as Christ had commanded. Besides this, the Jansenist heresy of the sixteenth century, which stressed the need of great personal holiness for Communion, discouraged frequent Communion. Christ's original purpose in giving the Eucharist—to heal sinners—was almost reversed.

With the return to Christian roots ushered in by Vatican II, people today receive Communion frequently. As in the early Church, the danger is to slip into superficial habits, as though the Eucharist were only ordinary food. Like all the sacraments, the Eucharist challenges today's Christians to practice reverence and thoughtful participation.

■ What would you consider a reception of Communion which dishonors Christ?

REQUIREMENTS OF RECEPTION

Because the Eucharist is a visible sign and source of unity, only those who have been baptized in Christ and

Full participation means receiving the Sacrament.

1 Corinthians 11:27–28

who are in full communion with his Church may receive Communion. Christians who are not in close friendship with God are not prepared to eat the food of Communion. No one who is guilty of serious sin, even though he or she seems to be contrite, may approach the Holy Eucharistic table without previous sacramental reconciliation.

A communicant should approach the altar with the right intentions. To receive the Eucharist routinely or because everyone else does, instead of for the purpose of coming closer to Christ, would be to ignore God's faithful love and the return of honest love he deserves.

Finally, the Communion fast should be observed. This fast requires that one neither eat nor drink anything other than water one hour before the reception of Communion. The sick and the aged need to fast only fifteen minutes, and they may take nonalcoholic beverages and liquid or solid medicine up to the moment they receive Communion. Respect for the Lord also suggests that one neither celebrate the Eucharist in immodest or disorderly clothes nor receive Communion while chewing gum.

WHAT NEXT?

No one can say for sure what lies ahead in the life of any living organism, but of one thing you can be certain: where there is life, there is growth and change.

■ What changes can you look forward to in the liturgy? Exercise your imagination and dream up some possibilities for the year 2000.

In the future, there will probably be more careful use of nonsexist language in the liturgy. The Our Father may also appear in more contemporary language, replacing "thee," "thou," and "thy" with "you" and "your."

New Eucharistic Prayers may be added to the current list for special occasions such as baptism, confirmation, marriage, ordination, and funerals. Perhaps such holidays as Easter, Pentecost, and Christmas will enjoy their own canons as well.

Certain rites or prayers may be omitted, especially if they are repetitious or of limited meaning. Songs of praise sung as part of the entrance rite could easily replace the standard Glory to God. The washing of hands, which symbolizes a repentance that has already been expressed in the penitential rite, may be omitted.

Some parts of the Mass may become movable. For instance, the penitential rite may follow as a response to the Scripture readings and homily, rather than as a preparation for them. The Glory to God could be placed after Communion. The sign of peace might serve as a welcome during the entrance rite or express our willingness to be reconciled to our brothers and sisters before the preparation of the gifts. It might also be a visible response to the "Go in peace" at the end of the Mass.

Finally, there will probably be bread that looks and tastes like bread.

You may be able to think of other changes to make the chief acts of worship more truly expressive of what is going on in the hearts of the People of God. Although

the outer form of the Mass may change, the inner core of the Eucharist—Christ's perfect worship of the Father through the sacrifice of Calvary—will never change.

- What do you see ahead for women in ministry?
- What are the remedies for parishes that are too large and the growing shortage of priests?
- What results may flow from the ecumenical movement?
- What would you tell a friend who confides that he or she neither understands nor likes one of the changes introduced in the liturgy of your parish?
- What changes have you witnessed? Which have added to the meaning of the liturgy for you? Why?
- Do you think factions would develop within a parish if different kinds of Masses suitable to its different groups were offered? Why or why not?
- Who should have a say in the planning of the liturgy? What opportunities for liturgy planning are available for you in your parish? How can you create opportunities?

COMMUNION OPTIONS

Today, there are several options for receiving Communion. It is recommended that the faithful receive both bread and wine whenever possible. "Amen," which can be translated "so it is," is the Christian's response of faith to the Eucharistic minister's declaration: "The body (blood) of Christ."

The Eucharistic bread may be received on the tongue or in the hand. Receiving on the tongue is the only way to receive the sacred species when it has been dipped in the wine (intinction). One who receives Communion in the hand should accept the Eucharist in his or her cupped hand, step to one side, pick it up with the other hand, and immediately consume it. Communicants should consume the sacred bread normally, even chewing it if necessary.

The cup should not be taken impersonally from the altar. It should be handed by the minister in a personal way to each communicant. After drinking, the communicant returns the cup to the minister. Courtesy for the health of others suggests that anyone who has a cold or some other orally communicable disease should communicate only under the sign of bread.

The priest is united with the community in consecrating the bread and wine. For this reason, the priest does not ordinarily offer Mass alone. We give external evidence of our priestly power to share in the Eucharist by receiving the bread and cup as our response to Christ's offer of love. Our Communion is a sign of our willingness to die to evil and rise with Christ to our true and best self in God's glory.

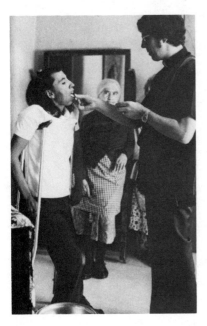

Intinction is the form of Communion in which the bread is dipped into the wine and then given to the communicant.

THANKSGIVING AFTER COMMUNION

Each person's union with Christ after receiving his sacramental presence is unique. It is appropriate to spend the moments after Communion sharing with Christ all that is in one's heart—thanking him, praising him, offering oneself to his love, renewing one's resolutions, asking for one's needs. Communicants may wish to use this time to sing or pray acts of faith, trust, love, contrition, humility, or gratitude, or to pray without words, communing with Christ heart to heart. Making the words of the Communion song or meditation one's own prayer is the best way to spend time in thanksgiving.

- Write a prayer that expresses your thanksgiving to God after Communion.
- Compose a prayer, song, drawing, or collage of sentiments appropriate to the Communion experience.

CONCLUDING RITE

After spending time following Communion in reflection and prayer, the celebrant then offers concluding prayers. Once more he greets the people, and then he gives them a blessing. Fortified with this blessing, the people are invited to "go in peace" and transform the world with Christ's presence.

- How can Christians carry Christ's blessings to the world?

Prayer

How gracious you are, Lord:
Your gift of bread from heaven
reveals a Father's love and brings us perfect
    joy.
You fill the hungry with good things
and send away the rich in their pride.

Body of Jesus, born of the Virgin Mary . . .
and offered for us in sacrifice, . . .
come at the hour of our death
as our living bread,
the foretaste of eternal glory:
come, Lord Jesus,
loving and gracious Son of Mary.

Antiphons from the Rite of Eucharistic Worship Outside Mass

SUMMING UP

Use the following questions to help you review the
main themes of this chapter.

1. What are the three main parts of the Liturgy of the Eucharist?
2. What is another name for the preparation of the gifts? Why is this part of the Mass no longer formally called by that name?
3. What prayer does the Eucharistic Prayer begin with?
4. How many Eucharistic Prayers are there? When may they be used?
5. Explain the eight parts of the Eucharistic Prayer. Give an example of each.
6. Why is the Great Amen so important?
7. When does the Communion rite begin?
8. What are the requirements for receiving Communion?
9. What options do you have for the reception of Communion?

Words to Know

acolyte, paten, preface, epiclesis, anamnesis, doxology, Great Amen, fraction rite, acclamation, Eucharistic Prayer, full participation, Communion fast, dismissal

Think/Talk/Write

1. Write a paragraph explaining what bearing these four small words—from, through, in, to (as they occur in Scripture and the liturgy)—have on your life.
2. The Eucharist is a sign of unity. Non-Catholic Christians are therefore not officially allowed to receive Communion in a Catholic service. But could the Eucharist be a sign of Christian unity (the belief in Jesus, despite church affiliation) and an expression of the desire for full unity? Give your reasons for your answer.
3. State your position, in an essay, on any one of the following statements:

Women should be allowed to be priests.

Divorced and remarried Catholics should be allowed to receive Communion.

Wine should be given only to adults during Communion.

The fast before Communion should be discontinued.

Activities

1. As a class, plan a Mass that develops a theme contained in the readings of the season, the saint of the day, or a Mass for the dead. Do the following:

   ■ Write a commentary that includes some aspect of the theme at these points: introduction before or after the priest's greeting, explanation of the readings, responses to the readings, introduction and conclusion to the intercessory prayers, meditation during the preparation of the gifts, and meditation after Communion.

   ■ Incorporate music that is appropriate to the theme of the Mass.

   ■ Inform the priest of the theme ahead of time, so that he can develop it in the homily and at other places in the Mass if he is willing.

   ■ Make banners to carry out the theme.

   ■ Get as many people as possible involved in the action: Mass planners, bannermakers, musicians, cantors, readers, persons to mimeograph programs or pass out songbooks, groups to form the entrance and offertory processions, and sacristans.

   ■ Decide on a practical project that will in some small way continue the theme of the Mass in your class, school, or neighborhood.

2. Create a slide presentation using nature or people to suggest the mood of each of the five main divisions of the Eucharist. Write your own script to explain what each part means and incorporate some of the most important Mass prayers. Add a musical setting or use songs that the class can sing during the presentation.

3. Depict the mood of each section of the Mass in a dance sequence, a series of paintings, or a collage.

In the Eucharist, Jesus comes with the message of God's love; in his personal presence he also makes his own tremendous power available to the Church for the spread of love in the world. The origin of the Eucharist is the Last Supper, where, in sacramental signs, Jesus gave himself to the people of the New Covenant as the source and center of their union with God and one another. After the Resurrection, the Apostles realized that in transforming the Passover supper of the Jews, Jesus had showed his intention to sacrifice his life that the world might be one with God in him. They repeated his action with high expectations of the coming of the kingdom as Jesus had promised.

Before the end of the first century, the basic form of the Eucharist had already been set. During the next several centuries, the books of liturgical prayers, the vestments, the furnishings, and the language of the liturgy evolved to add rich symbolic dimensions to the Mass.

Today, the single action of the Eucharist communicates God's Word and our response throughout the Liturgy of the Word. Our offering and thanksgiving to God and his communion with us are accomplished through the Liturgy of the Eucharist. This second part of the Mass has three important parts: the Preparation of the Gifts, the great Eucharistic Prayer, and the Communion Rite. While the external aspects of the Mass do change periodically, the essential element of the Eucharist never changes: the Paschal Mystery is made present for the believing community in every Mass.

PART III

SACRAMENTS OF RECONCILIATION

The Father has shown forth his mercy by reconciling the world to himself in Christ.

(INTRODUCTION, *RITE OF PENANCE*)

EIGHT

What is the meaning of sacrifice?

What did Jesus sacrifice?

How can the Last Supper, the crucifixion, and the Mass be perceived as the same event?

How does the bread and wine become Christ's body and blood?

Why is the Eucharist a sacrament of Reconciliation?

Healing Sacrifice

Every time you eat this bread and drink from this cup, you proclaim the Lord's death until he comes.

(1 Corinthians 11:26)

SACRIFICE: A GIFT TO GOD

One evening, a family was celebrating their mother's birthday. When the time arrived to present the gifts, the youngest child was instructed to sit in a chair and watch. One by one, the father and the two older children came in from the kitchen carrying their gifts on a tray. The little girl, too young to be in on the gift selection, had been left out of the joyous plans. But when the others thought the party was over, she appeared from the kitchen carrying an empty tray. Placing it on the floor before her mother, she stepped onto it and said, with a wriggle of delight, "Mommy, I give you me!"

- What demands or sacrifices does a self-gift entail?
- What gifts or sacrifices do children make for their parents? Parents for children?
- What message does a self-gift have?
- What are some things people sacrifice in order to give gifts to others?

From one point of view, sacrifice implies giving up something valuable. From another viewpoint, sacrifice can be seen as something positive. It can be a means to an even more valuable goal. For instance, athletes make many sacrifices in order to make the team. They continue to make sacrifices in order to keep winning. Some people sacrifice to lose weight or stay slim. Others sacrifice in order to get a good education. The word "sacrifice" derives from two Latin words, *sacra* (holy) and *facere* (to make). These words show that sacrifice has another shade of meaning. A sacrifice can be something set aside and publicly offered by an authorized representative for a holy purpose—to serve as a gift for the worship of God.

A SACRIFICE THAT RECONCILES

Because of sin, throughout history people have found it difficult to maintain their relationship with the divine. The ancient peoples employed rituals and sacrifices to reestablish contact with the offended gods by offering them gifts. Even the Chosen People of Israel strayed from God by failing to keep the promises they made in the Covenant. They needed a means of continual reconciliation with God. In Old Testament times, an animal was slaughtered as a sacrifice to God. Actually, the killing of the sacrificial victim was something secondary and preliminary in these sacrifices. The real purpose of the rite was reconciliation.

Still, the relationship between God and his People was incomplete because God had not yet fully revealed himself. The animal sacrifices of the Israelites could not ensure freedom from the burden of sin, nor could the sacrifices guarantee full access to the friendship of God. In the Paschal Mystery, Christ became the perfect sacrifice and made full reconciliation with God possible.

Through Christ, God's forgiveness of sin is complete and offered to all who accept baptism in the name of the Father, Son, and Holy Spirit. And because Christ is God, his sacrifice on our behalf is God's pledge of eternal friendship with humanity. That same reconciliation and friendship are made available to the Church in a special way in the Eucharist.

JESUS' GIFT OF HIMSELF

The Eucharist is more than just a meal; it is *the* great sacrament of reconciliation. It is Christ's sacrifice. Some Christians believe that it was Jesus' death that saved the world and brought about union with God. They wrongly hold that Jesus died because his Father, angered by the rebellion of the human race, demanded the death of his Son in order to make up for sin. Jesus' teachings say something different. He says time and again that his Father is a loving God, and such a Father would never destroy his Son.

See Philippians 2:8

Saint Paul writes that Jesus "walked the path of obedience." Jesus' obedience consisted in his perfect acceptance of all that was involved in being human. He willingly welcomed the pain of change needed for his growth and development. He accepted the suffering imposed by other humans, who were capable of mistaken judgments and of sin. Jesus faced the human situation that was his: the nation he was born into, the prejudices and misguided expectations of his people, and the bad will of some of the leaders who ruled in his day.

Jesus' loving obedience to God brought about forgiveness of sin and humanity's reconciliation with God. The role of Savior that Jesus accepted from his Father did eventually lead to death. It was not this death, however, that "made up" for sin. Rather, reconciliation was won by the attitudes and dispositions Jesus had throughout his life and that he embraced even in death.

Jesus' total cooperation with his Father's plan sprang from a deep inner attitude of absolute trust in God's goodness. Jesus' mind, heart, and instinct told him that God would never use his almighty power to inflict evil on his creatures. He lived in the confidence that God, as a divine Father, could and would bring good from every event. Jesus' response was profound thanksgiving and love, even in the unjust suffering he endured.

Jesus' inner disposition was revealed in the words he pronounced at the Last Supper over the bread "given for you" and over the cup "poured out for many for the forgiveness of sins." In these two simple phrases, Jesus showed that he was fully aware of what was ahead, and that he deliberately and consciously offered his life for the world's salvation. He, the divine victim, was also to be the priest, the human offerer of the sacrifice. His altar was to be the cross.

Luke 22:19
Matthew 26:28

The Jews regarded every innocent death as atonement to the Father. Jesus' perfect obedience in submitting to a death he did not deserve atoned for all human rebellion and established a New Covenant of friendship with God. The Father's acceptance was shown in the resurrection and glory of Christ, and in the outpouring of his Spirit on the world.

Atonement means making peace or bringing things that are separated into oneness.

If Jesus' inner attitude of obedience had remained only interior, it would not have been a sacrifice. By living out his inner attitude of perfect trust in God's love in the terrifying circumstances of the crucifixion, he set himself apart for God's worship. Jesus prayed to his Father at the Last Supper, "For their sake I dedicate myself to you." The Last Supper and Calvary were two moments of the same act of perfect love.

John 17:19

- What things are teenagers tempted to rebel against? Which of these "rebellions" are sinful?
- Submission is not always virtuous. Was Christ always "passive"? Was he a "rebel" in any way?

CHRIST'S SACRIFICE MADE PRESENT

Instead of offering an animal victim as Moses had done, Jesus set apart bread and wine as the signs of the gift of himself. But in naming them his body and blood, he did not create a merely psychological, spiritual, or symbolic memorial. By the power of his divine word, Jesus' presence took over the bread and wine completely. He changed their meaning so radically that they were no longer what they had been. They became, instead, truly his body and blood, signs of his actual presence.

Through the Eucharist, Jesus' sacrificial act becomes present, too. It is as if at a banquet celebrating the memory of a national hero such as Abraham Lincoln, the toast that everyone offered brought Lincoln—not just his memory, but his actual bodily presence—into the banquet hall to advise and encourage the people who honored him.

The Eucharistic meal is radically different from the Jewish Passover supper, which brought God into the midst of the Chosen People only in a figurative way. Christ comes to his People not merely in memory, but truly in his risen, bodily state. The Eucharist is the death, resurrection, ascension, and pentecost of Christ brought to believers under sacramental form.

To grasp somewhat how Christ is present, Christians must realize that although God is present everywhere, the risen Christ is, by his nature, only in heaven. But his risen life permits him to be present wherever he wills to be, in the way he wills. You may see Christ pictured in a host or chalice as an infant or as the crucified. But his presence in the Eucharist is not a physical confinement of his earthly body to the area of the bread and wine. When you receive the consecrated bread or drink the consecrated wine you receive the risen Christ really and truly present in the bread and wine, whole and entire, body and blood, soul and divinity, as he is in heaven. This is called being sacramentally present.

In sacramental presence, Christ is personally present under each form and in every part of both the bread and the wine. In sacramental presence, the bread can be multiplied and the wine divided without multiplying or dividing Christ, and many can receive his one body. It is a type of presence known only by faith because we experience Christ's Real Presence only through the signs of his presence. Christ's sacramental presence remains as long as the bread and wine remain—from consecration to the corruption of the sacred species.

Corruption of the sacred species is a technical term meaning the breakdown of the consecrated bread and wine by the body's natural digestive system.

LITURGY

In the Liturgy of the Eucharist, the Christ who offered himself on the cross is the same Christ who now, through the ministry of the priest, offers himself on the altar. Under the Eucharistic species (the exterior signs of bread and wine), he comes in the way that is most satisfying—as a human person. He is present in a unique way—whole and entire, God and man—as long as the signs of bread and wine last. This presence is also called *Real Presence,* not because the other ways of being present are not real, but because this way of being present surpasses all the others. It is the personal presence of Christ's glorified body. He makes himself truly present in a sacramental way in the Eucharist through the instrumentality of his Church.

When Jesus comes to us in Communion, he knows and loves each of us personally. As the food of divine life, he deepens his eternal life in us, transforming the human things we do into the true worship of God in the Spirit. Our words and actions become his proclamation of the Good News. Our service of others is both his service to them and our service to him, for "Whenever you did this for one of the least important of these, you did it for me." And so, through the Eucharist, the world is daily recharged with the current of Christ's love until the final day when God's love will be the light and warmth of both heaven and earth.

Matthew 25:40

- ■ Why is it impossible for someone who truly understands the Eucharist not to become involved with the needs of others?

THE LADY OF THE EUCHARIST

See Matthew 27:46

Luke 23:46

Acts of the Apostles 1:14

Mary had taught her Son to pray, giving him the human words. Now, under the cross, he taught her the secret of lived prayer. She saw that even when he cried out to God, he did not for one moment lose faith in the Father's goodness. One heart with him, she joined her perfect submission to his, hoping against all hope in God's faithful love.

In this, Mary is the Lady of the Eucharist—a model of participation in the Mass. Mary is mentioned in all the Eucharistic prayers. The more lovingly we accept God's will in our life, the more we, like Mary, participate in the saving of the world.

Human like us, Mary shows us how to glorify God in all our sufferings. Three days after she laid the mangled body of her Son in the tomb, she saw him gloriously risen. From her, we are given reason to believe ever more firmly that God's goodness cannot be conquered by suffering, death, or even sin. In Mary, we see that, by loving, God turns everything to good.

- ■ It is said that during their imprisonment in concentration camps many Jewish people shared their meager food and clothing with those more needy than themselves. What evidence have you witnessed of peoples' ability to transform suffering into beauty and love?
- ■ Mary's experience of the Paschal Mystery made her a strong influence on others: "They gathered frequently to pray as a group . . . with Mary, the Mother of Jesus." All true participation in the Eucharist leads to service of the Christian community and of the world. What forms of service to others are available in your parish? What additional services are needed by members of the parish and by others in the neighborhood?

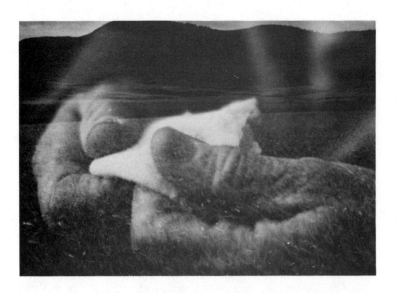

THE MYSTERY OF CHRIST'S PRESENCE

How the change in the bread and wine by the words of consecration takes place is a mystery. No explanation can clarify it completely, but, from the beginning of the Church, theologians have labored to find words that attempt to explain what Jesus did that night of the Last Supper.

While bread is an ordinary, basic food, it contains many meanings. It is the symbol of all God's gifts of creation and also all "the work of human hands." The crushing of the many grains to make flour is an image of human interdependence. It also signifies that while animals always eat separately, humans do not usually enjoy eating alone.

Jesus did not merely strengthen these meanings. He gave the bread an entirely new meaning. Jesus broke the bread to share it, to show that all present were one in spirit: Jesus with his disciples and they with one another. He changed the bread completely from a gift—a thing given—to the very giver himself. Although the appearances of the bread remain in the Eucharist, the reality of bread is changed into the personal, actual, and real presence of Christ himself.

To describe this change of bread into the body of

Christ, official Church teachings use the technical word *transubstantiation.* It means the change of the substance of bread into the body of Christ. The bread and wine are not annihilated or wiped out of existence. Instead, they are transformed. All their physiochemical properties—color, taste, bulk, minerals, carbohydrates—remain. It is faith alone that tells us that what we eat and drink is the risen Lord Jesus.

Because of developments in physics and philosophy in the last two hundred years, the word *substance* has undergone a shift in meaning. As a result, Catholic theologians of this century have been prompt to search for more suitable words to reinterpret the doctrine of the Real Presence. One of the new words is *transsignification,* which comes from *trans* (going beyond) and *signification* (the meaning). Transsignification validly describes the change in the meaning that takes place in the bread at the consecration. But many scholars feel that this word does not touch the change of purpose that comes about in the bread because of the changed meaning. The same is true of another word that has recently been coined: *transfinalization,* which comes from *trans* (going beyond) and *finalization* (the end or purpose). This word applies to the change in the purpose of the bread, but it does not reach to the change in its reality.

Thus far, no word is so helpful as *transubstantiation,* first used by the Council of Trent in the sixteenth century, to describe the "how" of the Eucharist. Although the term is not in the Bible and was never used before A.D. 1150, it has served for centuries to express what happens at the words of consecration. As Christians, we have the obligation to be careful of the words we use to express this mystery. The great truth that we must always remember is that in giving the Eucharist, Christ gave not merely a proof or symbol of his love, but his very self to be the sacramental food.

- ■ What makes wine a good symbol of God's gifts, your cooperation with God's plan, human unity, freedom and joy born of suffering, and Christ's blood?

Substance is a word that, in philosophy, always meant the total reality or essence of a thing. Today it can mean the physical material of which a thing is made or it can mean whatever is of importance, as in "You grasped the *substance* of the message, but not the fine points."

146   LITURGY

- What groups of people in your parish do you think are most lonely? What can you do to restore their sense of community?

SOURCE OF HEALING AND LIFE

All during his life, Jesus healed people by his presence. Now his sacramental presence brings healing to the people of every generation by making his supreme act of healing—the sacrifice of the cross—sacramentally present on the altars of the world. These symbolic actions do not repeat the death of Calvary; they continue it. Because of Christ's personal presence under the appearance of bread and wine, he—through the priest together with the laity—offers himself anew to the Father as he did on Calvary and as he does eternally in glory.

Through baptism, Christians become a priestly people, capable of worshiping the Father in Christ.

Although Jesus actively surrendered to death, all the emphasis in his sacrifice was on life. In submitting to death, Jesus actually chose resurrection. Jesus accepted death as the means to the greatly amplified life of union with God. It is for the sake of this life of love, this new wedding of humanity with God, that the Eucharist exists at all.

To be *amplified* means to be extended or enlarged in magnitude.

Jesus' sacrifice is an accomplished historical fact that can never be repeated. He will never die again. In the repeated consecration of bread and wine, Jesus does not relive or repeat his passion. Rather, he continually offers himself to the Father. Because of his divinity, Jesus' inner decision of obedience is a glorious, eternal act.

While Christ, the eternal high priest, has been victorious over evil once and for all, each Eucharist gives us a share in his offering. Every Mass is the bringing before God of Jesus' saving actions and a bringing to us of that one past action.

- The Eucharist is a great sacrament of reconciliation. What kinds of reconciliation does it accomplish?

SOURCE OF UNITY AND RECONCILIATION

Emphasis on Christ's bodily presence in the Eucharist may cause us to overlook the fact that Christ is present at worship in a very real way before the words of consecration over the bread and wine. He is present in the entire action of the Eucharist. The faithful themselves are a sign of Christ's presence. "Where two or three come together in my name, I am there with them," Jesus said. Baptized in Christ, Christians are a continuation of his risen life. Jesus also speaks personally to us through the Word of Scripture proclaimed in human words and explained through the minister as he preaches or explains the readings in the Liturgy of the Word.

Matthew 18:20

Eating is a natural sign of our unity. Food turns into body cells and even becomes part of our individual personalities. In receiving Christ, we are transformed into his body. And, since he has only one body, we are truly bound more intimately together through him. In this way, Christ in the Eucharist is the center of the entire Church and of each individual's life. He is the source of all Christian existence and unity. Because of him, reconciliation with God and with others is possible.

Christians partake of one cup and sing, "Because the bread is one, we are one." The early Church called this spiritual love of one another in Christ *ágape:* an unselfish love that was celebrated in the Church's love feast of unity and reconciliation. At each Eucharist, the priest represents Christ, the head. The members who are present at the Mass represent the entire Church, not only all over the world, but even those members who have already died. With Christ, the Christian longs for and works toward the day when all human beings will become one in God.

The Eucharist makes the Church much more than a religious organization, a social body, or a group with common teachings. Through Christ's actions at the Last Supper and Calvary, the Eucharist creates the Christian life itself. When Christ worships God through the Church, we live his life. As we see a new reality in consecrated bread and wine, the Eucharist helps us look at everything in a new vision of faith. Our eyes of faith receive power to see truth and love in their deepest reality. Like the cured paralytic, we can become more and more free, and gradually we are more able to choose good instead of sin. And, like the cured blind man, we are less afraid to tell the world what Christ has done for us.

See John 5:1–18

See John 9:30–33

Because the Eucharist unites us with Christ and his body, every Mass is a symbol of our glorious resurrection and union with creation that Christ's sacrifice has made possible. As we celebrate these mysteries in the liturgy, we are gradually being resurrected in faith, hope, and love.

Christ is the great reconciler of heaven and earth. As the supreme peacemaker of the world, he works each day to bring about the perfect fulfillment of the kingdom that Christians look forward to at the end of time.

- How does each sacrament originate in the Eucharist? How does each lead back to it?
- Do a drawing or painting, write a poem or letter, create a dance or a slide presentation expressing how the Eucharist is a preparation for heaven.

Prayer

Lord, God, in this mystery of the Eucharist, help us to possess one love and to be united in spirit and ideals. Help us never to act out of rivalry or conceit. Rather, let us think humbly of ourselves, looking to others' interests rather than to our own. Through this bread and wine, let our attitude be that of Christ:

Adapted from Philippians 2:1–8

> Though he was in the form of God, he did not consider equality with God something to grasp. Rather, he emptied himself, and became fully human. He humbled himself, obediently accepting even death, death on a cross.

Help us always remember that, as there is but one bread, we are members of his one body. We ask this through Christ, our Lord. Amen.

SUMMING UP

Use the following questions to help you review the
main themes of this chapter.

1. Why is it incorrect to say that sacrifice emphasizes destruction?
2. What did Jesus' obedience to his Father's will consist of? Why was he obedient?
3. What is a sacrifice? How is the Eucharist a sacrifice?
4. How is the Eucharist *the* sacrament of Reconciliation?
5. What actions make Christ's sacrifice on Calvary actually present?
6. Why is it incorrect to say that the Mass repeats Calvary? Why can you come in contact with Christ's sacrifice in every Mass?
7. What are the benefits of the Eucharist?
8. How is the Eucharist a source of unity for Christ's members?
9. What action of the priest represents your future resurrection with Christ?
10. In what ways is Christ present at the celebration of every Eucharist?
11. What does the bread at the Eucharist signify?
12. What happens at the words of consecration? What terms have been used to describe the change? Which is most appropriate, and why?

Words to Know

sacrifice, atonement, species, Real Presence, transubstantiation, substance, transsignification, transfinalization, *ágape*

Think/Talk/Write

1. In every Eucharistic acclamation, you affirm your faith in Christ's Second Coming. Several of Jesus' parables use the figure of a banquet to show what the joy of his kingdom will be like in the life beyond death. Read the following parables and answer the questions: Matthew 22:2–14; Luke 14:7–11, 12–14, 15–24, 16:19–31. From these parables, what "hints for happiness" does Christ give about the kingdom-banquet you experience in the Eucharist? Compose a "Dear Abby" letter asking for advice about happiness. Submit it to someone

else in the class who volunteers to answer your letter on the basis of the "hints for happiness" suggested in the parables above.

2. When the Israelites were dying of snakebite in the desert, Moses had a bronze serpent made and lifted up on a pole so that anyone who was bitten could look at it and be healed. To make sure that those healed understood that they were not worshiping the snake, the writer of the Book of Wisdom forbade a magical interpretation of the incident. What interpretation did he give it? Consult Wisdom 16:5–7. Saint John makes three references to this event in the desert. Look up each and tell what he teaches by it: John 3:14, 8:28, 12:32. Express your understanding of the parallel between the Old Testament incident and that of the New Testament in a composition, poem, prayer, drawing, pantomime, dance, skit, or any other form you feel comfortable with.

Activities

1. Do a research project concerning the place of sacrifice in the worship of prehistoric peoples, the Israelites, the Greeks and Romans, or present-day religions.
2. Organize a debate on the topic: "Sacrifice is necessary for true love."
3. Write a prayer service which thanks Jesus for his willingness to sacrifice for you.
4. Read the story or see the movie *Iphegenia*. What role did sacrifice play in the plot of the story? How did this sacrifice affect the lives of each of the main characters? How is this story similar to the Christ story?

NINE

What is original sin?

How does God respond to us when we sin?

What can we do to restore our friendship with God?

How can we live a life of conversion?

Daily Conversion

To err is human. To forgive, divine

(ALEXANDER POPE)

THE SIN OF THE WORLD

In one of Shakespeare's greatest plays, the Danish prince Hamlet, suspecting that his father had been killed by his present stepfather, says, "Something is rotten in the state of Denmark." Over the centuries, social commentators and philosophers have come to interpret "the state of Denmark" to mean "the world." Thus, Hamlet's deduction, when applied to present-day happenings, means that the world is basically rotten or crooked, that things just aren't right with individuals or society.

Sadly, there is more than a germ of truth to Hamlet's perspective. Many children come into families that lack harmony: tensions between parents reach a baby before birth; rivalries between brothers and sisters scar the young in their earliest formation; physical abuse turns a home into a prison of fear; hostile divorces or family ruptures can sow the seeds of lifelong emotional problems. About us, we see a society charged with negative values: infants are abandoned on random doorsteps or dumped in garbage cans; most cities cannot pass through a night without a robbery; fraud and deceit stain our highest circles of government; and, while adults may walk with confidence on the moon, too often their children cannot walk alone safely to the corner drugstore.

People who experience the "rotten" side of human nature are understandably appalled and often turned off by the world around them. They shake their heads and mutter that there must be something better (after all, there is a loving God!) than what they have encountered thus far.

- Do TV shows, ads, or other media suggest that something is wrong with the world? Name specific programs and commercials in your answer. What is your personal opinion about the state of the world?
- From your experience, reading, or study, would you say that people are generally good, generous, and concerned with others? Or are they more inclined to be cruel, greedy, and selfish? Give reasons for your stand.
- What things and characters in fairy tales symbolize the evil in the world? What part of the stories represent your longing for something better?

The world's web of disorder is the result of what is called "sin." Biblical writers defined sin as *hatta:* "missing the mark" or "being deceived by the evil one or by oneself." This understanding of sin still holds true in describing the disharmony we experience when we yearn to do what our best selves tell us to avoid.

Christians attribute the world's disharmony to original sin. Such sin is called "original" not so much because it was the first sin, but because it describes the original or root condition that separates people from God. Original sin is a complex term. It can mean the basic rebellion against authority and human unwillingness to accept God's commands. Original sin can

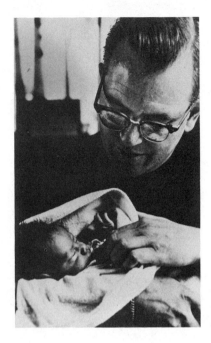

refer to the web of sin active in society, the disruption of nature that seems to act against good, and the personal lack of integrity that results from the failure to live up to one's best impulses.

- As a class or in groups, list any behaviors against society that you can think of within three minutes. (An example would be child abuse.)
- List the tendencies that draw you away from following the promptings of your conscience. (For instance, greed may lead you to avoid paying taxes or to ignore the needs of a neighbor.)
- How does the material universe seem infected by the corruption of human sin?

SENSITIVITY TO SIN

Television and radio news programs and daily newspapers seem to overflow with depressing news. But this does not necessarily prove that the world is more bad than good. It only shows that bad news is more attention-getting. If we open our eyes, we can point to dozens of fine people we know and hundreds of kind acts being performed all the time—in families, schools, hospitals, businesses, and other institutions. If we scan our acquaintances, we will definitely find people who are loving and good.

It takes sensitivity to see the good that is in the world, in others, and in ourselves. Likewise, it takes great sensitivity to recognize evil. Some people don't see anything wrong with abortion or other actions against life. Even highly developed peoples like the Greeks and Romans accepted infanticide, suicide, slavery, and illicit sensuality. Only a little more than a century ago, slavery was still a part of life in the United States. In this century, a supposedly Christian nation supervised the extermination of 6 million Jews.

Sensitivity to sin comes to the Christian through the vision of faith. Unless we have "eyes to see," as Jesus said, we will be blind to the sense of sin and its terrible

Infanticide is the killing of infants or young children because they are defective or unwanted.

power to destroy individuals as well as our society. People with a sense of sin are sensitive to the often invisible, but very real, destructiveness of anything that is contrary to God's design for the human race.

Besides recognizing the existence of original sin, persons of faith go further and take the giant step of admitting that they themselves are sinners. This disposition, which runs contrary to human pride, is a gift of the Spirit. It is in facing this truth that people find God, who is truth, and open themselves to receive his pardon and reconciliation.

This tremendous breakthrough doesn't happen just because people say "Lord, have mercy on us" or make an act of contrition. As Jesus said, "Not everyone who calls me 'Lord, Lord' will enter the kingdom of heaven." People must have a sincere inner conviction that things aren't completely right. They must know that they are torn and wounded and at cross purposes with themselves and their universe. And they must realize that they can't reach wholeness by themselves. They need God's help. They need a Savior.

Matthew 7:21

PERSONAL SIN

Sin is turning away from the love of God who, like the father of the prodigal son in the Gospel, is constantly waiting with open arms to welcome us to share in the good things of his house. Sin can be a partial turning away, a short detour, like a word of irritation spoken when we are tired. It can also be more serious, like a downright refusal to do chores, eat with the family, or show respect to our parents. Or it can be a complete "running away from home" with no intention of returning.

Sin does not begin with the external actions that others see, although these can reveal a person's basic attitude. Think of every person as possessing a core covered by many layers. Sometimes we all do unthinking, unintentional things that come from the outside layer. Such actions don't reflect our deepest self. For instance, you might angrily shove a boy into the locker next to yours because he is always in your way. But if his father were to be in a serious accident, you would forget this boy's thoughtlessness and express sincere sympathy—which was always a deeper part of you.

The more integrated we are as persons, the more we relate everything we do to our deepest core. That's why sometimes the saints considered their small faults to be serious failings. That is also why criminals who are disintegrated can experience no guilt for serious sin.

But no matter how grievous the sin, God's love never fails. Because of this, our very sins can be a way to increase our love. Jesus taught this lesson while having dinner with a Pharisee named Simon, who had criticized Jesus for allowing a sinful woman to wash his feet. From this story, we learn several startling facts:

See Luke 7:41–47

> The kind of sin we commit is not really the crucial issue.
>
> No one can make up for even one sin. God's forgiveness is a pure gift.
>
> Acceptance of God's forgiveness frees us to be truly kind, loving, and sensitive persons.
>
> As human beings, we tend to express inner attitudes, like sorrow, outwardly.
>
> Those who can open only a small part of their sinfulness to God's mercy will be only partially freed to be better persons.

■ If you know someone who "reformed" or converted from a life of sin, tell how he or she now reveals a deeper devotion to Christ. Is this person happier than before?

A FORGIVING GOD

Because people find it hard to forgive, they often picture God as having the same difficulty in burying injury. The problem is that human beings, who have never seen God, can only think of God as someone like themselves.

But there is someone who has actually seen God and who knows what he's really like. Jesus said, "No one knows the Father but the Son, and anyone to whom the Son wishes to reveal him." Jesus reveals the Father in human language, because he is God become human. What Jesus touches with his human hands, God touches. What Jesus cures, God cures. What Jesus speaks is the very Word of God.

Matthew 11:27

Before his birth, Jesus' name and mission were given by the angel. He was to be the "Savior," the one who would "save his people from their sins." John the Baptizer pointed him out as the "Lamb of God" who would "take away the sin of the world." Jesus' ministry of healing was directed against the ancient Jewish symbols of sin: sickness, leprosy, and possession by the devil. Repeatedly, Jesus claimed the power to forgive sin, sought the company of sinners, and acted out God's loving attitude of gentleness, compassion, and understanding toward wrongdoers.

Matthew 1:21

John 1:29

The heart of Jesus' message about his Father is contained in one word: forgiveness. From the first pages to the last, the Gospels proclaim God's desire to forgive sin. The parables of the Lost Sheep, the Lost Coin, and the Prodigal Son (or Merciful Father) show God's concern for and loving welcome of the sinner. Jesus' farewell gift of the Eucharist is his blood shed "for the forgiveness of sins." Even on the cross, he forgave both those who executed him and the repentant thief who died with him.

See Matthew 26:28

- Recall a time when you were worried about something you did. What effect did you experience when you learned that you had been forgiven?
- What kinds of things does lack of forgiveness cause people to do?
- Read the following passages: Matthew 9:9–13; Luke 7:36–50, 19:1–10; John 8:1–11. Which of these Gospel incidents of Jesus' dealing with "public sinners" appeals most to you? Why?

John 15:13

On the night before he died, Jesus told his Apostles, "There is no greater love than this: to lay down one's life for one's friends." Jesus not only said this, but he acted on it. In the Paschal Mystery—his suffering, death, and resurrection—we learn of God's great desire to forgive and be reunited with humanity.

Christ's submission to his Father redeems all sin. When we realize how much God has loved each of us and how impossible it is to truly appreciate such love, we may experience sorrow and a desire for conversion. Such love makes us want to keep returning to God in love, word, and example, to a place of harmony and wholeness with him.

- Read the parable of the Unmerciful Servant in Matthew 18:21–35. What is its main idea? What effect does someone's forgiveness of you have on your faith in God's forgiveness?
- What effect does the faith that God forgives you have on your relationship with others?
- Research these texts: Matthew 9:1–8; Mark 2:1–12; Luke 7:36–50, 19:1–10, 23:39–43. Copy the phrases in which Jesus proclaims power to forgive sin.

CONVERSION

The Greek word often used for "conversion" is metanoia.

When Jesus appeared on the banks of the Jordan, he asked only one thing as the proper response to God's merciful love. That one thing was conversion. In Aramaic, the word means "a turning" or "change." Jesus did not expect the Jews to change their religion. He expected something else.

Jesus summed up this expectation in two words: "Follow me." In this, he asked only for faith and for a complete dedication to himself. Unlike the religious leaders of the day, Jesus did not lay down a lot of small, isolated rules. He knew that once a person's heart was given to someone, everything else would follow. This is because a person operates as a unity. Everything we do and say reveals who and what we are. If we are dedicated to Christ, our actions will follow our heart. We cannot follow and not follow at the same time.

Just as an engaged person no longer feels interested in other possible mates, so the person converted to Christ experiences a certain settling and feelings of wholeness and healing. A conversion is a special moment, an awareness of a new direction in life. It may come as the result of some crisis, tension, failure, or problem.

Those who cannot pinpoint a definite turning point but who know that their lives are Christ-centered may find, upon close examination, that their conversion came about in small, almost invisible stages. Perhaps their conversion began with an enlightening word or perhaps a picture, prayer, program, or book opened the personal realness of Christ's love to them. Even those who have dramatic conversions can usually look back and recognize events that led to their peak moment of total acceptance.

The most mysterious thing about conversion is that, even though one definitely chooses Christ, the choice is more a form of "letting go" or surrender. It is an act of love expressed in trust and openness, a letting Christ in, rather than a "doing" of something specific.

Conversion, like human love, is God's love taking hold of us at so deep a level that we can't fully contain it at any given moment. A lifetime is not long enough to express it adequately. Nor can we know with certainty how complete our response to God is. The actions we perform are only signs pointing to the reality of our personal relationship with Christ. They are like the top of an iceberg that does not always reveal its true dimensions hidden underwater. However, if our actions are predominantly hateful, bitter, or self-centered, they reveal that our relationship with divine love is faulty. If tendencies of concern for others, joy, peace, and other good things come from within, we know that God's love is alive in us.

A LIFE OF PENANCE

Perhaps you feel that Catholics have more laws to follow than people of other religious denominations. Although this is not true, many Catholics take their moral obligations very seriously, because they understand the Covenant of love God has made with his new Chosen People. Those who sincerely try to respond to God find that complete conversion comes in God's good time and is not accomplished in a single moment. Conversion is not a one-shot deal; it is a way of life.

It is a fantasy to imagine that we can possess God forever and never be tempted by sin again. Jesus himself reminds people that the weeds will always remain with the wheat, the bad will always exist with the good. We will always be surrounded by sin and we will always be susceptible to temptation. Thus, we need to live a life of constant conversion, or turning toward God. In other words, we are called to a life of penance.

See Matthew 13:24–30

Many people associate penance with negative things such as sacrifice and self-denial. Penance may require some sacrifice and self-denial, but always in the context of something very positive. Penance is a loving response to the fiercely loving relationship God has with each of us. We are sorry for not loving. Through penance, we reaffirm our love for God. Love expressed in sacrifice and self-denial is never negative. Instead, it is a joyful, freeing experience.

By living lives of constant conversion, we are called to love again and again. All people thirst for love, but they don't always know where to look for it. It is too easy to buy the gospel of advertising, movies, or TV, which promises love from money, beauty, health, comfort, pleasure, and security. Jesus, on the other hand, says that he alone is the love that can quench our desire: "If anyone thirsts, let him come to me; let him drink who believes in me. Scripture has it: 'From within him rivers of living water shall flow.'"

John 7:37–38

The life-giving waters Jesus speaks of spring up at baptism where, by dying with Christ to the life of sin, we rise to his life, becoming his very body in his community, the Church. As each of us grows, we are required to make many decisions that affect our relationship with God and his People. Through these decisions, we either develop our unique gifts according to God's design and build up the community of faith, or we allow our faith to weaken.

Since we are attracted by both evil and good, living in the spirit of penance means developing a growing distaste for sin and a finer sensitivity to God in order to deepen our friendship with him. It isn't enough to go to confession from time to time to unload our guilt. Every action of our lives is meant to contribute to a basic Christian attitude of penance.

Specific acts of repentance can be shown outwardly by tears, bowing one's head, striking one's breast, fasting, abstaining, and using ashes on Ash Wednesday. The spirit of penance, however, is expressed in all daily actions. By these, we worship God, have our sins forgiven, and weaken the effects of sin. More important, in living lives of penance we replace evil with good and cooperate with Christ in reconciling ourselves and our world to God.

If the spirit of penance lives within us, we will want to express it outwardly from time to time. Here are some actions that express a spirit of penance:

Faithfulness to duties. You may have read stories of dramatic penances performed by the saints. Some had themselves whipped, while others wore itchy hair shirts or other instruments of torture. Even the jovial Saint Thomas More poured warm water in his beer as a penance. Today, spiritual directors favor consistent faithfulness to the duties of our state of life. Such penance is the surest way of doing God's will and inspires very little temptation to vanity.

A *hair shirt* is a cloth of coarse fabric, with the rough side worn toward one's skin.

■ What are the "duties" of your stage in life as a teenager?

Works of charity. Love of neighbor is a sign of love of God. Christ said that what we do to others we do to him. But love does not consist only in giving to others. The Anabaptists, for instance, take Jesus' words about

Anabaptists are groups of reformed Christians formed around 1500.

loving one's enemies with absolute literalness. They call this nonresistant love the "way of the cross of human relationships."

■ What do you think is the "way of the cross in human relationships"? Give some examples from your own life.

Forgiving others. In forgiving others, we are forgiven. To forgive is to let go of two things: our own hurt, and a sense of power over the offender who asks pardon. Only mature people—those whole enough to love—can truly forgive.

■ Why do you think forgiveness is so difficult?

Suffering. Suffering in itself is not good, but the way we deal with suffering can help us all to mature. Through suffering we can learn to be more sensitive to the pain of others. We can also grow closer to Christ, who suffered in order to redeem us.

■ List some positive ways to deal with suffering.

Prayer. Penance without prayer is meaningless. Prayer flows from the human need for friendship with God. In being called to a life of penance, we are also called to a life of prayer.

■ How does prayer relate to love? How does it relate to conversion?

Fasting and abstinence. In the United States, Ash Wednesday and Good Friday are days of fast and abstinence, and all Fridays in Lent are days of abstinence. The obligation to abstain from meat binds Catholics fourteen years of age and older. The obligation to fast, which means limiting oneself to one full meal per day, binds Catholics from twenty-one to fifty-nine. These disciplines are meant to sharpen our sensitivity to God and to make us more focused on him. They are also meant to increase our ability to love others.

■ How can fasting and abstinence practically help you love God and your neighbor more?

Use of sacramentals. Some sacramentals that are particularly penitential include the way of the cross, pilgrimages, parish missions, retreats, and days of recollection. Every year during Lent, the Church encourages all Catholics to foster a spirit of penance through such sacramentals.

- Make a list of the sacramentals you use. How do they help you turn toward God?

SACRAMENTAL FORGIVENESS

God loves each of us and forgives our sins. So why can't we just go to God to have our sins forgiven? We can tell God we are sorry in our hearts; why do we have to tell our sins to a priest? After all, what the Jews claimed is true: God is the only one who can forgive sin.

These questions, which are hundreds of years old, have been asked by almost every generation since Christ's coming. Questions that you may have now are a sign that you are beginning to truly accept the faith you received from your parents.

One Protestant minister, preaching over the radio, said that Protestants often envy Catholics the sureness of having their sins forgiven. Protestants, who ask God's forgiveness only in their hearts, often aren't quite as confident, he said.

This situation reveals God's wisdom in giving the sacraments, which—like Jesus' actions—are visible, external, human signs through which we may truly encounter God. When the priest hears our sins, we have given him a definite sign that we are sorry for them. The celebrant's hand extended in blessing and his words of pardon are concrete signs of forgiveness. In this way, the millions of people who live after Christ experience his forgiveness by seeing, hearing, and touching him in his Body, the members of the Church. We can approach God directly in our hearts, but because we have sinned outwardly and have affected others by our sin, we need to openly undo the evil.

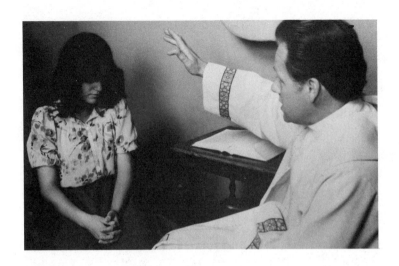

Another reason we don't just go directly to God for forgiveness is that Christ gave his followers the Church and the sacraments through which he willed to continue his actions on earth. When we confess to the bishop or priest, we confess to Christ because in a mysterious but real way the minister represents Christ. And through this official representative, Christ speaks to us and forgives us.

THE CHURCH'S POWER TO FORGIVE

Sometimes you may hear people ask how the Church can claim the divine power of forgiving sin. It is a matter of faith in Christ's word that Catholics believe in Christ's presence in the priest, but it is not an unreasonable belief. It would have been strange if God had gone to all the trouble of sending his Son into the world to cure only a handful of people in Palestine. After having entered his People's lives time and again to save them throughout the Old Testament, it stands to reason that God would create a way to continue his visible saving mission after the death of Jesus.

Saint John records that the first thing Jesus did on the evening of the Resurrection was to give the gathered Apostles the power to forgive sin: "As the Father sent

John 20:21, 23

166   LITURGY

me, so I send you. . . . If you forgive people's sins, they are forgiven them; if you hold them bound, they are held bound." This is basically the same commission given at the end of Saint Matthew's Gospel: "Full authority has been given to me both in heaven and on earth; go therefore, and make disciples of all nations. Baptize them in the name of the Father, and of the Son, and of the Holy Spirit."

Matthew 28:18–19

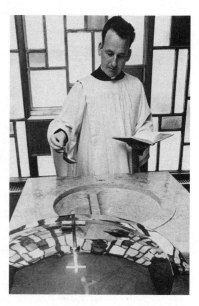

From the beginning, the main sacrament of the forgiveness of sin was baptism. This rebirth in Christ, which in the early Church followed a long training period, was a visible sign of a conversion so complete that Christians were expected never to commit serious sin again. But even in the early days of the Church there were individuals who sinned seriously after baptism. At first, the Church did not know what to do about this situation. Then, gradually, the Church developed a ritual that forgave the sins committed after baptism.

- Many psychiatrists highly recommend telling some trusted friend about your moral failures. Why do you think they do this?
- Some counselors send their non-Catholic clients to a priest to confess. What does the priest have to offer that the psychiatrist or a friend does not?

Prayer

Jesus, I have often sinned.
But when I see your nailed limbs,
    I realize what you were willing to do for love.
Your arms are open to reach out to me,
    to forgive what I have been,
    to forgive what I have done.
In your humble acceptance of suffering,
    you reverse my rebellion.
Your cross is the ladder set against the sky
    by which I can climb to God, our Father.
Your cross stretches across the world
    reconciling all things and all peoples.
Help me to forgive as I have been forgiven.
Help me to reflect your resurrection peace.

SUMMING UP

Use the following questions to help you review the
main themes of this chapter.

1. Name some evils that plague the world. What disorders also arise
   from within people?
2. How does the Bible describe sin?
3. Why is the penitential spirit so essential to the Christian life?
4. In what way is penance something positive?
5. What actions express a Christian spirit of penance?
6. According to Jesus, what is God's chief quality?
7. What response does God ask from his People?
8. What is conversion?
9. Why do you need an external rite for the forgiveness of sin?
10. How do you know that the Church has the power to forgive sin?
11. What is the basic sacrament of the forgiveness of sin?

Words to Know

sin, original sin, conversion, metanoia

Think/Talk/Write

1. Read Chapters 1 and 2 of Genesis. What is God's plan for human
   beings?
2. Read Chapter 3 of Genesis, and then answer these questions: What
   steps led to sin? What was the immediate effect of sin? What promise
   did God make to Adam and Eve? What punishments come into the
   world with sin?
3. Read Genesis 9:9–13. What promise did God make to Noah?
4. What promises does God make to Abram in Genesis 15, to Moses in
   Exodus 19:5–6, to David in 2 Samuel 7:16, and to Hosea in Hosea
   11:8–9?
5. What does Jesus do in Matthew 26:26–28 and John 20:22–23?
6. It is said that just as sin affects us outwardly, even the smallest inner
   experience of healing or conversion can touch off unexpected gen-

erosity or other acts that express change. Read Luke 19:1–10. What did Zacchaeus do when he experienced Christ's love?

7. At one time or another, everyone feels guilt, or at least a sense of uneasiness at personal wrongdoing. What actions in your experience relieve this uneasiness? What helps you to feel content, free, and whole again?

8. Some people say they don't receive the sacrament of Reconciliation because they commit the same sins again and again. The sacrament doesn't seem to do them any good. What answer, if any, is there to this problem?

9. Sometimes people can't bring themselves to apologize to the persons they have hurt. In what other ways, besides words, can they say they're sorry?

Activities

1. Interview a member of a religious community and ask what penances are woven into his or her life. Which seem the most freeing? Ask whether penance is a source of sorrow or joy, and why.

2. Research the life of any of these famous penitents. What problem did they overcome? What did they later do for Christ?
   Saint Ignatius of Loyola
   Matt Talbot
   Thomas Merton
   Saint Augustine
   Saint Margaret of Cortona
   Charles de Foucauld

3. As a class, adopt a concrete plan for carrying out one of the actions that express a spirit of penance. After a few weeks or a semester of doing this action, discuss what satisfactions and frustrations were involved.

4. By means of music, dance, art, or poetry, portray a person who goes through true conversion and begins to live in the spirit of penance.

TEN

What are the eternal and temporal results of sin?

How can we determine the gravity of sin?

How can we form a good conscience?

What are the benefits of confession?

Reconciliation

Nothing in this lost world bears the impress of the Son of God as surely as forgiveness.

(ALICE CARY)

SIN AND ITS RESULTS

Hugh McEvoy, age sixteen, a wild wit and school clown, died in the intensive-care unit of Manhattan's Saint Luke's Hospital. A respirator had kept him alive since the previous Sunday night, when a thirteen-year-old gunman had put a bullet in his head.

Six hours after watching his son die, Leo McEvoy faced the press. He knew that neither the thirteen-year-old gunman nor his sixteen-year-old accomplice had shown any remorse at having fired a pistol into the temple of his son as he was talking and laughing with a friend. Yet the victim's father, a state parole officer, said, "Toward the two boys charged with the crime, I have no hatred. They should be given an opportunity to rehabilitate themselves . . . I hope they can fulfill their lives. My son's attitude today would be one of forgiveness."

Mr. McEvoy's soft-spoken words seemed to touch the city's conscience. More than a thousand New Yorkers wrote consoling letters. The mayor and the governor attended the funeral. Cardinal Cooke, who had blessed the dying boy, later wrote his parents: "You have given New York a powerful witness on the meaning of forgiveness and compassion." Another noted Scripture scholar said, "I have learned more about Christianity from you in the past few days than from all my reading."

- What things do you think helped the elder McEvoy to forgive such a cruel hurt?
- If you were Mr. McEvoy, how would you respond in this situation?
- Someone has defined forgiveness as showing mercy even when the injury has been deliberate and there is no excuse for it. Do you agree or disagree with this definition? Explain what you think forgiveness is.

All people are expected to promote the general good of society, but the actions and attitudes of Christians carry an even greater responsibility. As representatives of the Church, they are to be signs to each other and to the world of God's special love. As "other Christs," their mission is to join together as a priestly people and to hasten the fulfillment of the deepest purpose of all creation—the worship of God and the building of his kingdom "on earth as it is in heaven."

But sin places an obstacle to this mission of the Church in the world; it promotes the power of darkness rather than of light. It tears apart, breaks down, and disunifies instead of reconciling all things in love as God wills.

Every act of evil, whether public or private, leaves its effect on the individual and society. Mortal sin destroys all relationships by seriously eroding the love and unity that God gives. If one were to die in such a state, he or she could be eternally alienated from God. Saint Teresa of Avila once said that hell is the inability to love yourself, others, and God. Traditionally, we call this the "eternal punishment of sin."

This effect is easy to see in the case of such criminal acts as murder, rape, and theft. However, it is not so clear how a person's secret suicide wish, inner jealousy,

or anger harms others. Even when interior sin itself never comes to light, it changes the quality of the sinner's life. Essentially a break with God, this kind of sin makes us less able to relate to others, to work within God's plan, or to cope with success or failure. Our personal defectiveness is carried into social life, affecting everything it touches. Traditionally, this effect has been called the "temporal punishment of sin."

- How does one family member thinking jealous or gloomy thoughts affect the other members, the plans and dreams of the group, and the things the family can do?
- Describe a time when someone you know added to your problems by moodiness, irritability, suspicion, or other negative attitudes.
- What effects do people with the Christlike qualities of patience, trust, and generosity have on you?

Conditions for Sin

If you are not free to act, if someone forces you to pull a trigger, or if, through no fault of yours, you do not realize that you are doing something wrong, you are not held responsible for your actions. Neither are you guilty if you do something that you didn't intend to do. For instance, no one would blame you if, in pushing someone to protect him or her from a falling object, you caused that person to fall and break an arm. These three things, then, are necessary for human actions to be virtuous as well as sinful: freedom, knowledge, and willingness.

For a sin to be serious, it must involve a complete rejection of a moral law. Our actions must show a serious neglect of the honor due to God, grave irresponsibility in family obligations or in the respect due to our own life or toward the life or property of others, or deliberate deceit on a grand scale. When we deliberately and knowingly choose to take or omit a course of action that wholly divorces us from God, others, or the Christian community, we sin mortally. The sin is in our intention. Even if we never get to carry out a scandal we deliberately planned, our decision to do so mars our character and harms our relationship with others and with God.

Serious and Venial Sin

The Old Testament describes different kinds of sin, including sins of commission, such as Cain's murder of Abel, and sins of omission, like Eli's failure to correct his sons. Serious sins—those done in open revolt against God—were distinguished from those of human weakness. All the sins listed below were considered serious by Jewish law. The sins that were considered serious enough to merit the punishment of death included murder, striking or cursing one's parents, kidnaping, adultery, incest, and homosexuality.

See 1 Samuel 3:13

- If you, a Jewish elder, were responsible for the welfare of the community, what punishments would you prescribe for each of the following sins?

idolatry	striking or cursing one's
blasphemy	parents
fortune telling	adultery
stealing	incest
murder	homosexuality
kidnaping	fornication
slander	

The gravity of sin is determined today by dividing all sins into three categories. Mortal sin is a complete break with God and his Church, and a personal, definite decision to do or not to do something that one knows for sure is a serious betrayal of loyalty to Christ. Every other sin is either serious or venial sin.

These three categories might be compared to degrees of fracture in a marriage relationship. After a difficult day with the children, a wife might slam a milk carton on the table in annoyance at her husband. That might be called a venial offense, one that is easily forgivable. It in no way seriously threatens the marriage.

If there is a bitter exchange of name-calling and physical assault during an argument, that would be more serious. Yet even that situation could conceivably be patched up and excused. However, in cases of long separation or divorce, the basic marriage relationship is ended completely. That is an analogy of how mortal sin breaks one's friendship with God. It is the whole self turned away from God in a rejection of his gift of love.

- One of the cruelest of human actions is the rejection of a gift. Describe a time when a gift you or someone else gave was rejected. Since, strictly speaking, God cannot be hurt by sin, why is rejecting his love such an evil?

FORMING A GOOD CONSCIENCE

To repair one's relationship with God, one must be able to recognize sin. Whether it is external or internal, sin is the consent to something less good than God's will. God's will for us is known as moral law. Following moral law will lead to our being better persons; failing to follow the moral law has bad effects.

The internal power that enables us to judge sin for ourselves is called "conscience." Conscience is not a separate sense like hearing or smell, but a power of the mind. Conscience can be considered in three ways:

1. The sense of right and wrong.
2. Our judgment of individual values, such as the morality of boxing or of abortion. This sense can be educated. It can make mistakes. We have the obligation to remain open to new knowledge and to obey the teachings of the Church.
3. The individual act of the conscience of a specific person judging the goodness or the badness of a particular action. What one sincerely judges in conscience, even if it is objectively wrong, holds true for that person. Thus if you do something you think is wrong but that is essentially right, it is wrong for you, and vice versa.

When we confess our sins in confession, the priest does not judge us, nor does God judge us. We confess our own judgment of the good or evil of our past actions and omissions as we saw them when we committed them—not as we see them at some other time.

It is obvious that the truer our conscience is, the better judge we will be of what can heal or harm us. A baby who guesses that a heater is cold when it is actually hot will suffer the consequences of the misjudgment. So we, too, will suffer the consequences of our moral misjudgments. Eating or drinking to excess leads to illness, even if we think it is not wrong. Allowing ourselves to think jealous, petty thoughts, rationalizing our actions if we cheat on an exam, showing disrespect to authority—all these things work to destroy us by making us less truly human. Conversely, the more closely we pattern ourselves after Christ, the more we become our true selves.

We can develop a right conscience by meditating on Scripture, by studying the Faith and the teachings of the Church, and by consulting books and experts. We also learn by doing. The sincere effort to follow our conscience and to be obedient to the good inspirations we receive is one of the surest helps. Prayer and the celebration of the sacraments are other indispensable aids to forming a right conscience. When we are in doubt and cannot obtain all the information we need from outside sources, we must decide for ourselves, using our best judgment.

■ To whom can you go if you are facing a tough moral problem?

Contrition

A well-informed conscience should lead one to have contrition for his or her sins. Contrition is, first, a recognition that we have sinned or done something that keeps us from becoming the person God intended. Contrition is not necessarily a feeling of hatred for sin; it is, rather, a cold, clear judgment that sin is evil. Second, contrition is sorrow for having allowed evil an entrance into our life. This sorrow, however, is not bitter like remorse or despair. It believes fully in God's love and mercy. Third, contrition is an act of the will, a determination to turn away from sin and to turn toward God. The sincerity of this determination is tested when we avoid those persons, places, and things that we know will lead to the same sins already confessed in confession.

In times past, it was believed that only perfect contrition—sorrow for sin springing from love of God—could restore the Christ-life lost by mortal sin. Sorrow arising from the fear of punishment (attrition) could not obtain the forgiveness of sin without the sacrament of penance. Today, some theologians think that all true sorrow for sin involves the love of God; this contrition leads to forgiveness of sin, reinstates us to God's friendship, and wipes out the effects of sin insofar as love dominates our life. However, Christ gave his followers the sacrament of Reconciliation as the ordinary way to have mortal sin forgiven.

Since we cannot grow in Christ's life so long as our friendship with God remains severed, each of us should try to repent—that is, to bring our mind and will around to God. Setting a time every day for personal prayer and meditation can help cultivate the habit of quickly returning to God. If we remember that God waits with open arms to receive us at every hour of the day or night, we will not waste time worrying about whether we are worthy to come to him. The fact is that God doesn't take us back because we are worthy, but because he loves us.

One important fact to remember is that God is not angry or hurt when we sin. God cannot hate anyone. He cannot be hurt. As God, he is perfectly happy and loving. What sin changes is the effect of God's love in us as we pull away or reject him.

Repentance is not necessarily an emotional thing. The Prodigal Son did not shed tears or throw himself on the ground. He thought the thing through, comparing his starvation with the better situation of the hired workers in his father's house. He remembered his father's goodness, and, most important, he was willing to admit his mistake. He resolved not to ask to be reinstated to his former position—only to be treated as one

See Luke 15:11–32

Luke 15:22–24

of the servants. He didn't mope around looking hungrily at the pig slop. Instead, "he got up and started back to his father." His hatred of sin was a conviction. He saw sin for what it was: an evil that destroyed his happiness and frustrated his father's wish to do him good. His faith in his father's kindness to his lowliest servants gave him confidence that his father might take him back.

It is interesting that when the son began the speech he had rehearsed for his father, he never got to the part about being willing to be treated like a hired hand. As soon as he admitted his sin, the father "called out to his servants: 'Hurry!' he said. 'Bring the best robe and put it on him. Put a ring on his finger and shoes on his feet. Then go and get the prize calf and kill it, and let us celebrate with a feast! For this son of mine was dead, but now he is alive; he was lost, but now he has been found.'"

It is not guilt feelings, shame at having been caught, or disappointment at the sadness sin brings that constitutes contrition, although these may help. Rather, contrition—from the word *conterere,* which means "to grind together or pulverize"—means to grind down that which is hardened. It is the opposite of what the Bible calls "a hard heart." A contrite heart is a heart that is melted down, broken, completely changed. It maintains no walls or other rigid structures that could keep God from coming in.

■ Compose a prayer or a poem of contrition that expresses Christian sorrow for sin.

BENEFITS OF CONFESSION

The sacrament of Reconciliation is the Church's way of expressing contrition. It brings about a reconciliation between the penitent and God through a visible reconciliation between the penitent and the Church.

Since every sin affects both the person and the community (others), it is not enough for the individual to

ask God's pardon in personal prayer. Neither is it sufficient to ask forgiveness of the particular persons our sins may have wounded or scandalized. Our reconciliation must be made in a way that the community or its official representative can see. Our encounter with the risen Christ in the sacrament of Reconciliation satisfies all these needs.

- What would you think of someone who seriously hurt you and felt sorry in his or her heart, but never showed this sorrow or any change of attitude in word or action?

People can experience deep comfort by the humble confession of their sins. It is psychologically helpful to talk over our intimate failures and self-doubts with someone who will not condemn us. We experience a sense of relief at sharing our burden of guilt. We receive encouragement in our efforts to overcome our selfishness and rebellion.

Modern psychology affirms that we reach our full potential through our relationships with others. The priest's acceptance of us as we confess our sins reflects Christ's acceptance. This religious dimension is perhaps the most healing of all. Even many secular psychiatrists recognize that they cannot get to the root of their patients' problems without superhuman assistance.

The famous psychiatrist Carl Jung, in his book *Modern Man in Search of a Soul,* wrote that healing could come to his patients who were over thirty-five years old only when they built a relationship with God. Alcoholics Anonymous has made a similar discovery.

Confessing our sins is, above all, a religious action. It expresses our love of God, which in itself forgives sin and remits some of its bad effects. Through admitting our guilt, we can grow in self-knowledge and humility. Humility does not mean putting ourselves down. Rather, it means facing our good and bad qualities in truth. Through confession, we begin to see the patterns our bad habits take and we can systematically work to root them out. We become better at recognizing the slightest whisperings of conscience. We more easily pray, do our work more responsibly, and see God in our daily joys and sorrows. As we grow in a sense of our own littleness before God, we worship him better, love and respect others more, and so become more Christ-centered persons.

Carl Jung (1875–1961) was a Swiss psychiatrist who founded one of the schools of analytical psychology.

- Just as it is best to have a regular doctor, it is advisable to have a regular confessor. What advantages can you see in such an arrangement?
- The encounter with the confessor is truly an encounter with the living Christ. Which three of the following qualities would you consider most Christlike in a confessor? Why?

    personal goodness   honesty
    experience   taking the penitent
    understanding   seriously

kindness	respect for the
youth	penitent
sense of humor	theological training
easiness	patience

- What three qualities in a penitent do you think a confessor would profit by?

openness	effort to improve
ability to make a	sense of humor
decision	respect for the
youth	confessor's
sincerity	advice
true sorrow	patience
personal goodness	careful preparation
	serious attitude

Two Kinds of Confession

The sacrament of Reconciliation can restore a serious break in our relationship with Christ. In this case, the sacrament is known as a *confession of necessity*. It is necessary because, under ordinary conditions, it is the only means for Catholics who have sinned seriously after baptism to be healed.

If one is in danger of death, an act of love for God—even an interior one—may forgive sin.

But penance is not only for sinners in need of "major surgery" for salvation. Christians may regularly approach this sacrament to confess their less serious sins, much as they would go to a doctor for a regular medical checkup. Such confessions are known as *confessions of devotion*.

The sacrament of Reconciliation preserves and builds spiritual health. Frequent self-examinations can deepen our life with God and lead to greater consciousness of our strengths and weaknesses. The graces of sorrow and repentance provide courage to cope with particular moral problems.

- Joan of Arc is said to have asked for the sacrament of Penance every day when she fought on the French battlefields with her soldiers. Why do you think she did this?

A GREAT CONFESSOR

The coach service operating from Paris in the middle of the nineteenth century had to arrange a special daily run to the tiny French village of Ars. The travel agency in Lyons was forced to issue tickets that were good for a week because the travelers always stayed in Ars longer than a few days. What brought so many people from all over Europe to a little town of a mere 230 people? The reason was one country priest who possessed the gift of reading hearts: John Marie Vianney, the Curé of Ars.

Beginning in 1827, penitents by the thousands flocked to the peasant priest's confessional. For thirty years, Ars had an average of 300 visitors waiting to consult the holy man who was almost refused ordination because he had left school in his childhood to tend cattle and couldn't master the required Latin.

From the time his cures and conversions began to attract crowds from outside his parish, the curé arranged a strict daily schedule to make himself available to the people. He would rise an hour after midnight and hear confessions until 11:00 A.M., with a break for Mass at 7:00. After a meager, fifteen-minute lunch of little more than boiled potatoes, he gave catechism instruction and visited the sick. He would then return to the confessional until 9:00 P.M., allowing himself only three to four hours of sleep each night.

Nocturnal is another word for nightly.

John Vianney's influence for good was so strong that he was the victim of strange nocturnal noises, cruel beatings, and, once, a fire in his bed—all of which he attributed to the devil.

Born in Dardilly, fifteen miles north of Lyons, John Vianney died in Ars in 1859, at the age of seventy-three. Four years after his canonization in 1925, he was named patron of parish priests.

LITURGY

What to Confess

When our confession involves mortal sins that have totally severed our relationship with God and others, then the sacrament of Reconciliation becomes a second baptism—with this exception: in baptism, there is no need to tell or make up for any sins that may have been committed before the sacrament. But, because we knowingly went back on our baptismal promises to Christ, we must now mention every serious sin that we can remember by its correct name, give the number of times we have committed it, as far as we know, and explain any circumstances that make it serious. If we deliberately omit some serious sin or fail to mention that the amount of money we took was very large, we would not be reconciled with Christ and his Church because our sin has not truly been confessed.

Unless we are confessing mortal sins, it is not the exact kind and number of sins that we should be concerned with so much as a growing understanding of what is keeping us from the wholeness that will attract others to us and, through us, to Christ. Because our venial sins have probably been forgiven by our sorrow before we confess them, the sacrament does not reforgive our sins. Rather, it gives us a deeper share in the life of the Spirit, making us better worshipers and more effective laborers in God's kingdom.

Deep sorrow and charity also forgive our mortal sins, but we cannot be reconciled with the Church community unless we publicly celebrate the sacrament of Reconciliation. This means that we cannot receive Communion unless we first confess our sins. The sorrow we express in confessing our sins and making an act of contrition, together with the celebrant's absolution, actually brings about the forgiveness of sin. We are then reconciled with God and can fully worship with the Church.

If you fall into serious sin, you can be forgiven as soon as you make an act of deep sorrow or love. You need not wait until your confession to regain your friendship with God.

There is no strict obligation to confess sins that are doubtful. For instance, if we are not sure whether we freely consented to thoughts that gave us sexual pleasure, we don't have to mention them. However, talking the problem over with the confessor may put us at ease. He may ask us questions about our intentions when we get into situations of temptation and then assure us that we really are doing the best we can to love God. This in itself will help us in the next temptation, by relaxing us and increasing our trust in Christ, who is with us as we struggle to act according to God's will.

If we forget to tell a serious sin after reasonably careful preparation, the forgotten sin is forgiven with all the others. If, later, we remember that we forgot to confess something, we should mention it in our next confession. We should never be phony, however, by accusing ourselves of things we know we are not responsible for.

Our confession can deepen our union with God and with our brothers and sisters. The closer we draw to God, the more we will realize what a great evil sin is and the more we will want to turn even more seriously to God for assistance.

Penance and Atonement

The prayers we are given to say in confession for the persons we have harmed change us so that we may be better able to relate to that person. But the limited prayers assigned to us as "satisfaction" are only a beginning. The point of penance is to launch us in the direction of genuine love, as a fulfillment of God's plan.

It is not the number or length of penances we are given to do, but the depth of our willingness and sincerity to do them that atones or makes satisfaction for our sins. If our heart is truly converted to Jesus, we won't feel limited by the penances given us. We will work until we arrive at a true "at–one–ment" with both God and our neighbor.

The best satisfaction for sin is doing whatever is necessary to correct the harm done by the sin. If we have been selfish in the use of our stereo, then lending that

same stereo or practicing some other act of unselfishness can correct the evil done.

Although we may perform the penance imposed in the sacrament anytime, we must have the *intention* of performing it at the time we confess. Without this intention, our sorrow would not be sincere. It is advisable to perform the penance as soon as possible, preferably in the church immediately after confession. Of course, some penances—such as the doing of good works or the saying of certain prayers daily—cannot be carried out at once. We sin if, through our own fault, we fail to do the given penance, because the willingness to do penance is at the very heart of the conversion that the sacrament brings about.

- Sin sets up ripples of fear in society. What changes would take place in your home or school if everyone suddenly discovered that someone within the group was a thief? A liar? Determined to murder someone?
- What things would be unnecessary in a city if there were absolutely no threat of stealing or murder?
- What penances do you find most unmeaningful? Why? Which seem most helpful?

Prayer

Opening Prayer, Revised Rite of Penance

Almighty and merciful God,
you have brought us together in the name of your
      Son
to receive your mercy and grace in our time of need.
Open our eyes to see the evil we have done.
Touch our hearts and convert us to yourself.

Where sin has divided and scattered,
may your love make one again;
where sin has brought weakness,
may your power heal and strengthen;
where sin has brought death,
may your Spirit raise to new life.

Give us a new heart to love you,
so that our lives may reflect the image of your Son.
May the world see the glory of Christ
revealed in your Church,
and come to know
that he is the one whom you have sent,
Jesus Christ, your Son, our Lord.

Amen.

MAKING A GOOD CONFESSION

As a child you may have confessed sins as if you were rattling off a grocery list: "I told three lies. I disobeyed five times." This cleared your conscience, but it didn't do much to improve you as a person. To grow spiritually, you have to "fly above" from time to time like a traffic helicopter so that you can see the patterns your sins and virtues are taking. If lying is one of your faults, the number of lies is less important that the reason *why* you are lying. Is it because you're not satisfied to be yourself and feel you have to exaggerate? To what extent do fear, envy, exaggerated independence, gluttony, greed, and sex influence you to lie? What good quality of character is God developing in you through this fault? (Often it is the exact opposite virtue.)

It may be that your bad habits are related to temperament. You should try to learn what type of personality you have. If you tend to be hot-tempered, your principal weakness may be anger and insensitivity to others, but you may have organizational leadership abilities. If you are basically gregarious—that is, one who enjoys the company of people—you may be tempted to excess in drink or smoking and find it hard to remain chaste. However, you may also be generous and forgive easily. If you tend to be introverted—that is, chiefly concerned with your own thoughts and feelings—your tendency could be to moodiness and self-pity, but your vivid imagination may make you sensitive to the suffering of those around you and capable of helping others through teaching or writing. If you are basically listless, you may lack ambition and tend to be miserly, but your emotional balance could make you a good counselor and you may have an abundance of perseverance and orderliness. Knowing what type of personality you have will help you to prepare against temptation and, at the same time, develop your good points.

Now that you are older and more capable of discovering patterns in your behavior, you may want to concentrate on one main weakness for a few months. If you've noticed that you lack generosity and can be selfish at home, concentrate on the faults that come from your inability to be generous. However, in your confessions, mention your successes as well as your failures.

Understanding your motive and your personality may light up the next step of your way and lead to the liberation you are looking for. Prayers to the Holy Spirit, nightly examination of conscience, and discussion with a confessor are helps to the inner conversion which is at the heart of penance.

- Think of your last three confessions or examinations of conscience. What sins did you repeat? What occasions triggered the sins?
- What patterns do you notice? What can you do about it?

An important thing for you to consider as you mature is the tendency you may have to avoid taking responsibility for your own weaknesses. Placing the blame for your bad habits on others or on circumstances beyond your control may be a way of camouflaging your own selfishness. Although it is true that external circumstances do affect your behavior, it is important for you to assume control of your life and accept responsibility for strengthening your virtues and overcoming your bad habits.

In confessing your sins to the priest, try to relax and realize that Jesus forgives you and wants to help you. Remember, too, that there is no need to be embarrassed to admit your sins. You are not the first person nor will you be the last to confess a particular sin to the priest.

Finally, keep in mind that the penance given to you by the priest is only a start in correcting your weaknesses. Like bad habits, good qualities need time to grow. Being eager to perform the penance is a great help. Meditating on the specific ways God has been good to you, on Christ's love, and on the power of the

Spirit will bring out your finest qualities. Earnest and honest confessions can result in a peace and joy that can make you a more attractive person than you ever dreamed you could be.

- Look over the pattern of a typical day or week. When are you usually at your best? At your lowest? When does "sin" seem to enter in? Chart your course in your journal.
- Think of each person who touches your life. When do your relationships tend to be at their best? What usually gives rise to friction? Why? Pray for each person. Ask God to change *you* enough to make getting along easier.

Summary of the Main Steps of Confession

1. *Prayer for Light.* Ask the Holy Spirit to help you look honestly at yourself.
2. *Examination of Conscience.* The main question is, "How am I responding to what God is asking of me at this time in my life?" This question includes reviewing your response to the commandments, beatitudes, laws of the Church, duties of your state in life, relationships with God, others, and your own body and mind.
3. *Contrition.* Reflect on God's love for you and his sorrow for your lack of generosity in return.
4. *Confession.* Make an honest confession centered around a main fault and try to see your hidden motives.
5. *Penance.* Perform your penance in a spirit of repentance, directing it toward correcting a particular fault.
6. *Thanksgiving.* Spend time in gratitude to Christ your Savior, and make a practical resolution to do one thing better.

SUMMING UP

Use the following questions to help you review the
main themes of this chapter.

1. Why can there be no such thing as "secret" sin?
2. What are some effects of sin?
3. What are the conditions for sin? What is the difference between serious, mortal, and venial sin?
4. What is sin? What is the internal guide God gives to deter you from sin? From what three viewpoints can this guide be considered?
5. Why is it inaccurate to say that the priest judges the confession of your sins?
6. Why is it important to form a true conscience? How can it be done?
7. What is contrition? If sin does not hurt God, why should you be sorry for sin? What is the main point of the parable of the Prodigal Son?
8. Why must every act of reconciliation be both personal and communal?
9. What benefits besides forgiveness of their sins do Catholics possess in the sacrament of Reconciliation?
10. Why is the sacrament of Reconciliation really a celebration?
11. What is the difference between a confession of necessity and a confession of devotion?
12. What is an example of "phoniness" in the confessions of one's sins?
13. What sins are you bound to confess? Must you confess doubtful sins, forgotten sins, and venial sins?
14. What is the best satisfaction for sin? Why do you sin when you deliberately fail to do the penance you've been assigned?
15. What are the main steps of confession?

Words to Know

eternal punishment, temporal punishment, mortal sin, serious sin, venial sin, conscience, contrition, attrition, confession of necessity, confession of devotion, satisfaction for sin, atonement

Think/Talk/Write

1. Invent three cases where a small amount of evil in a person's character brings on the total destruction of that person's life.
2. Does sin add evil to your life, keep you from your full development, or actually destroy you? Give examples and reasons for your answer.
3. A character in a novel published some years ago said that love is never having to say you're sorry. Do you agree? Why or why not?
4. Tell how a TV situation or commercial of your choice either fosters a spirit of penance or doesn't. Give specific examples.

Activities

1. By means of music, dance, art, or poetry, portray the entry of sin into the world and God's remedy for it. Include creation, God's plan for humanity, the first sin, God's early promises to Adam and Eve, Noah, Abraham, Moses, David, and Hosea, the coming of the Savior, and, finally, the gift of the sacrament of Reconciliation.
2. As a class, gather a number of plans suitable for teenagers to use in examining their consciences in preparation for the sacrament of Reconciliation. Precede the examinations with a number of ways to recall God's goodness. Follow them with some original acts of contrition.
3. Examine the newspapers over a period of a week or so for reports of people who sue others for injuries done to them. Discuss the evidence of Christianity in each case. When do you think it's right to sue? How much should you sue for? What effects does a suing society have on people like doctors and other public servants?

ELEVEN

How has the sacrament of Reconciliation changed from the early Church?

What does the sacrament emphasize today?

What are the three rites for receiving the sacrament?

Can forgiveness of sins be granted without confession?

Rites of Penance

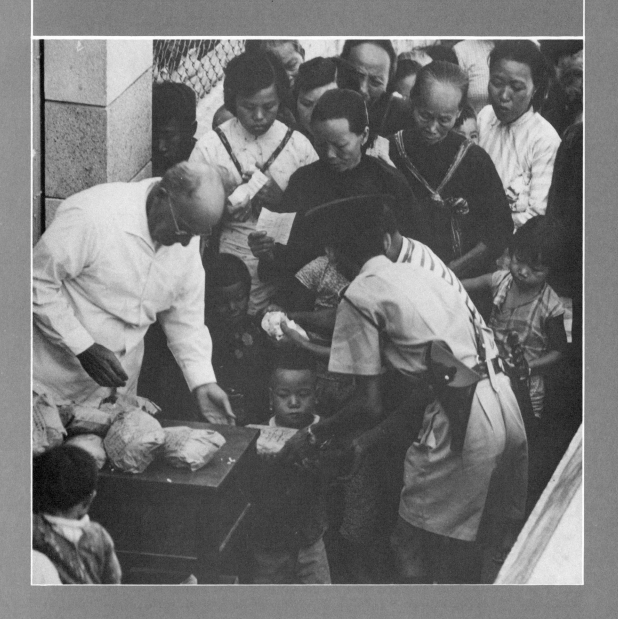

If we acknowledge our sins, he who is just can be trusted to forgive our sins and cleanse us from every wrong.

PENANCE: A HISTORICAL PERSPECTIVE

When some of Saint Paul's converts of Corinth allowed idol worship, greed, drunkenness, and sexual immorality to invade their community, Paul advised excluding the unfaithful ones from the common meals and worship. His purpose was not to condemn the guilty, but to save these people "in the day of the Lord." It did not seem too much to ask Christians to remain faithful to the Lord until his second coming—an event Paul expected at any moment.

For nearly a century and a half, the Church handled sin by simply encouraging converts to remain true to their baptismal promises. Sins were forgiven at the celebration of the Eucharist. There, too, Christians exchanged the sign of peace as a gesture of reconciliation with one another. The Church today continues to forgive sin in the action of the Mass and to exchange a sign of peace as a gesture of reconciliation.

From the second century on, when those who had denied Christ under the torments of persecution expressed a desire to return to the faith, the Church insisted on its power to forgive serious sin committed

The Church had to insist because those who had remained faithful under persecution resented the others being allowed back.

LITURGY

after baptism. As in the church at Corinth, the first step was to isolate the offender from the community in a kind of second catechumenate. This seven-year period of retraining, or "canonical penance," was required only of those who had completely cut off their relationship with God and the community through what were then considered the only three serious sins: adultery, murder, and apostasy. Reconciliation involved the following stages and could be undertaken only once in a lifetime.

The *catechumenate* is a period of instruction for those seeking to belong to the Church.

Apostasy is the sin of abandoning the Faith.

1. Interior admission and sorrow for sin.
2. Private confession to the bishop and enrollment in the Order of Penitents. This involved a laying on of hands and the penitent's acceptance of sackcloth and ashes as a sign of repentance.
3. A visible expression of sorrow by fasting and performing works of penance and charity, along with receiving instruction in virtue.
4. Solemn reconciliation with the community by re-admission to worship at the Eucharist on Holy Thursday.

The *Order of Penitents* was something like a religious order for those who sinned seriously.

Just as the entire local church was involved in encouraging and preparing candidates for baptism, the entire local community participated in and financially supported the reformation of penitents. Each had a sponsor and, although not admitted to full worship, penitents were treated with love, understanding, and encouragement. Their presence in the community served as a reminder that all are sinners and are in constant need of conversion to Christ.

Unfortunately, canonical penance resulted in abuses. Baptism was often delayed, sometimes until very late in life. Death-bed conversions seemed preferable to the possibility of sinning and then having to practice severe penances. Gradually, the entire practice of canonical penance fell into disuse.

Around the sixth century, in an effort to renew the fervor of the Church, groups of lay persons formed penitential monastic communities in the African desert in order to live the Christian life more intensely. Individuals went for guidance or spiritual direction to those

in the monasteries who seemed most gifted in understanding the human heart. These lay spiritual directors examined the lives of their penitents; noticed patterns of strengths, moral weaknesses, and sins; and reassured them of God's forgiveness.

In these sixth-century practices, there was no special liturgy, no public act of reconciliation, and no involvement of the official Church leaders. Many who flocked to the monasteries for direction were in need of sacramental forgiveness. This resulted in the practice of ordaining some of the monks for the purpose of hearing private, individual confessions. This is how the present-day Rite of Penance originated. The change in name at that time from "reconciliation" to "confession" reveals the shift in emphasis from the supportive role of the community to an individual listing of sins by the penitent.

By the ninth century, the practice of public, canonical penance had entirely disappeared and private confessions were urged. The name of the process now shifted from "confession" to "penance." *Penance* comes from a verb that means "to weigh," signifying the weight a person feels if he or she has sinned. Penance also implies the willingness to pay something heavy—a penalty, punishment, or fine—to make up for the sin. Confessors consulted penitential books that listed the proper penalty or penance for each sin.

In the sixteenth century, another shift in emphasis turned attention from both the community and the action of the penitent to the priest as the main element in reconciliation. Serious sin could no longer be forgiven without the penitent's perfect interior contrition, when confession was accompanied by priestly absolution.

Perfect contrition is sorrow for sin because of one's love for God instead of the fear of punishment.

The Council of Trent (1545–1563) officially declared penance as the sacrament of the forgiveness of sin and obliged Catholics to confess all mortal sins to an authorized priest. The priest became a judge, having the power to withhold absolution if the penitent's attitudes seemed faulty. Before this time, children never approached the sacrament of forgiveness because it was taken for granted that they were incapable of committing serious sin. Now, confession became compulsory once a year for all who had reached the age of reason and who had sinned seriously.

In the years preceding Vatican II, big parishes and the large number of confessions to be heard resulted in short, impersonal encounters where a stranger whispered to another stranger in a dark box. Penitents listed sins, expressed sorrow, and received forgiveness with very little practical conversion. "Going to confession" replaced living a life of penance.

- What does each name—penance, reconciliation, confession—reveal about the sacrament of forgiveness? Which name do you prefer? Why?
- Confessors are forbidden by Church law to make use of any knowledge gained in confession, even if it would not betray the penitent. What advantages can you see in such a law?
- Why is trust so important in the sacrament of Reconciliation?

■ Have you ever confided a secret to a friend only to discover later that this friend told others your secret? If so, what effect did this have on your relationship with this person?

PENANCE TODAY

Today, there are three rites of penance available to Christians. An overview of these rites reveals that the emphasis has been taken off the penitent's confession of sins and is now focused on the warm, human, and divine reconciliation the sacrament brings about.

"Penance" is still an acceptable name for the sacrament. However, the recent use of the title "sacrament of Reconciliation" and the new communal penance services once again focus on the role of the community in the sacrament. The basic structure of all three rites shows that this sacrament is a celebration of forgiveness and reconciliation.

The priest, who represents the community, greets the penitent in a bright room and begins reading the Word of God's mercy from Scripture. The option of face-to-face encounter adds a personal dimension. The stretching out or laying on of hands and the praising of God together reinstate part of the earliest ritual of the Church. The giving of a more personalized penance as satisfaction after confession once again points to the connection of the sacrament with the rest of one's life and highlights the reconciliation of the penitent with his or her neighbor.

The sacrament of Reconciliation may be pictured as the peak of all God's efforts through history to help individuals to repent. It restores the penitent who has turned away from God by sin to full participation in the purpose of the community—which is to glorify God through worship and the spread of the kingdom. For those whose sins are only the result of human weakness and not a full break with God, penance deepens the Christ-life, making the Christian more and more suited to carrying out the aims of God through the Church.

COMMUNAL CELEBRATION

Song—"Blest Be the Lord" by Dan Schutte, S.J., or another appropriate song.

All: God, our Father in heaven, send your Holy Spirit into our hearts. Point out our sins. Give us the courage to confess them honestly. Help us to believe in your readiness and willingness to forgive. Remove our sin and guilt; fill us with your peace. Then send us away strong and free, filled with your power to do better in the days ahead. We ask this through Jesus, your Son, our Lord and Savior. Amen.

Priest: We need forgiveness. We need to forgive. We must all admit that we have failed to love enough. We have sinned against God and against one another. It is fitting, therefore, that we join with one another as a visible expression of our real unity as members to Christ's Body to ask for forgiveness and to give forgiveness. From each other we receive the assurance that we are forgiven not only by Christ, but also by other Christians.

All: Lord, Jesus Christ, we believe that you are here with us. We rejoice in your presence. We have sinned against you and against one another. We have forgotten your presence, ignored your love, and have acted contrary to your laws and advice. We know also that in neglecting or hurting one another, we have rejected your love and have spoiled your plans for our happiness. Give us the grace to really hear your revealed Word so that we may turn more completely to you and be healed.

Reader 1: Matthew 9:1–8 (Jesus heals a paralyzed man)

(*Time for silent reflection*)

All: O Lord, your goodness, mercy, and love took human form in your Son. Help us grasp his gentleness and kindness toward sinners. Help us to accept others in spite of their failures. Accept us, in spite of our weaknesses and sins.

Reader 2: Luke 7:36–50 (Jesus at the home of Simon the Pharisee)

(*Time for silent reflection*)

All: Jesus, we have listened to your words of forgiveness. Help us to love you and all whom we have offended as intensely as the woman who washed your feet with her tears.

(*Homily*)

Priest: Let us publicly examine our consciences. The response after each phrase will be: "Lord, forgive us."

1. For our weak and unenthusiastic faith, and for our failure to pray . . .

2. For our irreverent and profane use of your holy name . . .

3. For the injuries we have done to Christ in our families, among our friends and acquaintances . . .

4. For our sarcasm, cynicism, insults, and gossip . . .

5. For misuse or irreverence to our bodies or to those of others—in thought, look, word, action . . .

6: For the bad example we have given to others, especially to the young . . .

7. For our unjustified and exaggerated anger, and for the misuse of our talents and gifts . . .

8. For the routine and thoughtless worship we have offered to you during the holy sacrifice of the Mass, or for our repeated failure to worship at all . . .

9. For not respecting the rights and property of others, and for refusing to help those in need . . .

10. For refusing to believe in your deep and personal love for us, and for our neglect in responding to your love . . .

All: My God, I am sorry for my sins with all my heart. In choosing to do wrong and failing to do good, I have sinned against you whom I should love above all things. I firmly intend, with your help, to do penance, to sin no more, and to avoid whatever leads me to sin. Jesus, your Son, suffered and died for me. In his name, show me your goodness and mercy.

Priest: My brothers and sisters in Christ, what do you ask of God and his Church here on earth?

All: We ask forgiveness of God and your blessing, Father, for we acknowledge that we are sinners. We

wish to renew our conversion to the Lord in and through his holy Church.

Priest: May the Lord be in your hearts and on your lips.

All: Amen.

Priest: May he give you a true spirit of repentance, and grant you the courage to properly confess all of your sins, in the name of the Father, and of the Son, and of the Holy Spirit.

All: Amen.

[During the individual confession of sins and granting of absolution, any of the following Scripture passages may be read privately: Matthew 9:9–13; Luke 15:1–7, John 8:1–11, 20:19–23; Daniel 9:4–23; Isaiah 55:1–12; Luke 15:11–32, 19:1–10; Romans 5:6–11; Ezekiel 18:20–32, 34:11–16; Joel 2:12–19.]

(Continue after all have received the sacrament of Reconciliation.)

Priest: Let us remember the peace and love we have just experienced. Do not fail to show others the new life that is already within you. Have the courage to hold on to what is good. Never return evil for evil. Strengthen those who fail, support the weak, honor all that God has created. Love and serve the Lord to the best of your ability. Always ask for and be guided by his Holy Spirit.

All: God, our Father, once again you have shown us your great mercy and restored us to union with you and with one another. Grant that our contrition be creative and that our resolution be genuine. This day give us the sacramental grace to rise refreshed, strengthened, and renewed in courage so that we may live more closely united to you. Amen.

Closing Song—"Day by Day" from *Godspell,* or another appropriate song.

THE THREE RITES

The first Rite of Reconciliation is for individual penitents. The person can choose to go to confession either anonymously behind a screen or face to face in a room designed for that purpose. The four parts of the rite are the same for all three: (1) Introductory Rite, (2) Liturgy of the Word, (3) Sacramental Celebration, and (4) Proclamation of Praise, and Dismissal.

To bring out even more clearly that penance is not merely the action of one individual seeking personal forgiveness, the Church has drawn up a second Rite of Reconciliation that involves communal penance. In this rite, common praying and singing draw attention to the fact that as every sin affects and alienates one from the community, every return to God is also a good that restores relationships among God's people. This rite follows the same order as the Rite for Individual Confession, except that most of the ceremony is performed together with others. Only the actual confession and absolution of each penitent is individual.

Communal celebration recognizes our need to associate with other Christians in prayer, song, and mutual concern. Actual contact and physical presence is necessary for community love.

■ It is said that indifference, not hate, is the worst sin. Do you agree or not? Why? What groups do you think are neglected by your school or parish?

A third Rite of Reconciliation involves general confession and absolution. It does not replace individual confession but may be used in cases involving danger of death or in places where confessions would be overheard. It may also be used if there are large numbers of penitents and an insufficient number of confessors or if people would otherwise be deprived of reconciliation or reception of the Eucharist for a long time. The general absolution is not effective without a person's proper disposition. This disposition includes sorrow for sins, a firm purpose of amendment, the intention

In general confession, the penitent substitutes an exterior sign of sorrow, such as striking one's breast, for the verbal confession of sins.

to repair any scandal or harm done, and the resolution to confess grave sins at the first opportunity. The common absolution does not relieve the penitent of the obligation to observe the precept of the Church that requires individual confession to a priest of all grave sins at least once a year. Common absolution, however, does point up the primary role of God in forgiving sin and the Church's power of intercession and forgiveness.

THE RITE OF INDIVIDUAL CONFESSION

Introductory Rite. Jesus portrayed the great willingness of God to receive the sinner back in the unforgettable picture of an elderly father watching every day at the top of the hill for his wayward son. "He [the son] was still a long way from home when his father saw him;

Luke 15:20

his heart was filled with pity, and he ran, threw his arms around his son, and kissed him."

In the reception of the penitent in confession, the priest greets him or her in warm welcome as a sign of God's readiness to forgive. After the penitent calls on the Trinity by making the sign of the cross, the celebrant invites him or her to trust in God's pardon and love.

Liturgy of the Word. Either the priest or the penitent may choose the Scripture reading. One or more readings that illustrate God's call to conversion and reconciliation may be used. If more than one reading is used, a psalm, song, or time of silence should be inserted between them. This response to the readings allows the penitent to more deeply understand God's Word and give heartfelt consent to it. Some possible Old Testament readings are the following: Deuteronomy 6:3–9, 30:15–20; Sirach 28:1–7; Isaiah 53:1–12, 58:1–11; Jeremiah 7:21–26; Ezekiel 11:14–21, 36:23–28; Micah 6:1–6.

The following psalms may be used as responses to God's Word: Psalm 13 (All my hope, O Lord, is in your loving kindness); Psalm 25 (Turn to me, Lord, and have mercy); Psalm 32 (Lord, forgive the wrong I have done); Psalm 51 (Give back to me the joy of your salvation); Psalm 90 (Fill us with your love, O Lord, and we will sing for joy); Psalm 95 (If today you hear his voice, harden not your hearts); Psalm 123 (Our eyes are fixed on the Lord); Psalm 130 (With the Lord there is mercy and fullness of redemption); Psalm 143 (Teach me to do your will, my God).

Some possible New Testament readings include the following: Romans 5:6–11; 2 Corinthians 5:17–21; Ephesians 5:1–14; Colossians 3:1–17; James 1:22–27; Matthew 25:31–46; Mark 12:28–34; Luke 7:36–50; John 20:19–23.

The celebrant usually spends a little time discussing one or more sins mentioned in the confession, or he may speak on a theme of the readings. This personal homily is another sign of Christ's immediate presence in the sacrament. As part of his comments, the priest may suggest or ask the penitent to suggest some prayers or actions that will "satisfy" for the sins committed.

Strictly speaking, you do not do penance to "make up" to God or to "satisfy" for your sins. God does not lay down certain conditions for accepting you back into his friendship. He remains ever ready to reach out to pick you up, to embrace you, to draw you near him. When the penitent accepts the penance given by the celebrant after the confession of sins, he or she shows a willingness to replace the evil done with good. It is a remedy for one's failure to reach out to God.

Sacramental Celebration. As a response to God's Word, which calls one to reconcile his or her life with God, neighbor, and self, the penitent performs three exterior actions as signs of interior repentance. These acts include *confession of sins* to a priest, *acceptance of a penance,* and an *expression of contrition.* The celebrant's absolution is the sign of God's forgiveness. Together, these actions make up the sacrament.

In confessing his or her sins, the penitent may begin with a simple formula: "I confess to almighty God." The penitent then confesses any acts that have destroyed or lessened his or her wholeness either since baptism (in the case of a first confession) or since the last celebration of the sacrament of Penance.

If necessary, the priest helps the penitent make a thorough confession. After appropriate counseling in which he urges the penitent to be sorry for his or her sins, the priest gives some kind of penance. The penitent agrees to accept this penance as a means to satisfy for the wrong done and as an aid in changing his or her life in the future.

The penance should correspond to the seriousness and nature of the sins.

The penitent then expresses sincere sorrow for the sins committed. This prayer can be spontaneous, memorized, or taken from a Scripture passage, such as Psalm 25:6–7, Psalm 51:4–5, Luke 15:18, or Luke 18:13.

After this expression of sorrow, the priest extends either his right hand or both hands over the head of the penitent and says a prayer of absolution. This absolution indicates that reconciliation between the penitent and God, and between the penitant and the Church, has taken place.

When the priest places his hand upon the head of the penitent, he is, in the eyes of faith, Christ inviting the sinner to return. He is also the Church reaching out to the sinner in a gesture of welcome. The words he speaks are the action of God's acceptance and forgiveness made visible in the earthly action of the Church.

Proclamation of Praise and Dismissal. In the concluding rite, the priest and the penitent together proclaim God's praise for the mystery of his mercy. Although the entire sacrament is an act of profound worship, all that precedes this moment leads to the celebration of God's goodness. This celebration does not end here, but finds its fulfillment in the Eucharist, *the* sacrament of thanksgiving and reconciliation. The priest then dismisses the penitent, who has been restored to or more deeply united with God and the Church. His final word is a most appropriate one: peace.

- Why is the final word "peace" an appropriate way to end the sacrament of Reconciliation?
- Write an original prayer of praise and thanksgiving to God for his mercy and love.
- Try to imagine what it would be like to go through life never being forgiven. What would you feel like? How would you act?

Prayer

Father of mercies
and God of all consolation,
you do not wish the sinner to die
but to be converted and live.
Come to the aid of your people,
that they may turn from their sins
and live for you alone.
May we be attentive to your word,
confess our sins, receive your forgiveness,
and always be grateful for your loving kindness.
Help us to live the truth in love
and grow into the fullness of Christ, your Son,
who lives and reigns forever and ever.
Amen.

Opening prayer, Revised Rite of Penance.

SUMMING UP

Use the following questions to help you review the
main themes of this chapter.

1. What was the Church's first way of dealing with people who turned
   their backs on the Christian way of life?
2. What was the thinking of the early Church regarding reconciliation?
3. What was canonical penance? List its main stages. What abuses
   accompanied it?
4. What big shift in the Church's Rite of Reconciliation took place in
   the sixth century? What brought it on?
5. When and why was confession made compulsory? What refine-
   ments on the sacrament did the Council of Trent make in the sixteenth century?
6. What was the characteristic of the sacrament of Penance from the
   seventeenth to the twentieth centuries?
7. What elements of community spirit as well as of attention to the
   individual does the new revised Rite of Penance have?
8. What are the four main parts of the sacrament of Reconciliation?
9. What dispositions must a penitent have in order for the absolution
   to take effect?
10. Briefly describe the differences among the Rite for the Reconciliation
    of Individual Penitents, the Rite of Communal Penance, and the Rite
    of Communal Penance with General Confession and Absolution.
11. What is the deeper significance of the priest's greeting as the penitent
    first arrives for confession?
12. What should be the theme of the reading of the Word of God in the
    sacrament?
13. What are four main elements of the sacramental celebration part of
    the Rite of Reconciliation?
14. Why is the statement "Penance makes up to God for sin" not really
    accurate?
15. Why does the sacrament end with a prayer of praise?

Words to Know

apostasy, Order of Penitents, perfect contrition, seal of confession, absolution, satisfaction, canonical penance, communal penance, general confession and absolution

Think/Talk/Write

1. Which of these Scripture texts best represents what the sacrament of Reconciliation does for you? Why? Psalm 7:9 (Stop the wickedness of evil people and reward those who are good); Psalm 6:4 (Come and save me, Lord: in your mercy rescue me from death); Psalm 32:1 (Happy are those whose sins are forgiven, whose wrongs are pardoned); Isaiah 11:6 (Wolves and sheep will live together in peace).
2. What is the difference between forgiving and forgetting? Is it necessary to forget in order to forgive? Must you forgive in order to forget? It is not always possible to deliberately forget a thing, especially a hurt. What does it mean to "bury the hatchet" and "forgive *and* forget"?
3. In which era of history would you have liked to celebrate the sacrament of Reconciliation? Explain why.

Activities

1. Write a communal penance service that you can celebrate with your class. Start with a theme, and then select appropriate readings and songs.
2. Make a chart or a slide presentation tracing the interior and exterior steps from a sin of commission or omission through all the stages of the sacrament of Reconciliation to the conversion of heart that is shown by one's changed actions.
3. Make a twenty-five-point examination of conscience for a teenager. Compare this with others in the class.

Everyone's experience shows that something is amiss in the world. The Bible lays the source of the problem to sin—the basic human tendency to reject God's commands. The resulting separation from God causes disharmony not only within oneself but among individuals and nations.

Christ prayed to restore all people to their original destiny of union with the Father in his own love. He accomplished this restoration by his obedience, even to death, on a cross. As the great high priest, Jesus made his life and death holy—a sacrifice—by the perfect love and trust with which he offered himself. The disposition he manifested at the Last Supper and on Calvary remain for all eternity.

By changing the substance of the bread and wine into his body and blood (transubstantiation), Jesus, in union with his community, makes himself truly present under the form of the Eucharistic species. As the victim of the sacrifice, he also makes Calvary really present, although in an unbloody manner. This one sacrifice, reenacted sacramentally, is *the* great source of reconciliation—the font of healing for all the ills of the world.

Although Christ redeemed all people, they may fall into sin after baptism and continually need to be converted. The Father waits with ready forgiveness for the return of his prodigal sons and daughters. Through the sacrament of Reconciliation, God offers healing for sin committed after baptism. The more we understand and live what we know about conscience, sin, and the Rite of Penance itself, the more we stand to benefit from the sacrament.

History shows that the sacrament of Penance has undergone many changes; the emphasis today is not so much on a person's confession of sins as on his or her reconciliation—with God and with the community that sin wounds.

PART IV

THE LITURGICAL YEAR

In the various seasons of the year . . . the Church completes the formation of the faithful by means of pious practices for soul and body, by instruction, prayer, and works of penance and mercy.

(CONSTITUTION ON THE SACRED LITURGY)

TWELVE

What are the seasons of the Church year?

How did the liturgical seasons come into being?

What is the purpose of the Church calendar?

What is the Liturgy of the Hours?

Liturgical Seasons

In the course of the year . . . ,   she [the Church] unfolds the whole mystery of Christ from the Incarnation and Nativity to the Ascension, to Pentecost and the expectation of the blessed hope of the coming of the Lord.

(CONSTITUTION ON THE SACRED LITURGY)

DEALING WITH TIME

"Year" is a term people invented to deal with the repetitious flow of the seasons. Nature divides itself naturally into four distinct "times." Spring, a time of increasing light and warmth, is known for its new life and regeneration. Summer, a time of maximum light and heat, is a time of growth and leisure. Fall, a time of decreasing days and longer nights, is a time of harvest and reaping. Winter, a time of darkness and cold, is a time of quiet and hibernation.

Some ancient peoples looked at the seasons as a continuing war between the gods of light and the gods of darkness. In spring, they celebrated the fullness of life and light in joyous festivals. In winter, toward the end of December, they marked the shortest day of the year and celebrated the triumph of light over darkness; from that day onward, the hours of light begin to increase. Only in spring, however, do the days become longer than the nights.

- Read Ecclesiastes 3:1–8. What time of year were you born?
- What is your favorite season? Why?
- What has been the best year in your life? The worst year? Why?
- What has been your happiest day? Your most sad day?
- Describe some moments when you have felt laughter, silence, love, and peace.

When Christians looked at the events of Jesus' life, they saw in them similarities to the pagan feasts of seasons. They celebrated the birth of Jesus—light coming into darkness—shortly after the winter solstice, the shortest day of the year. As Saint John describes this event, "The light shines on in darkness, a darkness that did not overcome it." John 1:5

Likewise, when Christians looked for a time to celebrate the great feast of Easter—the resurrection and new life of Jesus—they chose springtime, the season of flourishing life. This feast is marked with the exuberance of life eternal, the resurgence of hope, and the celebration of joy. Winter is over. Jesus has triumphed forever over the powers of death.

It is around these two great feasts—Easter and Christmas—that the liturgical year is built. Although Easter is the highest feast of the Church year, the liturgical seasons begin with the first Sunday of Advent. Advent is a four-week period of preparation for Christmas. It prepares for the celebration of Christ's first coming and also looks forward to his coming at the end of the world. Advent is followed by the Christmas season, which begins with Christmas and lasts until the Sunday after Epiphany.

The Church also spends time preparing for Easter. This time consists of forty days called Lent, which remind Christians of the forty days Jesus spent in the desert before his active ministry and of the forty years the Israelites spent wandering in the desert before entering the Promised Land. See Matthew 4:1–2

See Numbers 14:33 and 32:13

The last three days of Lent, known as the Easter Triduum, are the climax of the entire liturgical year. They *The week of the Easter Triduum (tri = three; duum = days) is Holy Week.*

commemorate the passion, death, and resurrection of Christ—his great passover from death to eternal life. The fifty days between Easter Sunday and Pentecost are known as the Easter Season. They are like one long feastday, sometimes called the "Great Sunday" of the Church year.

Besides the seasons of Easter, Lent, Christmas, and Advent, there are thirty-four weeks during the year that do not stress the Paschal Mystery. Instead, they dwell on the life and teachings of Christ and celebrate the fullness of grace gained by redemption. This season is known as Ordinary Time.

Ordinary Time begins on the Monday after the Sunday following Epiphany and continues until the beginning of Lent. It resumes again on the Monday after Pentecost Sunday and ends on the Saturday before the first Sunday of Advent.

The diagram shows the five seasons of the liturgical year and their length in relation to the entire year.

■ What season commemorates Christ's coming to earth to show God's will and to bring peace to all nations? The fullness of the Christian life in the Spirit? Christ's passover from death to life? The longing of all people for a Savior? One's repentance and desire to be converted to a wholehearted following of Christ?

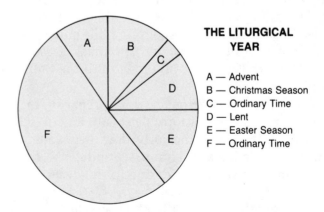

THE LITURGICAL YEAR

A — Advent
B — Christmas Season
C — Ordinary Time
D — Lent
E — Easter Season
F — Ordinary Time

VIEWING THE YEAR

Time is divided into different units. A year may be described as four seasons. It may also be defined as twelve months, fifty-two weeks, 365¼ days, or 8,766 hours. So, too, the liturgical year may be divided into smaller units than its five seasons. One subdivision is by weeks.

Of the fifty-two weeks in the year, four weeks are spent in Advent. The Christmas Season lasts two to three weeks. Lent comprises six Sundays, while the Easter Season takes up eight. The season in Ordinary Time can last from thirty-one to thirty-four weeks.

The liturgical year is the annual cycle of seasons and feasts that reenact the mystery of Christ. It is designed to instruct the faithful, to help them become an ever holier people, and to unite them in Christ, whom they encounter in the midst of their celebrations. While recalling the events of Jesus' life, these celebrations bring the effect of those events into the present. Christians actually encounter the risen Christ and are healed by his sacramental presence and action. Moreover, these celebrations look to the future, containing in themselves the promise of the eternal celebration in which all the faithful will share in the future resurrection. This threefold dimension of sacramental celebration is referred to as Christ's coming in history (time), mystery (sacrament), and majesty (at the end of the world).

From the Middle Ages to Vatican II, the Church looked at the celebrations of the liturgy as a historical representation of Christ's life and the years preceding it. The liturgical year was divided into four segments. The four weeks of Advent represented the thousands of years before Christ, in which people looked forward to a Messiah. The time from Christmas to Pentecost in the liturgical year represented the life of Christ from his infancy to his ascension and the sending of the Holy Spirit. The weeks after Pentecost represented the period from the birth of the Church to the second coming of Christ.

Vatican II introduced a sacramental dimension to the liturgical year. In this sacramental interpretation, it is easier to see that the Paschal Mystery, the great event of redemption, is the center of the Church year. All the seasons and feasts unfold that mystery, keeping Christ and his life, teachings, and saving action in the midst of his people always. The *Constitution on the Sacred Liturgy* explains it this way:

> Recalling the mysteries of the redemption, she [the Church] opens up to the faithful the riches of her Lord's powers and merits, so that these are in some way made present for all time; the faithful lay hold of them and are filled with saving grace.

CELEBRATING THE PASCHAL MYSTERY

The name "Sun-day" refers to the powers of light and warmth.

Each Sunday is a mini-celebration of the Paschal Mystery. From the time of the Resurrection itself, this day has been "the Lord's Day." Because a day has been traditionally measured from sundown to sundown, many Catholics begin their celebration of the Lord's Day on Saturday evening. They gather in community, listen to God's Word, and participate in the sacrament of the Eucharist. Through extra rest and time spent eating and relaxing together, they make Sunday truly a day of rest and family togetherness.

During the first several centuries of worship, Christians celebrated the Eucharist only on Sunday. Gradually, the Church discovered that the single annual celebration of Easter was not enough to express the mystery of Jesus' life, death, and resurrection, and so added a number of feasts, extending aspects of the Paschal Mystery throughout the year. The Church added special days to celebrate the way certain saints lived out the Paschal Mystery. Now Fridays, especially during Lent, remind Christians of the passion and death of Jesus. Saturdays are dedicated to Mary, the Mother of God.

The latest revision in the daily liturgical calendar was in 1969, by Pope Paul VI.

Because of the eternal and unending mystery of Christ, the Church celebrated the Eucharist every day. Somewhere in the world at all times, Christ's sacrifice

is being offered. Through the Eucharist, God continually lives among his People, revealing and communicating himself in Christ's one sacrifice. Although people are physically limited to the number of Masses they can attend, they can feel assured that, as members of Christ's Body, they are included in every Mass said throughout the world.

- Match the following feasts with the events they celebrate: the Annunciation, the Ascension, Christmas, Christ the King, the Epiphany, Good Friday, Holy Thursday, Pentecost, Easter Sunday.
- What particular feast celebrates Christ's institution of the Eucharist? His conception in Mary's womb? His reign over the entire universe? His death? His sending of the Spirit? His bursting the bonds of death? His return to share equal glory with the Father? His birth? His revelation of God's mercy to all nations?

TIME OUT

An *ostracon* is a piece of broken pottery with ancient inscriptions impressed on it. Ostraca were used the way we use paper to keep records and write letters.

Today people are good at taking time out—for coffee breaks, for medical appointments, for sports, and for vacations. If you could read the ostraca dug out of the dwellings of the talented artisans who decorated the tombs of the pharoahs, you would find that in ancient Egypt every tenth day was set aside as time out for rest and catching up on personal affairs such as preparing one's tomb. Highly valued for their specialized skills, the artisans were luckier than the slaves, who were required to work every day from dawn till dark without time off.

The Jews were the first to set aside one day in seven for rest. This custom was based on their belief that, after six days of creating, God rested on the seventh day. The Sabbath, as they called this seventh day, was not only a time of physical rest but also a time for acknowledging that God had entered their lives. They spent the Sabbath getting to know God better, reflecting thoughtfully on the purposes of life and creation, and giving thanks for God's saving action in the Passover. On this day, they studied Scripture and renewed their feeling of oneness with all fellow Jews. Special meals with blessed bread and wine, ceremonies, prayers, and songs prescribed by law and custom contributed to the holiness of the day, which began at sundown on Friday and ended at Saturday sundown.

Since most of the early followers of Jesus were Jews, they observed the Sabbath faithfully, although they also gathered in one another's houses each Sunday to remember the new creation in Jesus' resurrection. Coming together, they read the prophecies of the Messiah from the Old Testament and the letters from Paul and the other Apostles. They broke bread and passed around the blessed cup as Jesus had commanded them to do.

After the destruction of Jerusalem in A.D. 70, it became clear that Judaism and Christianity would go their separate ways. Christians, now numbering many Gentiles, dropped the Sabbath in favor of the Sunday celebration.

For nearly two thousand years Christians have kept the Lord's Day in their homes or parishes as a mini-Paschal feast by celebrating the Christian's highest act of worship to God—the Eucharist. Today, they rejoice to hear God's Word and to have it explained to them at Mass. They enter into close union with other members of the community by praying and singing together, and they renew their deep communion with Christ.

There is a human need for regular periods of rest and recreation. If we set aside such a time, we may enjoy the fruits of a balanced life. With family life threatened today by the many things that draw people away from the home during the week, Sunday is an ideal time to enjoy good meals and recreation together or to visit relatives and friends. Engaging in parish services or neighborhood activities can strengthen the life of the larger community as well. Thus refreshed in spirit, you will be better prepared to face whatever challenges the next week may hold in store.

In a growingly secular world, where shops are kept open on Sunday and people are expected to work straight through the week, the day of rest runs the danger of becoming extinct. Groups of Christians who understand the purpose of Sunday are gathering in one another's houses for Scripture study, holding religion classes for the young, and joining to pray the Liturgy of the Hours together on Sundays.

- How does your family celebrate Sunday? What can you do to keep its spiritual purpose uppermost?
- What are some things that keep you from observing Sunday as a day of rest? How can you overcome these obstacles?
- In your journal, record your deepest feelings about the Sunday observance.

LITURGICAL HIERARCHY

Each day of the year is ranked in order of its importance. Some days may have two or more coinciding feasts. Which one of these feasts will be celebrated is determined by certain rules regarding the liturgical year. Each feast is given one of the following ranks: Sundays, Solemnities and Feasts, Obligatory Memorials, and Optional Memorials. These ranks are given in the missal, the liturgical book for Roman Catholics containing the formulas and rites for the celebration of Mass.

Sundays are major days of the year. Each Sunday has its own readings and prayers that rotate on a three-year cycle. The liturgy of Sunday must always be celebrated, unless Sunday is also a Feast or Solemnity of the Lord. For example, the Baptism of Jesus, the Transfiguration, and Christmas would take precedence over the regular Sunday liturgy. However, the liturgies of the Sundays in Advent, Lent, and Easter take precedence over Solemnities. The liturgy of the Solemnity is then moved to the preceding Saturday.

Solemnities and feasts have their own proper (prayers and preface) and take precedence over weekday Masses.

Memorials are the Church's celebrations of the lives of saints. Prayers proper to the saint are inserted into

These ranks can also be found on the Ordo, a book giving brief directions for the religious celebrations of each year.

Feasts are the celebrations of events in the life of Jesus, Mary, and the Apostles and certain events in the history of the Church. Solemnities are high feasts celebrating important aspects of the Church's faith.

the regular Mass of the day. *Obligatory memorials* (important saints) must be observed unless they occur in privileged seasons, when the Mass of the day takes precedence, but the opening prayer of the memorial may be used. Privileged seasons include Advent weekdays, December 17–24, days within the Octave of Christmas, and Lenten weekdays, except Ash Wednesday and the days of Holy Week. Optional memorials list the saint's name in the calendar, but give no rank.

Weekdays in Advent and Lent have their own special readings. The Mass of the day or that of a saint may be said. Weekdays in Ordinary Time also allow Masses for special occasions or Votive Masses. For example, if your class graduation occurs on an ordinary weekday, you may select the theme and readings you want.

HOURLY CELEBRATION

Even the daily liturgical celebrations are not enough to express the fullness of the mystery of Jesus. The Church, also in obedience to Jesus' command to pray always, established a liturgy of the hours. This is a collection of psalms, readings, hymns, and prayers chosen to develop the themes for the seasons and feasts of the liturgical year. It is designed to be prayed with others at various hours throughout the day in order to consecrate time and all human activity and to foster a sense of Christian community.

See Luke 18:1

The "hours" covered in this liturgy are morning (Morning Praise), daytime (Daytime Prayer), early evening (Evening Prayer), and night (Night Prayer).

The following example is the Daytime Prayer for Wednesday—a typical short "hour" suitable for recitation at midmorning, noon, or midafternoon any day of the week. A leader reads the introductory verse, the psalm-prayer, and the reading. Another reader says the antiphons. The psalms are prayed by all those who are present. The community divides itself into two sections, alternating the praying of the stanzas.

DAYTIME PRAYER

Prayer of Christians, pp. 1008–1012

Leader: God, come to my assistance.

All: Lord, make haste to help me.

Leader: Glory to the Father and to the Son and to the Holy Spirit. As it was in the beginning, is now, and ever shall be, world without end. Amen. Alleluia.

Reader: *Antiphon 1*—Lord, may you be forever blessed; teach me the ways of holiness.

Leader: How shall the young remain sinless?

All: By obeying your Word.

Psalm 119:9–16

Section 1: I have sought you with all my heart: let me not stray from your commands.

Section 2: I treasure your promise in my heart lest I sin against you.
Blessed are you, O Lord;
teach me your statutes.

Section 1: With my tongue I have recounted the decrees of your lips.
I rejoiced to do your will
as though all riches were mine.

Section 2: I will ponder all your precepts and consider your paths.
I take delight in your statutes;
I will not forget your word.

Leader: *Psalm-prayer*—Lord, may we treasure your commandments as the greatest of all riches; never let us fear that anything will be wanting to us while you are at our side.

Reader: *Antiphon 2*—Lord, keep me steadfast in your ways.

Leader: Save me, Lord,

All: from those who hate you.

Section 1: Lord, hear a cause that is just,
    pay heed to my cry.
    Turn your ear to my prayer:
    no deceit is on my lips.

Section 2: From you may my judgment come forth.
    Your eyes discern the truth.
    You search my heart, you visit me by night.
    You test me and you find in me no wrong.
    My words are not sinful.

Section 1: I kept from violence because of your Word,
    I kept my feet in your paths;
    there was no faltering in my steps.

Section 2: I am here and I call, you will hear me, O
    God.
    Turn your ear to me; hear my words.
    Display your great love, you whose right hand
    saves
    your friends from those who rebel against them.

Section 1: Guard me as the apple of your eye.
    Hide me in the shadow of your wings
    from the violent attack of the wicked.

Reader: *Antiphon 3*—Rise up, O Lord, and rescue me.

Leader: My foes encircle me with deadly intent.

All: Their hearts tight shut, their mouths speak proudly.

Section 1: They advance against me, and now they sur-
    round me.

Section 2: Their eyes are watching to strike me to the
    ground as though they were lions ready to claw
    or like some young lion crouched in hiding.

Section 1: Lord, arise, confront them, strike them down!
    Let your sword rescue my soul from the wicked;
    let your hand, O Lord, rescue me from them,
    from people whose reward is in this present life.

Section 2: You give them their fill of your treasures;
they rejoice in abundance of offspring
and leave their wealth to their children.

Section 1: As for me, in my justice I shall see your face
and be filled, when I awake, with the sight of your
glory.

Leader: *Psalm-prayer*—Turn our eyes to see the truth
of your judgments, Lord, that, when our spirits are
tried by fire, the anticipation of seeing you may
make us rejoice in your justice.

Midmorning

Leader: *A reading from 1 Peter 1:13–14*—Gird the loins
of your understanding; live soberly; set all your
hopes on the gift to be conferred on you when
Jesus Christ appears. As obedient children, do not
yield to the desires that once shaped you in your
ignorance.
Lord, show me your ways.

All: Teach me to walk in your footsteps.

Leader: God of truth, Father of all, you send your Spirit
as you promised to bring together in love all whom
sin has driven apart. Strengthen us to work for
your blessings of unity and peace in the world.
Grant this through Christ our Lord.

All: Amen.

Midafternoon

> **Leader:** *A reading from James 4:7–8a, 10*—Submit to God; resist the devil and he will take flight. Draw close to God, and he will draw close to you. Be humbled in the sight of the Lord and he will raise you on high.
> God looks tenderly on those who revere him.

All: On those who trust in his mercy.

Leader: Lord Jesus Christ, to save all people you stretched out your arms on the cross. Let our work be pleasing to you: may it proclaim your salvation to the world, for you live and reign forever and ever.

All: Amen.

Leader: Let us praise the Lord.

All: And give him thanks.

Prayer

Come, let us sing joyfully to the Lord;
    let us acclaim the rock of our salvation.
Let us greet him with thanksgiving;
    let us joyfully sing psalms to him.
For the Lord is a great God,
    and a great king above all gods;
In his hands are the depths of the earth,
    and the tops of the mountains are his.
His is the sea, for he has made it,
    and the dry land, which his hands have formed.

Come, let us bow down in worship;
    let us kneel before the Lord who made us.
For he is our God
    and we are the people he shepherds,
    the flock he guides.

Psalm 95:1–7

Use the following questions to help you review the main themes of this chapter.

1. What is the liturgical year? How did it originate?
2. What three aspects of time do liturgical celebrations include?
3. What is the purpose of the liturgical year?
4. What is the greatest feast celebrated in the liturgical year? What is the second-greatest feast?
5. What are the five seasons of the liturgical year?
6. When does the liturgical year begin?
7. When is a Sunday liturgy selected over another one?
8. When is a Sunday liturgy not selected over another one?
9. What is a solemnity? Give some examples.
10. What is a feast? Give examples.
11. What is an obligatory memorial? Give one example.
12. What is an optional memorial?
13. What is a weekday in the liturgical year?
14. What is the Liturgy of the Hours? What hours does it include?

Words to Know

Paschal Mystery, Easter Triduum, solemnity, feast, obligatory memorial, optional memorial, Morning Praise, Daytime Prayer, Evening Prayer, Night Prayer, Liturgy of the Hours

Think/Talk/Write

1. In each of the following cases, select which of the two liturgies you should use. In some cases, either option is correct.
   Sunday liturgy or Saint John Vianney (obligatory memorial)

Saint Monica (obligatory memorial) or the Mass of the Blessed Virgin Mary on Saturday

The Twenty-Fourth Sunday of the Year of the Triumph of the Cross (feast)

Second Sunday of Advent or the Immaculate Conception (solemnity)

A weekday in Ordinary Time or Saint Albert the Great (optional memorial)

A weekday in Ordinary Time or Saint Anthony Abbot (obligatory memorial)

The last Sunday in December or Christmas

Monday in Holy Week or the Annunciation (solemnity)

Saint Rose of Lima (optional memorial) or a weekday Mass, or the Mass of the Blessed Virgin Mary on Saturday

The Sunday liturgy or the Assumption (solemnity)

Saint Benedict (obligatory memorial) or a Mass you plan yourself

Saint Jerome (optional memorial) or a Mass you plan yourself

2. Explain how each of the liturgical seasons celebrates some aspect of the Paschal Mystery. Do the same for any five feasts.

3. How important are religious celebrations to you? Are they becoming more or less important as you get older? Why?

Activities

1. Divide into small groups and research each of the solemnities. Find out when the solemnity was first celebrated, if possible. What does the solemnity celebrate? When does it fall in the liturgical year? Has it always been in this place on the calendar?

2. Divide into small groups and research each of the feasts. Ask the same questions as those relating to the solemnities in question 1.

3. Consult a Lectionary concerning the propers and readings of obligatory memorials. Choose one and then write an outline of the Mass. Include commentaries on the readings, music, and petitions.

THIRTEEN

How does the Church prepare for Christmas?

What is the meaning of Advent?

Why is the Incarnation important to you?

How can you experience the meaning of Christmas?

Advent/Christmas

See, the Lord is coming from afar; his splendor fills the earth.

(EVENING PRAYER, FIRST SUNDAY OF ADVENT)

SEASONS AND FEASTS

Celebrations such as weddings and graduations involve a considerable amount of planning and behind-the-scenes organizing. There are three stages to a celebration: the preparation, the actual celebration, and the period of grateful, quiet fulfillment following the festivities.

The liturgical year follows a similar pattern of buildup, high festivity, and fulfillment, particularly around the feasts of Christmas and Easter.

The Church year opens with Advent, a season of joyful preparation for the feast of the Lord's birth. In the first two weeks, the readings are directed to Christ's second coming at the end of time. The poetic and appealing passages used in the Masses of the third and fourth weeks are filled with longing for his birth. Mary's peace and interior reflection as she awaited her holy child are models for all people as they await the Savior.

The Christmas season brings this period of hope to fulfillment in Christ's birth at Bethlehem. His epiphan-

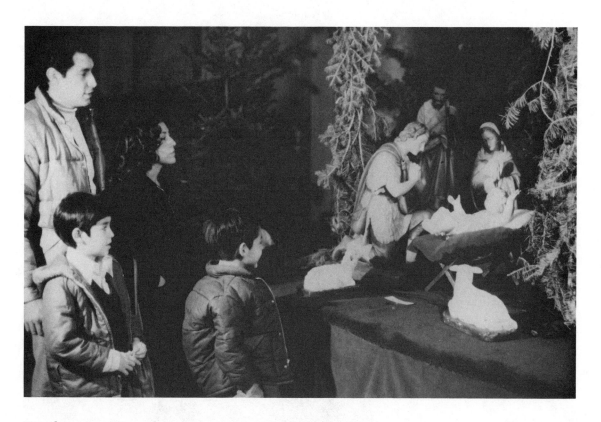

ies, the occasions when Jesus was revealed as the Messiah, are celebrated on the following two Sundays. The feast of the Epiphany celebrates the Three Kings, or Magi, who represent God's revelation of his plan of salvation in Christ to all the nations of the world. The feast of the Baptism of the Lord celebrates Christ's baptism in the Jordan when he was revealed as divine. During these three weeks of Christmas, the Church honors Mary, the holy God-bearer, and the Holy Family as the example of all Christian family life.

THE SEASON OF WAITING

When Notre Dame University's thirteen-story library was under construction, the surrounding area was a tire-marked stretch of reddish-brown earth filled with rubble. One morning shortly after the building was completed, the campus awoke to a beautifully landscaped library, complete with trees reaching to the second story. The students jokingly referred to it as the "instant forest."

Most people today like to see quick action and instant results. But God, to whom a thousand years are as one day, takes his time. Advent is the season of waiting. God waits for your response, even as you wait for his appearance. Mary's call at the Annunciation seems to have been a sudden revelation, yet Christ took his time—nine months to be born and thirty more years to prepare for his public life. He continues to wait for the response of each person.

THE JEWISH NEW YEAR

In late September or early October, Jewish people all over the world observe their High Holy Days. Rosh Hashanah, the Jewish New Year, opens a period of ten Days of Awe, during which the devout enter into a spirit of repentance and self-renewal. The penitential season closes with Yom Kippur, the Day of Atonement, which consists of twenty-five hours of strict fast. During this time, as an expression of penance for sin, observing Jews do not eat, drink, engage in sex, or bathe.

Five days later, the Jews hold another religious celebration of a very different character. The Festival of the Tabernacles, called *succot,* is a week of joyful thanksgiving, commemorating God's gift of food to the Israelites when they lived in tents in the desert.

To observe the occasion, Jews build booths *(succots)* in which families take their meals for the week. The booth is a permanent or temporary slatted structure, often built in the family's backyard or connected with the patio. The booth is covered with pine or fir branches and hung with fruits and vegetables. The top of the booth must allow some open spaces to allow the people to look up into the heavens.

Songs, ancient chants, and the praying of psalms accompany the festive meals. Jewish children sometimes construct miniature *succots* out of shoe boxes, decorating them with crêpe paper and fruits made of construction paper. To commemorate the gift of the Law in the desert, the Sacred Torah is carried in procession in the synagogues where the celebrants wave branches in a "Hosanna" procession. On the last day of the festival, there is a joyful ceremony in which the people celebrate the last solemn reading of the Torah for the old year. Amid music and song, the Sacred Scrolls are honored in procession before they are opened once again to begin the study of the texts in the new year.

The Torah is composed of the first five books of the Bible: Genesis, Exodus, Leviticus, Numbers, and Deuteronomy.

- What is it like to wait for someone if the person you're waiting for is someone you don't care for and he or she is late? What is it like if you are early and the person you're waiting for is someone you like?
- What do you wait for in Advent?
- What qualities did Mary need to respond as she did to her call?
- How must Mary have prepared for Christ's birth after her great life's mission was announced?
- When do you think most people are prepared to begin their life's work?
- What things can teenagers do to prepare themselves for their life's mission?

Advent is not only a time of waiting for Christ to come but also a time for finding and worshiping him. We find him not in the poor stable of Bethlehem but in our own cities. Jesus may be found everywhere: in the sick members of our family or neighborhood, in our brothers and sisters, and in our parents.

- Name others in whom you might find Christ.

Advent is a time when Jesus is born and grows within us—in the wisdom we gain from mistakes and in our service to others. Advent is a time of following the magi's star: in Scripture, which tells us Christ will come again, in daily inspirations to do good, and in friendships that develop our best assets.

- How else can Christ be born in you?
- Where are you likely to encounter Christ?

AN ADVENT PRAYER SERVICE

The following is a prayer service on Advent that may be prayed alone, at home with one's family, or in the classroom with one's friends. If it is prayed in a group, divide into two groups. One group will be Section 1 and the other will be Section 2.

Song—"Let Heaven Rejoice" by Bob Dufford, S.J., or another appropriate song.

Leader: Advent is the season of the seed.

Section 1: The seed is the Word of God sown in the human heart.

Section 2: The Advent, the seed of the world's life, was hidden in Mary.

Leader: Advent is the season of the secret.

Section 1: The secret of the growth of Christ.

Section 2: The secret of Divine Love growing in silence.

Leader: Advent is the season of silence.

Section 1: The silence of a child growing in the womb of its mother's body.

Section 2: The silence of a mother preparing for motherhood.

Reader 1: What did Mary have to give him?

All: Nothing but herself.

Reader 1: What did he want her to give?

All: Nothing but herself.

Reader 1: What did she really give?

All: Nothing but herself.

Reader 2: We have to give our humanity to be changed into Christ.

Section 1: We must not disturb this time of growth. We must believe he is growing in our lives.

Section 2: We must willingly choose good and perform our daily tasks as perfectly as possible.

Section 1: We must listen to others with understanding and use our hearts for life.

Reader 1: Sometimes, it may seem there iş no purpose in life. The routine monotony of sleep, school, meals, work, and study sometimes seems without meaning. But God has sent us here so that he would be here. That alone makes life worthwhile.

Section 1: The mystery of life, of the Christ-life, is growing in us.

Section 2: All we need do is give ourselves to this life and become more aware that Christ is being formed in our lives.

Section 1: We must trust him, because we cannot see his face.

Section 2: We must possess him secretly in darkness, as the earth possesses the seed.

All: We must fold our concentrated love upon him, like earth surrounding, holding, and nourishing the seed.

Leader: We live in an age of impatience.

Section 1: An age in which everything tries to cut out and do away with the natural season of growth.

Section 2: That is why so much in our life is abortive.

Reader 2: Why don't we let everything grow, as Christ grew in Mary?

Section 1: Quietly.

Section 2: Peacefully.

Section 1: Joyfully.

Reader 1: Certain things in this life refuse to be violated by speed. They demand a proper time for growth.

Section 2: Such as an angel food cake.

Section 1: An American Beauty rose.

Section 2: Or a child.

Leader: This is the hidden meaning of Advent.

Section 1: A new awareness of God.

Section 2: An increase of life, the light shining from our darkness.

Leader: Advent is the season of the seed.

Section 1: The seed is the Word of God sown in my heart.

Section 2: Advent is still the seed of my life today.

Leader: Advent is the season of the secret.

Section 1: The season of the growth of Christ.

Section 2: The secret of his Holy Spirit within us.

Leader: Advent is the season of silence.

Section 1: The silence of Christ growing in my heart and mind—all of me.

Section 2: The silence of a teenager preparing for Christ in adulthood.

Reader 2: What do I have to give?

All: Nothing but myself.

Reader 2: What will I really give?

All: Nothing but myself.

Song—"Wood Hath Hope" by John Foley, S.J., or another appropriate song.

THE INCARNATION

The word *incarnation* means "to become flesh." Christ, who is also God, became physically human on Christmas. This fact has important implications for the way one views one's self and Christianity.

To illustrate the implications of the Incarnation, a small comparison is in order. For centuries in the liturgy, the prayer before Communion recited by the congregation read: "O Lord, I am not worthy that you should come under my roof. Speak but the word, and my soul shall be healed." Today's liturgy reads: "Lord, I am not worthy to receive you, but only say the word and I shall be healed."

The word to notice in the second version is the *I* that replaces "my soul." Jesus did not come to save our soul. He came to save us as a total person, body and soul.

Our union with Christ in Communion is bodily. Our worship at the Eucharist must likewise be whole. It is meant to involve our mind and will, body and emotions, smell, sight, taste, touch, and hearing.

- What elements of the liturgy appeal to each of your senses? What elements appeal to your emotions? To your mind?
- How do people express their wholehearted devotion to Christ at public ceremonies?

AN ONGOING BIRTHDAY

Jupiter, Atlas, Hercules, Venus, Cupid, Helen of Troy, and Pandora are fictional characters in the ancient Greek and Roman myths. Their stories dramatize certain universal truths of life.

That's where the stories of Christianity are different. When we commemorate Christmas, we remember the actual birth of a real baby. He was the son of a Jewish girl named Mary whose carpenter-husband was called Joseph. All three belonged to a people whose stories were not fantasies, but the real history of their human ancestors. In God's designs, these stories contain the deepest truths known to the human race: God's love, his self-revelation, and the Incarnation of his Son.

It all began with the historical fact of Christ's birth, but the most amazing thing is that Christmas is still going on today. The Son of God takes on new flesh with every human being who accepts him. What is more, the process will never end until every last person is born. Only then will the birth of Christ be complete—when everything in heaven and on earth is brought back to the Father to praise him forever.

- What sins does Saint Paul warn against in 1 Corinthians 6:12–20?
- In what three ways is Christ born?

Prayer

You wait for us
until we are ready for you.
We wait for the Word
you send in our everyday lives.
Make us open, receptive,
attentive to your voice
whenever you speak.
Teach us to listen.
Bring Jesus, your Son, to us,
our Word of peace.

ADVENT TRAINING

Most athletes go through rigorous physical training to prepare for their sport. The preparation needed for the Christian life is spiritual rather than physical. Nevertheless, it is a training and it does involve discipline.

A good way to start off the Church's new year and "get into shape" for the coming of the Lord is to spend five minutes a day with him in meditating on Scripture. If your school has a chapel, this can be done before school, during the lunch hour, or right after classes. Just before climbing into bed is another good time for this practice.

Begin by taking a minute to quiet yourself. Close your eyes. Remember that God is present within you. Next, look up the reference of your choice from those given below, reading only the line given, no more and no less. Read it about three times. Let each word penetrate your mind. Think of its meaning for your life. Let your heart pray about it. Give the passage a final reading before you close the Bible.

Isaiah 49:14–15; Isaiah 6:3; Isaiah 9:2; Isaiah 9:6; Isaiah 9:7; Isaiah 11:1–2; Isaiah 11:5–6; Isaiah 12:5–6; Isaiah 22:22; Isaiah 25:1; Isaiah 28:16; Isaiah 30:18; Isaiah 33:17; Isaiah 33:23; Isaiah 35:4; Isaiah 40:31; Luke 1:28; Luke 1:32–33; Luke 1:35; Luke 1:38; Luke 1:45; Luke 1:52; Luke 1:54; Luke 1:78–79; Luke 2:4–6; Luke 2:7; Luke 2:9–11; Romans 8:22–23; 1 Corinthians 1:4–9; Ephesians 1:3–4; Ephesians 1:5–6; 1 Timothy 1:15; Philemon 2:6–7.

- ■ Which passage did you select? How does it relate to Advent? To Jesus?
- ■ How does this passage apply to your own life?

THE CHRISTMAS CRIB

Today, almost every Catholic home puts up a Christmas crib during the season of the nativity. This was not always the case. Although the Christ Child and the Madonna and paintings of Christ's birth were used in churches from the earliest centuries of Christianity, the crib scene was the inspiration of Saint Francis of Assisi.

In a famous Christmas Eve celebration, Saint Francis created a life-size representation of the nativity scene, including live animals. In a vivid and deeply moving sermon, he made the events of Christmas come alive for the villagers. Since then, cribs of every size, material, and style have been used in churches and homes.

This happened in Greccio, Italy, in 1223.

The importance of this religious symbol lies in its power to remind people that humility and poorness need not spoil their peace. The message of the angels that holy night—"Peace, and good will to all!"—is a most valuable revelation: God is good. He cares, even when things don't appear to be going very well from our point of view.

What do the following aspects of the Christmas scene mean to you?

- Jesus was born in an inconvenient setting, away from his own home.
- Jesus' first visitors were poor uneducated shepherds.
- The magi came a certain distance by following a star. They had to consult the Scriptures to find the exact location.
- Jesus' bed was straw; his means of warmth was the breath of animals.
- Jesus was immediately made the object of a hunt by those in power.

SUMMING UP

Use the following questions to help you review the
main themes of this chapter.

1. What stages constitute a celebration?
2. Why is waiting so difficult?
3. What is the spirit of each of the stages of the Advent-Christmas season?
4. Of which two events in history does Advent remind Christians?
5. How is Advent like an athletic training period?
6. What is meant by the Incarnation? How does this event relate to your
   salvation?
7. When was the Christmas crib first used? Who started this practice?

Words to Know

Advent, Christmas season, magi, Incarnation, *succot,* Torah, Yom Kippur, Festival of the Tabernacles

Think/Talk/Write

1. Christmas is a time when people spend a lot of time shopping, and
   they often become irritable. What do you think is the best way to
   handle someone who cuts in front of you in line? The clerk who
   makes a mistake? Someone who dents your car?
2. Is the mildness of the Christ Child an impractical ideal for today's
   world? Why or why not?
3. On a practical level, what does it mean to you to be saved both in
   body and soul? What effect does this have on your decisions and
   actions?

Activities

1. Write a paragraph, a poem, or a prayer, or draw or paint a picture that makes "sense" of Christmas.
2. Make up a list of guidelines for Christmas shoppers that includes tips for maintaining the real spirit of Christmas.
3. It is estimated that more than 2 billion Christmas cards are sent annually in the United States. Investigate and report on the origin of the custom of sending Christmas greetings by card. Look up the influence of Louis Prang.
4. Find out why people use poinsettias, holly, ivy, evergreens, and mistletoe at Christmas.
5. Where and when did the Christmas tree originate, and what is its symbolism?

FOURTEEN

How can self-denial be a positive thing?

Why is Lent a time for self-examination?

What is the message of the Scriptures during Lent?

What happens during Holy Week?

Lent

I tell you truly: you will weep and mourn while the world rejoices; you will grieve for a time, but your grief will be turned to joy. When a woman is in labor she is sad that her time has come. When she has borne her child, she no longer remembers her pain, for joy.

(JOHN 16:20–21)

A SEASON OF SELF-DENIAL

Nobody likes a headache, a humiliation, or a thorn of any kind, and yet most good things seem to involve pain. If you want to pass a certain subject, you have to submit to the daily grind of homework.

In Lent, Christians reflect on the tremendous courage with which Christ entered into his passion and death. It wasn't that he didn't understand or feel the pain, and he certainly didn't want suffering. He prayed so long in the garden to be relieved of it that his disciples fell asleep and the guards had to carry torches when they came for him. His prayer was an agony in which his whole body sank to the ground, sweating blood at the thought of the torture and humiliation that lay ahead. Jesus did not appreciate pain. He was not in love with the idea of his death. But he believed in God's promise of eternal life.

■ Think of some duties you do on the job, in school, or in your family that involve pain. Why do you accept the suffering involved in doing them?

- How would you classify your acceptance of the pain involved: very willing, willing, tolerant, grudging, or resentful?
- What were the values that made Jesus accept his passion and death?
- What other things must have added to Jesus' suffering besides the thought of the physical pain he would endure?
- The only way you can respond to Christ's personal love is through your love of others. Who might you be called to love (suffer for) today?

Lent is a season of self-denial and penance that culminates in the Easter joy of Jesus' resurrection and victory over death. The first Lent was only three days long—the time between Jesus' capture and death and his reappearance among his followers in a new and different life.

Today, Lent stretches over forty days, not including Sundays, which are considered separate from the forty-day period. They are called Sundays *in* Lent, not *of* Lent. Lent is not only a period of sorrow and mourning such as the Apostles experienced, but it is a period of self-examination. It is meant to result in the conversion of our minds and hearts to Christ so that we become our true selves.

- Why do you think Sundays are not included in Lent?

Ash Wednesday marks the beginning of Lent. The blessed ashes placed on each person's forehead are a call to "turn away from sin and be faithful to the Gospel." They remind each person of his or her humanness and of his or her eventual death. The ashes set the tone for the annual forty days of Christian renewal before Holy Week.

The Gospels of the Sundays in Lent include the accounts of Jesus' temptation in the desert, the transfiguration of Christ, and incidents in which Jesus condemned sin, cured sinners, raised the dead, and predicted his own death and resurrection.

A *catechumen* is someone who is taking instruction in the Faith in order to become baptized.

Hosanna means "Lord, please save."

A cross has no corpus (body) of Christ on it, while a crucifix has.

The Lenten season has three purposes: (1) to be an immediate preparation for catechumens asking to be baptized at the Easter Vigil, (2) to call sinners to return to the Church by means of the sacrament of Reconciliation, and (3) to deepen the spiritual life of the devout by a renewal of their baptismal promises.

Holy Week, which brings Lent and the liturgical year to a climax, begins with the Gospel of Jesus' entry as Messiah into Jerusalem amid waving palm branches and shouts of "Hosanna" by the crowds. During the week, the passion account is read in its entirety on Passion Sunday and Good Friday. The week moves solemnly from a commemoration of Jesus' gift of the Eucharist on Holy Thursday to the celebration of the Lord's passion on Good Friday. Good Friday is the only day of the year when Mass is not celebrated; there is a Communion service, however.

A TIME OF CONVERSION

Lent is a good time for repentance and conversion of heart. One way to help you see what turns you away from and back to God is to read Scripture regularly, meditatively, and prayerfully. The following texts, drawn from the prophet Isaiah, are especially appropriate to stir up repentance and conversion of heart. Consider each day's reading as a message addressed by God directly to you, meant only for you.

1. Set aside five minutes at any convenient time of day, preferably at the same time each day. Choose a place where you have easy access to a Bible.
2. Settle yourself in a place relatively free from the possibility of interruption and where a cross or crucifix is within easy view. Remain still and breathe deeply until you find that you can center your attention on God's presence.
3. Find the passage suggested for the day and read it slowly, repeating it aloud several times if possible.

4. Let the Word sink into your mind.

5. Respond with your heart as long as you can remain attentive to God. Close with a brief prayer to the Father.

Ash Wednesday—Isaiah 53:8; Thursday—Isaiah 53:5–6; Friday—Isaiah 54:8; Saturday—Isaiah 55:1.

First Week of Lent. Monday—Isaiah 55:12; Tuesday—Isaiah 55:5; Wednesday—Isaiah 54:10; Thursday—Isaiah 53:10a; Friday—Isaiah 54:5; Saturday—Isaiah 54:2.

Second Week of Lent. Monday—Isaiah 12:3; Tuesday—Isaiah 12:2; Wednesday—Isaiah 9:2; Thursday—Isaiah 9:6; Friday—Isaiah 1:18; Saturday—Isaiah 26:4.

Third Week of Lent. Monday—Isaiah 12:3–4; Tuesday—Isaiah 26:3–4; Wednesday—Isaiah 53:10b; Thursday—Isaiah 40:29a; Friday—Isaiah 40:1; Saturday—Isaiah 40:9.

Fourth Week of Lent. Monday—Isaiah 40:5; Tuesday—Isaiah 40:3; Wednesday—Isaiah 40:9a; Thursday—Isaiah 38:17; Friday—Isaiah 41:17; Saturday—Isaiah 31:1.

Fifth Week of Lent. Monday—Isaiah 35:4; Tuesday—Isaiah 53:5; Wednesday—Isaiah 61:10; Thursday—Isaiah 64:8; Friday—Isaiah 58:6; Saturday—Isaiah 57:14.

Sixth Week of Lent. Monday—Isaiah 49:22; Tuesday—Isaiah 63:7; Wednesday—Isaiah 40:29b; Thursday—Isaiah 12:5; Friday—Isaiah 59:12; Saturday—Isaiah 59:9.

Easter Sunday—Luke 24:1–53.

If the Old Testament doesn't appeal to you, you may wish to pray using the New Testament. You might read one chapter of Matthew every night from Monday to Friday for the six weeks of Lent. Another option is to read one chapter of Mark for the first sixteen days of Lent and then read one chapter a day from Luke for the remainder of Lent, or about seven verses of John beginning with Chapter 12 each day for the duration of Lent.

A TIME FOR FASTING

Before his entrance into a Carthusian monastery in Spain, Thomas Verner Moore had achieved a brilliant career in teaching, writing, and the practice of medicine. Ordained a priest in 1901, he left his Kentucky birthplace to study philosophy and medicine abroad. During the next thirty years, he became successively a psychiatrist, a major in the United States Army Medical Corp, and head of the Department of Psychology and Psychiatry at the Catholic University. He also published several highly successful books.

Why would a man leading so productive a life and so obviously intelligent want to enter the strictest contemplative order in the Church? He entered a monastery where he spent twenty years as a hermit, absolutely silent and alone except for daily community celebrations of the Eucharist and common prayer, and three or four hours of "brisk walking" with other Carthusians every Sunday afternoon. The mortifications of the life he undertook included many hours of private prayer, reading, and manual labor. Only one meal a day was eaten, and meat was never allowed, even to the sick. In addition, there was a black fast of bread and water once a week.

The decision of this famous man prompted many Christians and non-Christians alike to reexamine the value of mortification—the "dying to self" that Christians voluntarily undertake for religious reasons.

The tradition of a "strict life" involving fast, abstinence, and solitude goes back to John the Baptizer, who lived in the desert, wore rough clothes, and fasted on locusts in order to be a better instrument for preparing the way for the Savior. Jesus himself spent forty days in the desert fasting and praying before he began his life work. As a human being, he needed to strengthen his purposes and unite himself completely with God. Once, when the Apostles complained that they could not expel a demon, Jesus said, "This kind does not leave but by prayer and fasting." Matthew 17:21

During Lent, the Church reminds Christians of the age-old importance of fasting. On Ash Wednesday and Good Friday, all Christians over twenty-one and under sixty years of age are required to fast—that is, to eat only one full meal a day. During these forty penitential days, all persons over fourteen are bound by the law of abstinence, which forbids the eating of meat on all Fridays of Lent.

But these small mortifications relating to food are not all God asks. Rather, they are only a symbol of the real fasting of the heart that the Spirit calls for: abstinence from everything that may lead to sin and the control of such wayward passions as greed, selfishness, and lust.

- ■ As a class, make a list of mortifications that God might ask of an average high school student during Lent.

LENT AND SPRING CLEANING

Strange as it may seem, the annual shakedown we give our houses every spring has its origins in an event that took place 3,200 years ago.

Today, people buy dehydrated or compressed yeast in packages in order to raise homemade bread and rolls. In ancient times, women kept yeast or leaven in a mass of fermenting dough in a corner of the kitchen at all times. By pinching off a part of the dough and mixing it with their bread batter, they could have raised bread at any time.

At the time of the first Passover, the Hebrew families had to be ready to leave Egypt at an instant's notice. Because they did not have time to allow their dough to rise, they ate matzo—unleavened bread that looks like crackers. For centuries, as a remembrance of the hasty getaway, at the annual Passover Jewish families made a thorough search of their households to remove all leavened dough *(hametz).* Only unleavened bread was allowed at the most solemn supper of the year.

The ritual of cleaning one's house from top to bottom for Easter is a carryover of the custom of getting rid of all old fermenting dough. Of course, it is also linked with the spring mood of new growth after the lifelessness of the long winter.

1 Corinthians 5:7

As we chase away the dust and grime of winter, we can see a parallel with purification called for by Lent—the cleansing of sin from our hearts. Saint Paul says, "You must remove the old yeast of sin so that you will be entirely pure." Repentance is at the very core of Lent, which opens on Ash Wednesday with the words "Repent and believe!"

Turning away from sin is important, but it is only the beginning. The second word "believe" is a word of growth and life and is more important. Lent is the season to deepen our faith.

LITURGY

HINDU DEATH AND REBIRTH

In an annual Hindu celebration, families honor a home-made clay statue for the ten days of Durga Puga by placing before it flowers, rice, incense, and fruits. At the end of this time, the statue, which may represent anything in creation—an animal, a plant, a bird, or a reptile—is taken in procession down to the Ganges River. There, to the words "Oh, I return you to the Source from which you came," it is thrown into the water. These words express the Hindu belief that God is the soul of everything, that underneath all our various forms is Brahman—the ultimate living force. The action of drowning the image represents the countless deaths all things must pass through before being reborn to the highest state—a life of pure good deeds—when they merge into the great soul of God. This eternal state of peace is known as *moksha*.

Durga is the name of a Hindu god who reigns over the harvest. Puga is the name of a Hindu worship festival.

■ Non-Christian religions contain some of the truths that Jesus came to reveal fully to the human race. During what season do Christians celebrate the truth revealed by Christ that we share God's life when we are united with Jesus in his passage from death to eternal life?

LENTEN PALMS

Palms are found in tropical climates where lush fruit and balmy weather predominate. The early Egyptian and Semitic peoples prized these stately trees of graceful trunks and majestic height. Providing people shelter from the desert sun, as well as delicious fruit, palms became a symbol of success and well-being. Palm branches were used in liturgical feasts, in processions of royalty, and as trophies of victory in public games. As is still true today, a flourishing metropolis in which these princely trees grew was sometimes named after them.

When the Jews, in the festive mood of the Passover, waved palm branches as Jesus rode into Jerusalem, they showed clearly that they regarded him as the expected Messiah, the royal king who would liberate them from Rome.

The palm is also used as a sign of victory in the Book of Revelation: "I saw before me a huge crowd which no one could count from every nation and race, people, and tongue. They stood before the throne and the Lamb, dressed in long white robes and holding palm branches in their hands."

The tombs of the early martyrs had palm decorations as a sign of their victory over death. Mosaics and stone coffins used the palm as a symbol of paradise, showing Christ amid palms in heaven. In ancient churches, the Lamb and the Apostles appeared amid palms.

In the Middle Ages, palms symbolized Sunday, the day of the Lord's triumphant resurrection. During the Renaissance, palms were used as signs of virtue, a good marriage, or a long life.

Today, people carry palm branches home to be used as sacramentals, placing them over beds, entwining them in crucifixes, or displaying them near holy pictures or statues. Often, palms are decorated with ribbon and worked into a pattern such as a cross.

Semitic refers to Babylonians, Assyrians, Arabs, and Jews, all of whom were said to be descended from Shem, one of Noah's three sons.

See Leviticus 23:40 and Nehemiah 8:15

See John 12:12–13

Revelation 7:9

The liturgical procession of palms on Passion Sunday originated in the fourth century to reenact Jesus' entry into Jerusalem. The bishop rode a mule through the congregation as the people waved branches and shouted "Hosanna to the Son of David!" In the Middle Ages, the procession went from church to church. The presence of Christ was represented by the book of Scripture, the cross, an image of Christ fastened to the back of a donkey, or by the Blessed Sacrament itself. As more and more attention was focused on the blessing of the palms, the procession fell into disuse.

Since 1955, the procession of palms has been revived. Because Christians relive Christ's mystery in the liturgy, they join in the procession, which begins outside the church door or in another building. The priest wears a red vestment as a sign of victory. The cross, the emblem of Christ's conquest over death, leads the way.

Once inside the church, however, the Palm Sunday liturgy suddenly changes to a mood of sorrow, just as the fickle crowd's glad welcome changed to a treacherous call for Jesus' death in that first Holy Week. The Sunday is fittingly called Passion Sunday.

■ Try your hand at making a small decorative cross out of palm. Work while the palm is still soft and flexible.

THE POSITIVE SIDE

The cross, the main sign and greatest mystery of the Christian life, is the symbol of the seeming contradictions that make up life. Its vertical bar, pointing to the heavens, represents God and eternity. The horizontal beam stands for the things of this world—time and humanity. Some of the opposites symbolized by the crossing of the two bars are the following:

God and human beings are made one.
Every moment of time is bisected by eternity.
Death is the door to life.
Victory comes in defeat.
Love is born of hate.
Highest joy comes through deepest suffering.
The negative contains the positive hiding within it.

■ What other apparent opposites does Jesus' cross stand for?

Sometimes when Christians are thinking over what they should do for Lent, they consider only penances that seem negative—giving up fighting at home, giving up shows or games, giving up desserts or snacks. These things seem worthwhile because people concentrate on the difficulty of the penance. Yet all these negative things have a positive value: they express one's love of Christ.

If negative penances have a plus value, positive penances are helpful in a different way. In doing a positive penance, we concentrate on how it will affect the other person, rather than on how much it costs. Here are some positive penances to try for Lent.

Pray night prayers before going to bed.
Read from a spiritual book every day.
Read Scripture every day—alone or with someone else.
Play a game with a younger or older member of the family.

Visit a shut-in.

Collect, mend, and wash all the old or outgrown clothes in the house, and then send them to a charitable organization.

Make your own Easter cards.

Do something helpful around the house.

Attend Lenten services in your parish.

Participate in the Eucharist several times a week, or daily.

Make an Easter banner or design Easter placemats for the table.

Surprise the family by preparing a meal.

Help with spring cleaning.

Say grace before every meal.

Give to the missions any money you save from denying yourself something.

■ What are some other "positive" penances you could do during Lent?

HOLY WEEK

Holy Thursday

At the Mass of the Lord's Supper, Christians celebrate and thank God for his gifts of the Eucharist and priesthood. The liturgy focuses on the Last Supper. Dramatically, it brings out the institution of the Eucharist. We hear Christ's loving words to his Apostles. We see him humble himself by washing the feet of his friends. We share with him the last precious hours before his passion. At Communion time, we receive his own body and blood, recalling the love that prompted him to give us this great gift.

After Mass, the Blessed Sacrament is removed from the tabernacle and taken to a side altar. After midnight, the church will be empty and bare. Christ has left the Upper Room for the Garden of Gethsemane. His hour of passion and death is about to come.

Good Friday

Good Friday is not really a day of mourning. Although Christians commemorate the death of Christ, they know that Jesus rose from the dead. Good Friday is a time to ponder the meaning of Christ's suffering. It is a time to think about how great God's love must be that he would undergo this type of torment. How great must be the evil of sin that made such a death necessary! Good Friday is a day of prayer and soul-searching.

The liturgy in the afternoon consists of four parts: (1) readings from Scripture, (2) prayers, (3) the veneration of the cross, and (4) a Communion service. There is an awesome silence in the liturgy on this day of reflection.

- What meaning does Good Friday have for your life?

Holy Saturday

Holy Saturday is the holiest night of the year. At the beginning of the liturgy, the congregation is enveloped in darkness, the darkness of sin and death. Suddenly, the new fire is lit. The Light of Christ blazes forth, shattering the darkness of evil and death, and restoring life. The Paschal Candle is lit from this fire, another symbol of the victorious risen Christ. From this candle, people light their candles, signifying the victory they share with Christ through baptism.

The Holy Saturday Mass celebrates the Easter event. All evil, all sin, all eternal death is destroyed by Christ. The Resurrection fills Christians with praise, hope, and joy. The liturgy ends with an alleluia; the congregation leaves the church, praising God.

Lenten Meditation

A ragged cloak on his shoulders
a crown of thorns on his head—
"Here is the Man!"
Whipped and mocked and falsely charged
"Here is the Man!"
Abandoned by his friends
cast off by his people—
"Here is the Man!"
Look at the loser, the victim,
the scapegoat.
He has no armies, no advocates,
scarcely a friend.
"Here is the Man!"
Alone—but not lonely.
Beaten—but undefeated.
Crushed—but calm.
"Here is the Man!"
And in that one Man, see all of us.
In his defeat, see our victory.
"Here is the Man!"

Ecce Homo

SUMMING UP

Use the following questions to help you review the
main themes of this chapter.

1. What is the spirit and purpose of Lent?
2. How can penance during Lent be something positive?
3. What is the holiest night of the year?
4. What prevents Good Friday from being a day of mourning?
5. What event in the life of Jesus is celebrated on Holy Thursday?
6. What two things do Christians thank God for on Holy Thursday?
7. What is the one day of the year when Mass is not celebrated?
8. What do the ashes on Ash Wednesday symbolize?
9. What is the climax of Lent and the liturgical year?
10. What is the origin of spring cleaning?
11. What were palms used to signify throughout history?

Words to Know

moksha, Ash Wednesday, catechumen, Hosanna, crucifix, unleavened
bread, abstinence, fast, Passion Sunday, Holy Thursday, Good Friday,
Holy Saturday

Think/Talk/Write

1. Is fickleness a sin or is it a weakness? Or is changing one's mind
   simply a human right? Defend your position.
2. List a time when you, your parents, or your friends have changed
   their minds about something. Is this the same as being fickle? Explain.
3. Why do you think Mass is not celebrated on Good Friday or during
   the day of Holy Saturday?
4. What are some positive things you can do as a class to increase
   individual motivation to persevere in a penance throughout Lent?
5. What is the significance of Lent being forty days long?

Activities

1. Study the readings for Ash Wednesday. Then make up a prayer service, using the same theme and ideas. Incorporate appropriate songs, and then pray this service with the class.
2. Study the Mass of the Lord's Supper. Are the readings different for the three cycles? What is the significance of the washing of the feet? What is the structure of the Mass? How does this Mass end?
3. Study the liturgy of Good Friday. What are the parts of this service? How many readings are there? Why do people venerate the cross? What groups of people are prayed for this day? Why do you think the Church prays for them at this time?
4. If possible, attend the Eastern Orthodox Holy Week services and compare them with the Roman rite.

FIFTEEN

Why is the Easter season the climax of the liturgical year?

Why does the word "alleluia" express the Church's thanks to God?

What is the meaning of the Ascension?

What is the message of Pentecost?

How does the Church celebrate Christ's life during Ordinary Time?

Easter/Ordinary Time

Do not be frightened. I know you are looking for Jesus the crucified, but he is not here. . . . He has been raised from the dead and now goes ahead of you to Galilee, where you will see him.

(MATTHEW 28:5, 7)

THE EASTER SEASON

The Easter season officially begins with the Easter Vigil on Holy Saturday. The glorious alleluias of the Easter Sunday Mass ring throughout the fifty days of the festive Easter season. During this time the risen Lord is kept before the minds of the faithful through the Gospel readings of Christ's appearances after the Resurrection.

Although Christ was glorified at the instant of his death, the feast of the Ascension commemorates that glorification. At the same time, it launches ten days of prayer in preparation for the coming of the Holy Spirit.

The Easter Vigil

A *vigil* is a period of watching. In ancient times, sentries were stationed on the walls of a city to watch for enemies.

The Easter Vigil, which is held late evening on Holy Saturday, is the most glorious celebration of the Church year. It opens with the beautiful light service at which new fire (the symbol of Christ in his transformed state) is blessed and the Paschal candle (which represents the dazzling appearance of the risen Lord) is carried into the darkened church. This first portion of the four-part service climaxes in the joyful singing of the *exsultet,* an ancient hymn proclaiming Christ's resurrection.

Light was a symbol of God's presence for the Old Testament People of God. Similarly, fire is a symbol of Christ the Light and of one's response to him. This symbolism is expressed in the prayer over the fire: "Let us be so inflamed with desire for heaven that we may attain with pure souls to the feast of everlasting brightness."

In the Easter Vigil service, the Paschal Candle is carried forth in solemn procession to be enthroned on the altar. The procession itself reminds Christians of the Hebrews who were led by a pillar of fire through the Red Sea toward the Promised Land. In the Easter Vigil liturgy, the pillar of light represents Christ, who leads the new Chosen People through the waters of baptism to the promised land of heaven.

Each person bears a candle enkindled from the light of the Paschal Candle as they stand to hear the deacon proclaim the Easter message in the thrilling words of the *exsultet.* In this moving song of joy, they hear of the Christian mysteries first enacted by Christ long ago but ever renewed among them in the paschal celebrations.

In the second part of the service, the Liturgy of the Word, the Church meditates on all the wonderful saving actions of God since the creation of the world. Christians reflect on God's saving action that rescued the Hebrews from Egypt and led them to the Promised Land. Christians recall that they, too, are the People of God, and on this night are called to share even more completely in his saving action.

In the third part of the liturgy, the Baptismal service, all who have been instructed in the faith are sacramentally joined with Christ in baptism. It is in baptism that Christians are made members of Christ and sharers in his death and resurrection. In baptism, Christ rescues us from the kingdom of darkness and raises us into his own kingdom of light. Therefore, it is on this great

night, looking forward to the dawn of resurrection, that the Church welcomes new members and invites Christians to renew the promises of their baptism.

Baptism is both an individual and a social affair. For the individual, baptism is a new birth, a dying and rising with Christ. But it is also an initiation into the Church. In the new Passover from death to life, baptism makes Christians the new People of God. Thus the Easter Vigil is a celebration of the Christian community. In the renewal of baptismal promises, Christians testify to each other that they explicitly and corporately undertake the obligation of their baptism. They then join in the Christian prayer, the Our Father.

The fourth part of the liturgy, the Eucharistic service, is a perfect conclusion to the drama of the night. Emulating Mary Magdalene in the Gospel of the Vigil Mass, Christians seek Jesus, who was crucified and who has risen, and find him in their Easter Communion.

In the prayers after Communion, Christians pray that all who have taken part in this night will be filled with the Spirit and may live together in love and peace. The service closes with the glad chanting of the alleluia.

Alleluia is a Hebrew exclamation that means "praise to Yahweh."

Alleluia

The greatest event that is celebrated in the Church is the Resurrection. It is a historical event that is beyond our powers of comprehension. The experience of meeting the risen Lord can never be put into words, but the word that came closest to expressing the wonder for the early Christians was the Hebrew word *alleluia.*

This exclamation of joy and almost uncontrollable gladness is really a combination of two words, *hallelu* (a cry of praise) and *Yah* (Yahweh). This word begins with the outgoing breath of the *H* sound. To pronounce it aloud or to shout or sing it, as the Israelites did in their liturgies, literally sucks the breath out of one's mouth. By means of this expressive word, the Israelites poured themselves out in admiration, adoration, and awe before their God in return for all he had done for them.

The Easter alleluias are the response of the joyfully grateful new People of God at the greatest saving action God has performed for them—raising Jesus from the dead. For in that resurrection, those who are joined with Christ know that they too will rise gloriously. They too will know the *shalom* of Jesus.

When Saint Augustine said that "Christians must be an alleluia from head to toe," he meant that Christians are people of profound adoration to God who has given them reason for the most exhilarating gladness. The Easter liturgy rightly repeats again and again, Alleluia! Christ is risen! Alleluia! Alleluia! Alleluia!

- Why do you think so many martyrs went to their deaths singing and full of joy?
- Why don't more Christians radiate their alleluia vocation?
- What are some practical ways in which teenagers can be alleluia people?

EASTER SYMBOLS

Many symbols of Easter go back a long way. The symbol of the Hebrew paschal lamb is three thousand years old. The good luck and prosperity connected with the pig (ham) is rooted in pre-Christian times. Anyone who has raised rabbits, especially snow-white cottontails, is well acquainted with their fertility. Rabbits symbolize the superabundant life of the Resurrection. Pre-Christian people saw in eggs the symbol of spring's rebirth. Easter eggs speak to Christians of the risen life born out of the tomb. In the Middle Ages, people dressed in their best clothes and took an "Easter walk" after the Easter Mass, a custom that developed into the Easter parades once held in the big cities of America.

The use of lilies as an Easter symbol goes back only a hundred years, to 1882, when W. K. Harris, a florist, brought a new variety of lilies to the United States from Bermuda. Larger than the Madonna lily, it flowered around Easter. For this reason, churches began to adorn their altars with the lily that came to be known as the Easter lily.

For centuries, Gospel translations used the phrase "lilies of the field" for the wild flowers Jesus referred to when he said, "Learn a lesson from the way the wild flowers grow. They do not work; they do not spin. Yet, I assure you, not even Solomon in all his splendor was arrayed like one of these." Today, scholars know that the dull brown Palestinian hillsides were lit up not by white Easter lilies but by a profusion of colorful flowers that bloomed everywhere. Jesus used the natural beauty of his environment to illustrate the care the Father has. It is easy to see in the spotless fragrant white Easter lily, shaped like a trumpet, a reflection of the glory of the Resurrection—a regal announcement of profound joy and peace.

Ascension Thursday

The word *ascension* means "a going up." The feast seems to celebrate Jesus' being "lifted off the earth," as Luke puts it in the Acts of the Apostles. Painters through the centuries have pictured Jesus ascending into a cloud.

See Acts of the Apostles 1:9; Mark 16:19; Luke 24:51

Since you know that heaven is not up or out there beyond the farthest star, what are the evangelists and artists saying about this feast? To human beings, going up—an action that defies the pull of gravity and suggests heavenly ascent—is different from what people are naturally used to. Ordinarily, things fall down. People constantly experience their own heaviness. But the ability to rise shows another side, another potential.

In Mark's Gospel we are told that "the Lord Jesus was taken up into heaven and took his seat at God's right hand." The evangelist is trying to express in human terms what is really inexpressible: that Jesus, the very man whom the Apostles knew and loved and lived with, was glorified—that he was somehow equal with God.

Mark 16:19

That is a mystery Christians will never fully comprehend, but it has a corollary that is even more mysterious. We too shall one day join Jesus in this glory. Ascension Thursday is the day we praise the Father for the glory of Christ. It is the day we remember our own destiny in Christ. It is the day we dream what heaven will be like. Jesus sits at the right hand of the Father eternally praying for us. He told his followers simply to ask, and they would receive.

A *corollary* is a proposition that follows another one already given, with little or no proof.

- ■ If you knew you would get any three wishes you asked for, what would you ask?

Firebird and the Message of Pentecost

The third Person of the Trinity, the Holy Spirit, may seem less a person than the Father and the Son. Christians tend to think of the Spirit as a rushing wind, a burning flame, or a dove. The Bible does not say the

Holy Spirit is these things, but that he is like them. Some of his qualities include: power—the strength of a mighty wind; spirit—the gentleness and peace of a dove; and fire—the brightness and cheerfulness of a cozy fireplace drawing all to its warmth.

■ List five things you associate with the Holy Spirit.

Beneath all these symbols arises one single quality that is more personal than anything known—the very heart of God himself: love. The Holy Spirit is love as a person. As God's gift to the world, the Spirit lives in the midst of believers to bring out in them their potential to love.

In the letter of Saint Paul, the Holy Spirit teaches the characteristics of genuine Christian love of neighbor: "Love is patient; love is kind. Love is not jealous; it does not put on airs; it is not snobbish. Love is never rude, it is not self-seeking, it is not prone to anger; neither does it brood over injuries."

1 Corinthians 13:4–5

In the letter to the Ephesians, Saint Paul says that what binds people to one another is not their love, but actually God's own love—the Holy Spirit himself: "Make every effort to preserve the unity which has the

Ephesians 4:3–4

LITURGY

Spirit as its origin and peace as its binding force. There is but one body and one Spirit."

Pentecost—the celebration of the presence of the Holy Spirit in the followers of Jesus—teaches that unless we love with God's love (that is, in the Spirit) it will be hard, even impossible, to love truly and consistently.

- In Ephesians 5:1–7, 15–21, what dignities does Saint Paul insist that Christians maintain in their love of themselves and one another in the Spirit? What sins should they avoid?
- The Holy Spirit brings the fullness of life and love. What gift would he give to heal each of the following kinds of brokenness: tension, turbulence, anxiety, fear, bitterness, emptiness, pride, lukewarmness, lust, wounds, darkness, coldness, night, winter, crookedness.

ORDINARY TIME

On the day after Pentecost, Ordinary Time begins again and extends until the Saturday before the first Sunday of Advent. This is a period of deepening one's life in the Gospel spirit by prayer and service to others. The Sunday readings of this time bring out many themes that serve as an instruction on God's plan of salvation.

Three feasts are prominent in the period of Ordinary Time after Easter. Trinity Sunday, the first Sunday after Pentecost, celebrates the mysterious revelation Christ made of the Father's mercy. It points out his own divine Sonship and the Holy Spirit's presence in the Church as well as in the hearts of all people who love God. Corpus Christi (Body of Christ), celebrated on the following Sunday, worships the real presence of Christ in the Eucharist. On the last Sunday before the beginning of Advent, the feast of Christ the King commemorates the coming reign of Christ over the entire universe and in all hearts.

MEDITATING DURING ORDINARY TIME

Ordinary Time concentrates on Jesus' public ministry. But during the weeks following the Christmas season, you may prefer to reflect on the mysteries of Jesus' hidden life. Below are five meditations for you to reflect upon during Ordinary Time.

The Boyhood of Jesus. "Jesus," Joseph called, "let's go fishing. We'll surprise your mother with some big fish for supper." As they walked to the lake over the hills, they talked about how together they could make Mary happy and about Jesus' future as a carpenter. Jesus loved Joseph. The two were more than just companions, more than friends, more than father and son. They were God's chosen ones—Son of God and the strong, good man who taught Jesus to be a man.

■ What is your relationship with your parents?

Jesus the Carpenter. As time passed, Jesus grew in wisdom and age. A carpenter by profession, he worked with wood and stone, remolding and recarving the very substances he, with his Father, had created from nothing. What must have gone through his mind as his hands passed over and over the rough wood, sanding it to make it beautifully smooth! He loved creation so much. The fragrance of the sawdust reminded him of his Father in heaven.

■ What work do you love to do? How does it put you in touch with God?

Life in Nazareth. As a young man of Nazareth, Jesus was known by all his neighbors, both because of his skill as a carpenter and because of his way with people. He was known as the "son of Joseph," "the carpenter," and "Mary's son." But to those who saw deeper than the surface, he possessed an unusual wisdom and knowledge of the ways of God. Before Jesus went out on the road, people must have looked to him for advice

LITURGY

and for leadership. And he gave help without their asking. To those who saw him with their hearts, he began to unfold the mysteries of God's love.

- Whom do you turn to for advice and leadership? Why?

Death of Joseph. Mary and Jesus knelt beside Joseph. No words were necessary. No words existed that could express their hearts' desires at that moment. Jesus looked into the eyes of the man who loved him as no earthly father had loved before or since. The promise that was in that look opened into eternity.

- What feelings do you have about death? What would you need to make your death peaceful?

Jesus Prepares for Public Life. Jesus had always loved the Scriptures, studying them daily as a child in the school taught by the local rabbi. Now, during his manhood, they took on even deeper meaning. They were as a lamp lighting up his path. Mary sensed his intention to proclaim his Father's word and stood by him with silent encouragement. When the Spirit led him down the road, she let him go, knowing she could never lose him.

- How easily do you "let go" of others who move away? How is "letting go" different from "not caring"?

Here is a prayer service for you and your class to pray together. Its theme is the Light of Christ.

Leader: The Law of Moses commanded that the first-born son be returned to God as his own possession forty days after birth. At that time, the mother was to be purified after childbirth. Accordingly, Mary and Joseph took their child to Jerusalem to present him to the Lord. Today we celebrate this mystery of Christ's life.

Song—"Earthen Vessels" by John Foley.

Leader: Mary and Joseph, while holding the cages of the turtle doves they had brought for their sacrificial offering, waited for the priest. Simeon, a God-fearing and prayerful man, came over to the young couple and took the child into his arms. His face suddenly lit up and a prayer of thanksgiving burst from his heart—for, by the power of the Holy Spirit, he recognized in the child the Savior of Israel.

Luke 2:29–32

All: Now, Master, you can let me die in peace,
For your promise to me has been fulfilled!
This day you have shown me your saving power
Made public for all the people to see—
Here in my arms is the light to reveal your name
  to all the nations
And the one who is to be the glory of your people
  Israel.

Leader: Father in heaven, you have fulfilled your promise to us in Jesus.

All: Father, we thank you for the light of our faith.

Leader: Lord Jesus, you have come to enlighten our darkness.

All: Lord Jesus, we thank you for the light of faith.

Leader: Holy Spirit, you give us power to recognize Jesus as our Savior.

All: Holy Spirit, we thank you for the light of our faith.

Reader 1: Who is the light of the world? The Gospel of Saint John tells us: "Jesus spoke to them once again: 'I am the light of the world. No follower of mine shall ever walk in darkness, no, he shall possess the light of life. . . . While I am in the world, I am the light of the world.'" John 8:12; 9:5

All: Rise up in splendor! Your light has come, the glory of the Lord shines upon you! Isaiah 60:1

Leader: God our Father, source of eternal light, fill our hearts more and more with the light of faith. Enlighten us to know your will, and strengthen us to do it.

All: Christ, you are the light of the nations and the glory of your people Israel.

Reader 2: In Saint Matthew's Gospel, we read that Jesus went up on the mountainside where he taught the people in these words: "You are the light of the world. A city set on a hill cannot be hidden. People do not light a lamp and then put it under a bushel basket. They set it on a stand where it gives light to all in the house. In the same way, your light must shine before others so that they may see goodness in your acts and give praise to your heavenly Father." Matthew 5:14–16

All: Christ, you are the light of the nations
And the glory of your people Israel.

Leader: God, our Father, source of eternal light, may we become living lights to everyone we meet. Christ, bring your light to all who sit in the darkness of error, of ignorance, or of sin. Be our hope until we see your radiant glory, face to face in your eternal kingdom of light.

All: Amen.

Song—"Those Who See Light" by Osuna, or some other appropriate song.

SUMMING UP

Use the following questions to help you review the main themes of this chapter.

1. When does the Easter season begin?
2. What does the word "alleluia" mean?
3. How long does the Easter season last?
4. What are the four parts of the Easter Vigil service?
5. How does fire symbolize the risen Jesus?
6. Why do Christians renew their baptismal promises on the vigil of Easter?
7. Why is the Easter Vigil considered the holiest night of the year?
8. What is the relationship between Christ's death, resurrection, ascension, and his sending of the Spirit? Why are there several feasts to commemorate the Paschal Mystery?
9. When does the Church celebrate the Ordinary Time?
10. What three feasts occur within the Ordinary Time after Pentecost? What does each feast celebrate?

Words to Know

Easter Vigil, *exsultet,* Paschal candle, alleluia, *shalom,* Ascension, Trinity Sunday, Corpus Christi, Ordinary Time, Christ the King

Think/Talk/Write

1. Ordinary Time is the longest season in the Church year. The Church seems to be saying that Christ can be found in ordinary times and events. Make a list of the ordinary things you do. How can you find Christ in each of them?
2. What do you think your own resurrection will be like?
3. If the Spirit had not come to the Apostles, how do you think the Church would be different today?

4. Find out when the feast of Christ the King first originated, and why.
5. What are the symbols of Pentecost? The Trinity? Corpus Christi? Christ the King? Explain what each means.

Activities

1. Many parishes have the custom of blessing food during the last days before Easter. Find out what this ritual means.
2. Read a book about a career or vocation you've been thinking about recently.
3. Interview by letter or in person any of the following to find out why they chose their work: mother; monk; truck driver; military person; priest, brother, or sister; writer; teacher; doctor.

SIXTEEN

Why does the Church honor saints?

Who are some of the saints honored in the liturgical year?

What qualities did some saints possess that made them holy?

Were the saints always close to God?

Saints

Rid yourself of all that is worn out and old, for you know a new song, a new covenant. He himself provides you with a way of singing. Do not search for words as if you could find a lyric which would give God pleasure. . . . Sing to him with songs of joy.

(SAINT AUGUSTINE)

HEROES AND HEROINES

You can't drive through any city without encountering at least one statue of a founding father or some hero or deity from mythology. One of the most famous statues of recent years commemorates the raising of the American flag at Iwo Jima during World War II.

Likewise, families often have certain pictures of relatives and members on display somewhere in the home. It seems to be a human need to put up images and symbols of those who are admired.

- Why do you think people erect statues of their heroes?
- Whom does your city or town honor by means of a statue?
- What pictures of people do you have on display in your home? Why?

THE SANCTORAL CYCLE

Although the liturgical year focuses on the Paschal Mystery and the life and teachings of Jesus, it includes many feasts of the saints. These saints are honored because although they were human they were able, with and in Christ, to become free of the slavery of sin and become the free people God intends all to be. They exemplify the power of the Paschal Mystery.

There are more than 150 saints honored in the present liturgical calendar. The cycle in which they are honored is sometimes called the sanctoral cycle. There are many more saints who are no longer honored on this calendar. This does not mean that these persons are not saints, only that the scant knowledge we have of their lives makes it impossible for them to serve as models for Christians.

The feasts of Saint Valentine and Saint Philomena, for instance, were dropped.

The saints were not people set apart from their own times. Each one was a unique individual and became a saint in his or her own way. Like all of us, they had their heroes and heroines, found good in people around them, and struggled with day-to-day problems.

- ■ Spend some time pondering what you would like to do with your life. Think big, remembering that, with God, all things are possible.
- ■ Find out the anniversary of your baptism and celebrate it as you do your birthday.

In restructuring the feasts of the saints for the Roman rite, there was an effort to balance ancient saints with modern ones and, as far as possible, to represent each geographical area where saints of the Roman rite have lived. In the revised calendar, there are sixty-four saints who lived between the first and tenth centuries and seventy-nine who lived between the eleventh and twentieth centuries. Of these saints, 126 are from Europe, fourteen are from Asia, eight are from Africa, four are from America, and one is from Oceania.

Other rites of the Catholic Church, such as Maronite and Byzantine, honor their own saints.

The feasts of saints are celebrated on weekdays. In most cases, they may not replace Sunday celebrations or other proper feasts of Christ.

CALENDAR OF SAINTS

Among the greatest saints are the Apostles, who were closely associated with Christ during his public life and who had a privileged role in God's plan of salvation.

The feasts of the Apostles are as follows: May 3—Saints Philip and James; May 14—Saint Matthias; July 3—Saint Thomas; July 25—Saint James; August 24—Saint Bartholomew; September 21—Saint Matthew; October 28—Saints Simon and Jude; November 30—Saint Andrew; and December 27—Saint John. Saints Peter and Paul have two feasts each: June 29 commemorates their martyrdom; the Conversion of Saint Paul is celebrated on January 25; and February 22 is the feast of the Chair of Saint Peter, which honors the election of Peter as head of the Church and first bishop of Rome.

The two feasts of Saint Joseph occur on May 1 and March 19. On the latter feast, Saint Joseph is honored as the husband of Mary. On May 1, Joseph is honored as The Worker. He is held up as an ideal for Christians because of his prompt obedience to God's will, his loving care and concern for Mary and her child, his observance of the Mosaic law, and the faithful fulfillment of his religious duties.

- Saint Joseph is also included in the Feast of the Holy Family on the Sunday after Christmas. Examine the liturgy of that feast. For what reasons is he honored that day?

John the Baptizer ranks high in the Church's liturgy because of his important role as Christ's precursor. His two feasts are on June 24 and August 29. They celebrate his birth and his martyrdom.

- Read Matthew 14:1–12. How did John the Baptizer die?

The Feast of All Saints, November 1, celebrates all who have died and are now enjoying the vision of God. All Souls, November 2, honors those dead who still need healing before experiencing the joy of heaven.

November, the season of falling leaves and the coming of winter, is a good month for these two celebrations because nature "goes to rest" and the life-giving process of photosynthesis slows. The saints and all other members of the Church who have died can no longer work on earth. The Church speaks of them as having gone "to their eternal rest."

Feasts that are celebrated only in the United States are: January 4—Saint Elizabeth Ann Seton; January 5—Saint John Neumann; May 15—Saint Isidore; September 9—Saint Peter Claver; October 19—Saints Isaac Jogues, John de Brebeuf, companions, and martyrs; and November 13—Saint Frances Xavier Cabrini.

■ Look up one of the feasts celebrated only in the United States. What is the theme of the liturgy? Try to find out about the life of the saint(s).

A POOR MAN'S RICHES

"The man most like Christ!" This is the compliment that has been paid to Francis of Assisi. In his youth, this son of a wealthy cloth merchant enjoyed all the comforts of his times, being very popular with the well-to-do young people of his town. Francis reached a turning point at twenty-five, after he was taken hostage in a battle. In a dream, Christ called Francis to serve the sick; later he heard God tell him to rebuild the Church.

See Matthew 19:21

At first Francis began to lay a new brick wall at Saint Damiano's, the village church. Then he realized that God was asking him to renounce his wealth and reform the Church. By example, Francis was to inspire others to follow Christ's poverty in order to counteract the scandal given by the great wealth of some of the clergy.

Within ten years, several thousand young men had joined "the Poverello." Today, Franciscan priests, brothers, nuns, sisters, and lay associates are still the largest order in the Church.

The nuns are the Poor Clares, a contemplative branch of the Franciscan order.

The feastday of Saint Francis is October 4.

- Francis understood Christ's role in the world so deeply that he saw all nature linked in Christ. Write a poem or short essay about your view of nature.
- Make a modern-day litany of natural objects that especially move you with awe or wonder. Include praise and thanksgiving to God.

THE TRAVELER

See Matthew 28:18–20; Luke 9:1–6

Basques are a people living near the western Pyrenees in Spain.

Francis Xavier wasn't interested in studies, but he liked school because he was very sports-minded. He put his natural Basque temperament to work by being super-aggressive and determined in the contests he engaged in.

At nineteen, at the University of Paris where he had begun college, Francis met a man much older than himself who was to have an immense influence on his life. It took some time for Ignatius of Loyola, another Basque, to win Francis over from his original goals and get him to join the Society of Jesus. But in 1534, Francis Xavier was one of the first six, including Ignatius, to take vows in the new order.

Once "converted," Francis gave himself to winning the world for Christ. By the time of his death in 1552, he had traveled the greater part of the Far East. He died on a lonely island, waiting to obtain entrance to China, where he had visions of spreading the gospel.

Considering the condition of travel, the means of transport, and the delays and difficulties Francis Xavier encountered, his adventures seem like epics. But the flourishing Christian communities he left behind are the real miracles of his life. It is said he had the power of prophecy and healing.

Saint Francis Xavier, co-founder of the Society of Jesus with Saint Ignatius of Loyola, is co-patron, with Saint Therese of Lisieux, of all missions. His feast is December 3.

- What qualities of temperament do you see in Francis' life?
- Ask someone who knows you what qualities you have that might be used in God's service.

RICHES TO RAGS

One of the most courageous women who ever lived was Elizabeth Ann Bayley. She was born into wealth and position in a prominent family of New York two years before the Declaration of Independence was signed. Related to the Gothams, Barclays, Delanceys, and Roosevelts, she was reared by her mother and stepmother as a member of the Episcopal Church. From them, Elizabeth learned to pray and to love the Scriptures. Her father, the respected Dr. Richard Bayley, was not a reg-

See John 15:9–17

ular churchgoer even though he was genuinely involved in humanitarian efforts.

At nineteen, Elizabeth married the handsome and wealthy New York merchant William Magee Seton and later bore him five children. Nine years after they married, her husband became gravely ill with tuberculosis. Elizabeth nursed him faithfully, sailing with him to Italy for a rest.

After his death, Elizabeth was taken in by a Catholic family in Italy whose kindness and devotion to Catholicism attracted her to the Church. But it was the real presence of Jesus in the Blessed Sacrament—the central love of her life—that led Elizabeth, against the opposition of her minister and friends, to enter the Catholic Church on her return to New York.

It was the turning point in her life. As Elizabeth's spiritual life grew deeper and more intense, external circumstances caused her more and more suffering. Her former wealthy friends sneered at her for joining an "immigrant" church. Her family abandoned her, and she lacked even the necessities of life. Because of sexual prejudice, she could not get a job to support her family.

At the invitation of her friend Father Dubourg, Elizabeth left New York to live in Maryland, where she formed a school for Catholic girls. Later, gathering other young women around her, she founded the first religious congregation of women in the United States, the Sisters of Charity of Emmitsburg. She is credited with founding the American Catholic school system. Elizabeth suffered for her courage. Her own serious illness, the death of two daughters, a wayward son, and misunderstanding from the community of sisters she founded all weighed heavily on her mind.

Elizabeth's journey was not one of rags to riches, but the opposite. Yet her diary shows her great inner happiness even as she suffered. In 1975, Pope Paul VI canonized her as the first American-born saint of the Roman Catholic Church. Her feastday is January 4.

■ What advantages have come to Catholics in America through the Catholic school system?

- One widow who joined a religious community said that the hardest part of the transition was giving up all the possessions she and her husband had worked a lifetime for. The rich young man See Mark 10:17–31 who wanted to follow Christ also found his possessions an obstacle. Why is living in poverty so hard? What answer does Jesus give when the Apostles ask how anyone can do it?
- When should children first be taught to pray?

DETERMINED LOVERS OF CHRIST

A teenager once acquired a medal with Saint Agnes on See Matthew 19:12 one side and Saint Thomas Aquinas on the other. The craftsman who struck the medal saw in the virginal purity of the two saints a common bond. Agnes was once approached by a man who wanted her to have sexual intercourse with him. She resisted, despite his threats, and insisted on her desire to remain a virgin for the sake of Christ. Insulted, the man reported Agnes as a Christian to the Roman prefect. He, in turn, had her placed in a house of prostitution and then killed.

Saint Thomas displayed a similar determination to remain celibate. When he decided to become a Dominican friar, his wealthy family, shocked that Thomas was joining a begging order, sent a beautiful woman to seduce him. Legend has it that, seizing a red-hot poker from the fire, Thomas drove the woman from the room, insisting on his right to remain unmarried for the love of God.

Saint Agnes is honored on January 21. January 26 is the feastday of Saint Thomas Aquinas.

- What is the difference between the decision of a priest, a religious brother, or a sister to remain celibate for the sake of Christ and that of a person choosing to remain single for the sake of a career or to care for parents? Or is there a difference?

THE SIMPLE LIFE

See Matthew 6:19–21, 7:1–5

Oriental philosophers say that you can get to the heart of humanity by reaching into your own heart. In other words, deep understanding of yourself will give you hints about what makes everyone else tick.

Saint Patrick, the Apostle of Ireland who lived from 389 to 461, discovered a similar secret. He found that by getting to the heart of things, he could reach the heart of God. In the middle of his sermons explaining the doctrine of the Trinity, he would reach down to the beautiful green clover that carpets most of the Emerald Isle and hold up a shamrock as a symbol of three persons in one God.

A wealthy Roman in his youth, Patrick and some of his father's servants were captured by pirates and transported as slaves to Ireland, where he herded swine. Holding to his Christian faith, he learned humility. He wrote in his *Confessions* that he changed from a person who was "as stone lying in the deep mud" to "a stone placed by God's mercy on the very top of the wall." His experience taught him wisdom. Patrick escaped, returned to his homeland for his education, and became a priest. At age forty-three, after a dream calling him to return to Ireland, Patrick did indeed return to convert the pagans. He often preached the gospel at the risk of his life.

Like Christ, this bishop used the things all around him to explain the love of God to the people he served for thirty years. When he died, the Church in Ireland flourished with its own native clergy. No one loves Saint Patrick today more than the Irish, many of whom emigrated to America and became leaders of the Church during the last century. Saint Patrick's Day is March 17.

- Saint Patrick saw Christ in the heart and mind of every person, in everyone, and in all things. List the things that remind you of Christ.
- Use a concrete object to explain some doctrine to a child you know, such as the presence of Christ in the Blessed Sacrament, Mary's freedom from sin, or Jesus' being both divine and human.

LITURGY

A DEVOTED HUSBAND AND FATHER

Many people today are afraid to get married because they see so many marriages ending in divorce.

See Matthew 1:18–25; John 6:42

- Describe your idea of a happy family life.
- Who is the most important contributor to a happy family?

The best way to guarantee a good marriage later is to become a good family member now. If you bring a determination to go 100 percent of the way in loving other family members, your family relationships are bound to improve.

Saint Joseph gives the example every family member needs. Far from being the old man he is sometimes pictured, he was most probably a young, strong person with a fine mind, skilled hands, and a warm heart. He loved Mary and would not allow her to be stoned for infidelity when she announced her miraculous pregnancy. To accept Mary as his bride with a child he knew was not his own took humility and courage, but above all it required trust in God and in the woman he loved. It was important for him to care most attentively for her child, to be the human reflection of the Father Jesus so often referred to in his teachings, and to earn an honest living as a carpenter in order to provide for his family—and Joseph did all this until his death.

No wonder he is so highly honored in the Church as the husband of Mary, the "just" man, and the patron of a happy death. His feasts are March 19 and May 1.

- What qualities should you develop to become a good spouse?
- When should you begin to work on these qualities?

THE SAINT WHO GOT INTO SCRAPES

Saint Mark seems to have gotten into a few scrapes in his youth. There is a mysterious episode at Jesus' arrest described in Mark's Gospel. A young man covered with

See Acts of the Apostles 12:12–17, 15:37–39

See Mark 14:51–52

only a linen cloth left the cloth behind and ran away naked when the guards tried to seize him. Scholars are not sure the evangelist was speaking of himself, although the details and vividness of the incident strongly point that way.

The understanding and love of Christ reflected in Mark's writings must have come from his association with the Apostles. In Acts 12:12, Saint Luke says that after Peter's escape from prison he went to the house of John Mark's mother, where everyone was gathered.

Mark also associated with Paul, and was to have accompanied Paul and Barnabas on their first missionary journey. Because Mark had backed out at the last minute for some reason, Paul refused to let him sail with them on their second journey even though Barnabas pleaded in Mark's behalf. It is evident that either there was some friction between Mark and Paul, or Paul thought that Mark was still unreliable.

See 2 Timothy 4:11

In his maturity, Mark left a wonderfully realistic proclamation of the Good News of Jesus. By his martyrdom, he gave proof of his deep love of Christ. His life shows that a person who makes a shaky start can become a strong character in the end. Mark's feastday is April 25.

- Discuss the reasons why children are sometimes mischevous without being bad. What is the difference?

THE MONK WITH A TEMPER

See Exodus 2:11–16

Although many saints have been held up for public veneration, there are many more saints whom people either don't know or whose cause has not come up for canonization.

One example of an uncanonized holy man is Brother Joachim, a saintly monk who spent only a little more than ten years at the Abbey of Gethsemani in Kentucky. During his last years there, it is said he worked miracles. Once, it seems, he walked calmly for ten minutes through a torrential downpour carrying his infant nephew who had just recovered from pneumonia. Both remained bone dry. Since his death, Brother Joachim has answered many people's prayers.

But Brother Joachim wasn't always close to God. As a teenager, before running away from home in Lebanon, Kentucky, he burned down the tobacco farm in a fit of anger at his father. He stayed away for nine years, never letting his family know whether he was dead or alive. During this time, he lost his faith and became known in the West as the cowboy "Kentucky Jack." Because of his vicious temper, he was also nicknamed "The Quick One."

After his mother's death, he experienced a change of heart. He delayed his wedding a year. Then he broke off the engagement completely after visiting the Trappist monastery. He felt drawn to the monastic life.

Inside the monastery, his hot temper was not put off as quickly as his secular clothes. Several times, he lashed out against other monks who annoyed him, and, because of his impatience, he frequently broke things.

Eventually, however, the monk with the temper became one of the holiest men of the order. Maybe it was because he redirected his excess energy into loving God.

■ Tell how the following faults could be converted to virtues: a tendency to worry; the habit of bossing others around; constant complaining.

Prayer

Lord, make me an instrument of your peace; where there is hatred, let me sow love; where there is injury, pardon; where there is doubt, faith; where there is despair, hope; where there is darkness, light; and where there is sadness, joy.

Saint Francis of Assisi

O Divine Master, grant that I may not so much seek to be consoled as to console; to be understood, as to understand; to be loved as to love; for it is in giving that we receive, it is in pardoning that we are pardoned, and it is in dying that we are born to eternal life.

SUMMING UP

Use the following questions to help you review the
main themes of this chapter.

1. If the Paschal Mystery of Christ is central to the liturgical year, how
   can the feasts of the saints be justified?
2. How many saints are presently honored in the liturgical calendar?
3. Why were some saints taken off the calendar?
4. Which saints receive greater honor than others? Why?
5. What does the feast of the Chair of Saint Peter commemorate?
6. When are the two feastdays of Saint Joseph? What is his title on
   each day?
7. Why does the Church celebrate both the birth and the death of John
   the Baptizer?
8. When is the feast of Saint Francis of Assisi?
9. Who was Saint Francis Xavier?
10. Which feasts are celebrated only in the United States?
11. Who founded the Catholic school system in America?
12. What do Saint Agnes and Saint Thomas Aquinas have in common?
13. Who was Saint Blase?
14. When is Saint Patrick's Day? Why do the Irish particularly honor
    this saint?
15. Who wrote the earliest Gospel?

Words to Know

sanctoral cycle, calendar of saints

Think/Talk/Write

1. What, in your opinion, are the "ingredients" of sanctity?
2. Find out why Mark's Gospel is symbolized by a lion's head.
3. List the eyewitness details you find in Mark's account of the passion
   (Mark 15:21–31) or in the story of the storm at sea (Mark 4:35–41).
4. Look up the life of Miguel Pro, who, like Saint Mark, was not a saint

when a child, but grew to love Christ so much that he eventually gave his life in martyrdom.

5. Many people—saints and nonsaints—have dreams that influence their lives. Discuss the authenticity of following "voices" or dreams.
6. Make a list of people you would like to submit to Rome for canonization. What qualities in these people do you admire?
7. Ancient and recent saints are included in daily celebrations of the Eucharist. Look up the liturgy of any three of the following. When and for what are these saints remembered in the liturgical year?

Saints Ann and Joachim	Saint Blaise
Saint Anthony of Padua	Saint John Neumann
Saint Stephen	Saint Maria Goretti
Saint Julie Billiart	Saint Pius X

Activities

1. Write a part of the life of Christ for a child you know. Illustrate it, if you can.
2. Read the life of Brother Joachim in *The Man Who Got Even with God* by M. Raymond, O.C.S.O.
3. Research and report on the missionary activities of the Society of Jesus.
4. Find out where missionaries are being persecuted and martyred today.
5. See what "missionary" acts are available to you right in your own neighborhood.
6. Place yourself in the year 2080. You have been declared a saint of the Roman Catholic Church. Write the Mass you would like to see used in your honor. Compose the opening prayer, the prayers over the gifts, and the prayer after Communion. Choose the readings, antiphons, and responses that would express your unique contribution to the holiness of the world. Find two or more songs that express your favorite religious sentiments. Finally, write an introduction to the Mass and prayers of the faithful.
7. Find out what various kinds of blessings the Church gives.
8. Select three saints for further study. Research their lives and be prepared to share your findings orally.

SEVENTEEN

Why does the Church honor Mary?

What are the feasts of Mary celebrated in the liturgical year?

What is the difference between a Church feast and a civil feast?

What are some of the American civil feastdays?

Mary/Civil Feasts

The Holy Church honors the Blessed Mary, Mother of God, with a special love. She is inseparably linked with her Son's saving work. In her, the Church admires and exalts the most excellent fruit of redemption and joyfully contemplates, as in a faultless image, that which she herself desires and hopes wholly to be.

(CONSTITUTION ON THE SACRED LITURGY #103)

THE MARIAN CALENDAR

The Church honors Mary, the Mother of God, as Christ's closest follower and most graced human being. There are a variety of feasts in her honor. The Marian calendar throughout the liturgical year is as follows:

December 8	Immaculate Conception
December 12	Our Lady of Guadalupe
January 1	Solemnity of Mary, Mother of God
February 11	Our Lady of Lourdes
March 25	The Annunciation
May 31	The Visitation
June —	Immaculate Heart (first Saturday after the feast of Sacred Heart)
July 16	Our Lady of Mount Carmel
August 15	The Assumption
August 22	The Queenship of Mary

September 8   The Birthday of Mary
September 15   Our Lady of Sorrows
October 7   Our Lady of the Rosary
November 21   The Presentation of Mary

Three of these feasts—the Immaculate Conception, the Solemnity of Mary, Mother of God, and the Assumption—are holy days of obligation. Catholics are obliged to celebrate Mass on these days. Seven more feasts—the Annunciation, Mary's Birthday, the Visitation, the Queenship of Mary, Our Lady of Sorrows, Our Lady of the Rosary, and the Presentation of Mary—are celebrated by the universal Church. Catholics are not obliged, however, to celebrate Mass on these days.

Several other Marian feasts are observed locally, in the nation or place where the feast is known. These feasts include Our Lady of Lourdes, Our Lady of Fatima, the Immaculate Heart of Mary, Our Lady of Mount Carmel, Our Lady of the Miraculous Medal, and Our Lady of Guadalupe.

- Find out what event or aspect of Mary's life is commemorated in each of the above feasts.
- How is Mary a great model for all Christians?

The Immaculate Conception

During Advent, the Church celebrates Mary's freedom from original sin and all its effects from the first moment of her conception. Under this title, Mary is the patroness of the United States.

This feast is not to be confused with the Annunciation, which celebrates Christ's conception in the womb of Mary nine months before his birth.

- How does sinlessness free you?

Solemnity of Mary

During the Christmas season, the Church solemnly honors Mary as the Mother of God. She has the greatest privilege possible to a human being. The readings of

Luke 2:16–21

the day focus on the birth of Jesus and on Mary, who "treasured all these things and reflected on them in her heart."

■ Read Numbers 6:22–27. How does this text apply to the feast of the Solemnity of Mary?

Annunciation

See Luke 1:38

In this feast, the Church rejoices that Mary pronounced her great act of consent, which brought the Son of God to earth. This feast shows God's reliance on human cooperation for carrying out his plan of redemption. It is celebrated nine months before Christmas.

■ Read Luke 1:26–38. What are some things in your own life where God is asking your consent?

Mary's Month

From the earliest days of the Church, people have created paintings, mosaics, and statues honoring the greatest people and events connected with redemption. Perhaps no one besides Christ has been more honored by artists than Mary, his Mother.

For centuries, people of the Eastern rite have had Marian shrines in their homes. Lighting candles before icons, they pray there alone or gather as a family to offer prayers. People of wealth sometimes expanded these shrines into churches where the local villagers could join them in their devotions.

In the United States, the custom developed of placing flowers before a statue or picture of Mary in homes and schools during May. The May altar, as it is called, may be a simple statue placed on the window ledge, a larger shrine backed with drapes and adorned with candles and flowers, or a full-grown grotto in the garden or backyard.

The purpose of the Marian shrine is to cultivate a habit of turning to Mary, the woman whose response of perfect obedience to God's proposal to the human race allowed God's entire plan of redemption to come about.

- How does your family honor Mary in your home?
- In what ways can your class foster devotion to her?

The Assumption

This most recently established Marian feast honors Mary for what all who die in God's favor will experience—the transformation of the whole person, body and soul, in the glorious life of eternity. Because of her privileged role in God's plan, Mary's glory is more apparent in this mystery of faith. Artists picture this event by showing Mary's body being taken up (assumed) into heaven.

Mary's Birthday

Waiting 365 days to celebrate your first birthday is a common practice in the Western world, but people in the East consider themselves a year old on the very day of their birth.

■ Which custom is closer to the truth?

With three exceptions, the Church never celebrates the birthday of the saints. The reason is that before their baptism, saints lacked the full union with God that Christ came to restore. The three exceptions are: Christ, who is, always was, and always will be the Son of God; John the Baptizer, who at six months was baptized by the presence of Christ when the pregnant Mary visited her cousin Elizabeth; and Mary, Christ's Mother.

The birth of every child is a source of wonder, but the birth of the holiest human being ever to live is something to celebrate until the end of the world. Although Mary's birthday was not celebrated until the eighth century, her birthplace has been venerated in Jerusalem since the sixth century. In Hebrew, Mary's name was pronounced *Meer Yahm.*

■ What forms of Mary's name do you know?

Nine months after the celebration of her Immaculate Conception, the feast of Mary's birthday is celebrated and the Church praises God for choosing her of all the women on earth to be the Mother of his Son. Although she is the loveliest and most lovable of persons, she did not stand out as different from the people of her day. Like the other Galilean women, she probably wore colorful clothes—blue, brown, and crimson—and perhaps even earrings, gold rings, bracelets, and ankle chains.

Mary drew water from the common well and shared a common oven, exchanging news with the villagers. But she was different. Free from the least sin, she nursed deep within her a flame of love that would one day flare out as the Light of the World. Her birthday is celebrated on September 8.

A MATTER OF HEART

A professor who had been teaching at a state university for many years said that he was continually amazed at the number of mature adults who would place rabbits' feet, figurines, and other good-luck charms on their desks during their tests. It seems that even in this modern age people can be superstitious.

You may smile at the fears of those who won't go on a journey, engage in a contest, or undertake something dangerous without their special omen of good fortune. But it's a very human thing to give one's beliefs outward expression. The same need to express one's beliefs outwardly shows itself when people fold their hands to pray, extend their arms to someone they love, and choose certain ornaments and clothes to wear.

During the Middle Ages, many religious wore a length of cloth over their shoulders about sixteen inches wide with a hole in it for the head. Forming an apron, this scapular hung to the knees or ankles in front and back, and was fastened under the wearer's arms.

When devout lay people wanted to associate themselves with the spirit and good works of the friars, they joined a "third order" and wore a part of the religious habit, either a cord, a cloak, or the scapular. After 1500, as fashions became more fitted to the body, the scapular was reduced to two small pieces of cloth about two inches square that hung around the neck by a thin string.

The most popular scapular was the brown Carmelite scapular, which, according to a legend, was given by our Lady to Saint Simon in 1251 with the promise that all who would devoutly wear it would enjoy her protection and a happy death. In 1910, the Church permitted the wearing of a medal representing the Sacred Heart on one side and our Lady on the other to replace the small cloth scapular.

A *scapular* is the part of a habit that covers the scapula, or shoulders.

The first order was for men, the second order was for nuns, and the third order was for lay persons.

CIVIL FEASTS

There are a number of civil, secular, or national feasts that may also be celebrated in the liturgy. Among these days are the following;

January 1	New Year's Day
January 15	Martin Luther King Day
February 2	Ground Hog Day
February 12	Lincoln's Birthday
February 14	Valentine's Day
February 22	Washington's Birthday
March 20	First Day of Spring
April 1	April Fools' Day
May 1	May Day
May —	Mother's Day
May —	Memorial Day
June 14	Flag Day
June —	Father's Day
July 4	Independence Day
September —	Labor Day
October 12	Columbus Day
October 24	United Nations Day
November 11	Veterans Day
November —	Thanksgiving Day

And, of course, there are always birthdays and anniversaries to celebrate. These, too, may be celebrated in a special liturgy with selected readings, prayers, songs, and petitions.

■ Write a Mass for your birthday. First choose a theme, and then arrange everything else accordingly.

Halloween

Say "Halloween," and children everywhere think of dressing up in costumes and going out for trick-or-treat.

Before the Church calendar was simplified, October 31 was observed as the vigil of All Saints. In Brittany, All Hallow's Eve was a scary time. Superstition held

Brittany was a former province of France.

that the poor souls were freed from Purgatory and allowed to roam their old haunts for forty-eight hours before joining the company of the saints for All Saints Day.

The Irish and Scots turned this alleged "soul power" into a source of merrymaking by dressing up as "poor souls." They would knock at doors to beg for a "soul cake," in return for which they promised to pray for the dead. Refusal was supposed to bring on terrible revenge in the form of "tricks," allegedly perpetrated by the poor souls themselves.

Some of these "soul cakes" were shaped in a circle to remind those who ate them of eternity. This is how the donut originated.

- Today, there is much complaint about Halloween vandalism and the meanness of a few people who give children poisoned treats. Do you think trick-or-treating should be outlawed? Why or why not?
- When do Christians as a whole Church pray for the relief of the poor souls?
- If the dead are in close union with God, what is their mission to the living?
- Plan a liturgy to celebrate Halloween as the Eve of All Saints.

Thanksgiving

The average person spends twenty-five years of his or her life working for food. If one lives to be seventy-five, he or she will have put in at least 250,000 hours around a table.

Everyone can appreciate the human cooperation it takes to get the smallest raisin or a TV dinner. Thanksgiving meals are in part a recognition of this dependence on others, but even more so upon God. He gives not only food but health, clothing, shelter, and, best of all, families and friends.

The Jews were commanded by God to celebrate feasts of thanksgiving. Similarly, the Pilgrims ate turkey, wild geese, and harvest vegetables at an annual meal of thanksgiving. America's first president, George Washington, proclaimed Thanksgiving a national feast in

See Exodus 23:14–17; Deuteronomy 16:13

1789, acknowledging "the providence of Almighty God." In 1863, Abraham Lincoln, the sixteenth president, reaffirmed the observance. On this day, people everywhere admit they can't survive alone and show their gratitude for God's gifts.

- ■ How does your family celebrate Thanksgiving? What contribution do you make?
- ■ What is the perfect thanksgiving meal offered to God for his providence?

Martin Luther King

Martin Luther King had a strong conviction and a vision—a dream, he called it. He didn't deny the things that were. However, he was committed to a vision of how things could be if someone would exercise "a little leadership."

Dr. Martin Luther King (1925–1968) was a clergyman and civil rights leader.

Leadership for the blacks was what Martin Luther King supplied. The blacks were legally freed after the Civil War, but in 1955, almost a hundred years later, public-bus transportation in Montgomery, Alabama, was still segregated. King organized a boycott that alerted all U.S. citizens to the lingering effects of slavery.

It was significant that Dr. King did not encourage the people to throw rocks at public buses or bomb the homes of city officials. His dream was to be achieved without violence, he said, and within the structures of the establishment.

In this, he was like Jesus, who allowed violence to crush him. King's method was nonviolent resistance. Working through the Southern Christian Leadership Conference, King's dream led him to speak out for civil rights for all citizens. He led a massive march on Washington, D.C., in 1963, and won the Nobel Peace Prize the next year.

A champion of the rights of all disadvantaged Americans, King was beginning a national campaign against poverty when he was cut down by an assassin's bullet in Memphis, Tennessee, on April 4, 1968. His memory is celebrated in the United States during the month of January.

- What qualities of leadership did Dr. King show?
- Do you think only certain people can be leaders, or can anyone be a leader where a need for leadership exists?

Valentine's Day

Valentine cards, candy, flowers, and gifts will never go out of style, in spite of the fact that Saint Valentine has been dropped from the liturgical calendar.

The giving of a Valentine originally meant: "I offer to be your loving and affectionate comrade for the next twelve months, and I am willing to consider marriage if our companionship works out well." Today, anyone for whom you feel a special affection is a fitting candidate for a valentine.

Christian love can be encouraged by red hearts and paper lace, but it goes far deeper, joining people in the very love of God himself.

- What Christian value is there in sending valentines?
- Surprise someone with a homemade or simple gift on a day other than Valentine's Day.

Prayer

O Mary, my dear Mother, how much I love you. You teach me what I ought to know, for you teach me what Jesus is to me and what I ought to be for him. How close to God you are and how utterly filled with him! Mother of God, obtain for me the grace of loving Jesus; obtain for me the grace of loving you. Amen.

Merry del Val

SUMMING UP

Use the following questions to help you review the main themes of this chapter.

1. What are the three Marian feasts that are also holy days of obligation? When are they celebrated? What does each day commemorate?
2. What are the seven universal Marian feasts?
3. Name two Marian feasts of local interest.
4. Under what title is Mary the patroness of the United States?
5. Briefly explain the Annunciation, Visitation, and the Birthday of Mary.
6. What feast shows God's reliance on human cooperation?
7. When was Mary's birthday first celebrated?
8. Give three examples of a civil or secular feast.
9. How did the customs of Halloween originate?
10. When was Thanksgiving Day proclaimed a national feast?
11. What is a scapular? What is its religious significance?

Words to Know

Immaculate Conception, Annunciation, Marian calendar, Solemnity of Mary, Assumption, scapular

Think/Talk/Write

1. How would you define a hero or heroine?
2. What is the difference between a sacred feast and a secular one? Should there be a difference?
3. Jesus said, "The poor you will always have with you." What does this mean to you? Should you resign yourself to the fact that there will always be disadvantaged people around? Or should you as a Christian work primarily to help the poor? Or does Jesus mean something else?
4. The United States has hit the $2 trillion mark in its Gross National Product. Compare the U.S. per-capita income as given in the latest

almanac with that of the other countries of the world. What ideals or values does the result of your research inspire in you?

5. Read the Declaration of Independence and the Emancipation Proclamation. What Christian values do you find in them?

6. Make a list of ten famous people you would most like to invite to dinner. They may be from the past or the present. Why would you invite them?

7. Scripture is filled with references that prefigure and tell about the life of Mary. Here are some of the texts the Church has chosen as readings to celebrate events in Mary's life. Match up each reading with the appropriate event.

Scripture Text	Event in Mary's Life
1. Genesis 3:9–15, 20	____ Mary is taken up into heaven
2. Luke 2:16–21	____ Mary finds out she is to have a child
3. Luke 1:26–38	____ Mary's birthday
4. Psalm 45:10–16	____ Our Lady of Sorrows
5. Luke 1:39–56	____ Feast of Mary, Mother of God
6. Micah 5:1–4	____ Mary visits Elizabeth
7. John 19:25–27	____ Mary is conceived without sin

Activities

1. Visit the National Shrine of the Immaculate Conception in Washington, D.C.
2. Make a Marian shrine in your room or another place during May.
3. Write a poem to our Lady that stresses one of her gifts.
4. Compose a prayer in the form of a psalm or litany of thanksgiving to be used as grace for the Thanksgiving meal.
5. Send a thank-you to someone whose service you take for granted during the rest of the year.
6. Read Martin Luther King's "I Have a Dream" speech, delivered on August 28, 1963. What was his dream?
7. Identify someone poor or disadvantaged in your neighborhood or school and do what you can to help him or her in a practical way that is not degrading.

Time plays a decisive role in every life. By celebrating the events of Jesus' life, passion, death, and resurrection, the Church rhythmically unfolds the mystery of Christ every year. The purpose of the liturgical year is to instruct the faithful, to build them into a holier people, and to unite them in Christ, whom they encounter in the midst of their celebrations.

The Church is divided into the seasons of Advent, Christmas, Lent, Easter, and Ordinary Time. Every Sunday is set aside as the Lord's Day—a mini-celebration of the Paschal Mystery. Daily Masses offer God unceasing worship and are ranked according to whether they celebrate Sundays, solemnities, or obligatory or optional memorials of the saints' feastdays. The Church prays night and day always through the Liturgy of the Hours.

When we understand and enter into the various seasons and feasts, pray over the assigned scriptural readings, and become acquainted with and celebrate the lives of the saints as well as other holidays in a religious spirit, we enter more deeply into the mystery of Christ.

Acknowledgments

The authors wish to thank Sister Mary Raphaelita Boeckmann, S.N.D., Superior General, Rome; Sister Mary Christopher Rohner, S.N.D., Provincial Superior of the Sisters of Notre Dame, Chardon, Ohio; and Sister Margaret Mary McGovern, S.N.D., High School Supervisor of the Chardon Province, who supported and encouraged the writing of the Light of the World series.

Humble gratitude is also due to all who in any way helped to create the Light of the World series: parents, teachers, co-workers, students and friends. The following deserve special mention for assisting to plan, organize, test, or critique the series: Notre Dame Sisters Mary Dolores Abood, Ann Baron, Karla Bognar, Peter Brady, Mary Catherine Caine, Virginia Marie Callen, Deborah Carlin, Naomi Cervenka, Reean Coyne, Mary Dowling, Dorothy Fuchs, Margaret Mary Gorman, Jacquelyn Gusdane, Mary Margaret Harig, Joanmarie Harks, Nathan Hess, Sally Huston, Christa Jacobs, Joanne Keppler, Owen Kleinhenz, Jean Korejwo, Leanne Laney, William David Latiano, Aimee Levy, Nadine Lock, Mary Ann McFadden, Inez McHugh, Louismarie Nudo, Donna Marie Paluf, Helen Mary Peter, Phyllis Marie Plummer, Eileen Marie Quinlan, Anne Marie Robinson, Patricia Rickard, Mark Daniel Roscoe, Kathleen Ruddy, Kathleen Scully, Dolores Stanko, Melanie Svoboda, Louise Trivison, Donna Marie Wilhelm; Ms. Laura Wingert; Ms. Meg Bracken; Sister Mary Kay Cmolik, O.F.M.; Mr. Robert Dilonardo; Rev. Mark DiNardo; Ms. Linda Ferrando; Mr. Michael Homza; Sister Kathleen King, H.H.M.; Ms. Patricia Lange; Mr. James Marmion; Mr. Peter Meler; Rev. Herman P. Moman; Rev. Guy Noonan, T.O.R; Ms. Nancy Powell; Ms. Christine Smetana; and Ms. Karen Sorace.

The following high schools piloted materials: Bishop Ireton H.S., Alexandria, Virginia; Clearwater Central Catholic H.S., Clearwater, Florida; Elyria Catholic H.S., Elyria, Ohio; Erieview Catholic H.S., Cleveland, Ohio; John F. Kennedy H.S., Warren, Ohio; Notre Dame Academy, Chardon, Ohio; Regina High School, South Euclid, Ohio; St. Edward H.S., Cleveland, Ohio; St. Matthias H.S., Huntington Park, California.

The following parishes piloted the Abridged Lessons: Corpus Christi, Cleveland, Ohio; St. Anselm, Chesterland, Ohio; St. John Nepomucene, Cleveland, Ohio; St. Thomas More, Paducah, Kentucky.

Special appreciation to Sister Mary Roy Romancik, S.N.D., for management of all production and testing as well as for careful reading of the original draft.

Deep appreciation to Mrs. Anita Johnson for research; to Sisters of Notre Dame Linda Mary Elliott, Mary Regien Kingsbury, DeXavier Perusek, and Seton Schlather, and to Robert Clair Smith for special services; and to typists Sisters Mary Lucie Adamcin, Catherine Rennecker, S.N.D., and Josetta Marie Livignano, N.N.D.

Photographs
American Stock Photos 215; Barbara Baker 78; Marshall Berman 153; H.A. Bullard 94, 144, 198; Kathy Busch 267; Barbara Carroll 44, 249, 262; Dwight Cendrowski 109, 127, 137, 203; Chicago Historical Society 283; L. Cremonie 148; Vivienne della Grotta 35, 57, 187; Jon Erikson 62; FAO 28; Glencoe Library 17, 31, 139, 143, 167, 199, 252, 259, 270, 286, 293; Glennstock 79; Tony Heim 23; Iran Information and Tourist Bureau 30; Israel Government Tourist Office 32; Joseph Mancuso 85, 86, 243; Stephen McBrady 102, 125, 145, 166, 181, 255; Methodist Missions 60; Monkmeyer Press Photo Service 59, 111, 130, 161, 176, 235, 302; National Gallery of Art 82, 236; NC Photos 309; Popperfoto 14; Religious News Service 65, 156, 185, 221; Jerome F. Riordan 75, 80, 91, 98, 206; St. Patrick's Cathedral 27; Paul M. Schrock 50, 55, 114, 129, 177, 218, 224, 228, 233, 240, 260, 288, 306; Southwest Museum 18; A.E. Stewart 299, 301; Stockmarket 9, 39, 174, 257; Bob Taylor 26, 42, 191; Three Lions 171; United Nations 47.

Index